B

MARSALIS, W.

P9-DWE-823

WYNTON MARSALIS

Skain's Domain

A BIOGRAPHY

LESLIE GOURSE

SCHIRMER BOOKS
NEW YORK

Schirmer Books
An Imprint of Macmillan Library Reference USA
1633 Broadway
New York, NY 10019

Library of Congress Catalog Card Number: 99-27954
Printed in the United States of America

Printing number   1   2   3   4   5   6   7   8   9   10

Library of Congress Cataloging-Publication Data

Gourse, Leslie.
    Wynton Marsalis : Skain's domain : a biography / Leslie Gourse.
        p.   cm.
    Includes bibliographical references (p. 291), videography (p. 288),
discography (p. 273) and index.
    ISBN 0-02-864863-3
    1. Marsalis, Wynton, 1961–   . 2. Jazz musicians—United States—
Biography   3. Jazz—History and criticism. I. Title. II. Title: Skain's
domain.
ML419.M3G68 1999
788.9'2'092—dc21
    [B]   99-27954
                                                              CIP

Permission for text excerpts in *Wynton Marsalis: Skain's Domain.*

"Wynton Marsalis," by Howard Mandel, *Down Beat* magazine, July 1984.
Used with permission of Howard Mandel. This article was reprinted in its
entirety in Mandel's book, *Future Jazz*, Oxford University Press, 1999.

"Encounters With Jazz," by Jeffrey J. Taylor, Institute for Studies in
American Music Newsletter, Volume XXIV, Number I, Fall, 1994. Used with
permission of Jeffrey J. Taylor.

Piano Jazz, with Marian McPartland, host, and guest Wynton Marsalis,
recorded January 11, 1995, broadcast for the first time January 6, 1996.
Excerpts used with permission of Miss McPartland.

Excerpts from *Black Genius and the American Experience*, Carroll and Graf Publishers, New York, 1998, used with permission of Carroll and Graf Publishers.

This paper meets the requirements of ANSI/NISO Z.39.48-1992
(Permanence of Paper)

TABLE OF CONTENTS

This book is dedicated to:
Ellis and Dolores Marsalis
and to Zelda Gourse
and in memory of
Harry, Norman,
and Sydney Jane Gourse
and Maureen Zusy

AUTHOR'S NOTE

This is the story of trumpeter Wynton Marsalis, who, while still in his twenties, rose to become one of the most famous and influential jazz and classical musicians in the modern world. In 1997 he became the first Pulitzer Prize winner for jazz, ostensibly for his oratorio, *Blood on the Fields*, but actually for his entire body of work.

A prodigy as a teenage trumpeter in his native New Orleans, he was raised by exceptional parents. He revered his father, an accomplished jazz pianist and teacher, as a role model; he respected his mother, who stubbornly set standards for her family of six sons. And he used all his God-given talents to catch his parents' attention and worked very hard to please them. He loved, admired, and competed with his elder brother, Branford, also a talented musician, who was, in some ways, Wynton's opposite and, in other ways, a virtual soulmate. Whether as a result of his New Orleans environment, his natural inclinations, his family upbringing, his early successes and the terrific attention he was accorded, or all these elements, Wynton drove himself relentlessly to achieve his twin goals of establishing himself as a masterful musician and elevating jazz to its rightful place as a revered art form created by African Americans.

When the opportunity arose for him to become artistic director of Classical Jazz at Lincoln Center in 1987, he took hold of the brass ring and became an ambassador and spokesperson for jazz. Classical Jazz evolved to become a full constituent, Jazz at Lincoln Center, in 1996. Wynton has shaped the country's perception of jazz by imposing his own traditional priorities, and sometimes controversial taste in jazz, and profound understanding of music in general for Lincoln Center's presentations. Despite some controversial choices he has made, it is probably safe to say that the music Wynton has selected is the main reason many jazz lovers fell in love with the music in the first place.

The rest is history, or it will be, for at this writing, Marsalis has just turned thirty-seven years old. But he has already done a full life's worth of work.

LESLIE GOURSE
October 1998

PREFACE

Wynton Marsalis was twenty-one years old in 1982, when he first came to the notice of the jazz and classical worlds as a prodigious player of the trumpet. By 1996 he was one of the most influential people in jazz, rising to the prestigious position of artistic director of Jazz at Lincoln Center. Controversies have arisen around how he has presented himself and his music from time to time. But, in making this climb from star performer to jazz spokesperson, he has used his considerable personal charm and his musical brilliance to answer his opponents. He has always focused on his music as his primary, organizing purpose.

As a child, he had loved sports and showed little interest in music. His father's struggles to make a living as a jazz musician made an impression on him. Ultimately, it was his father's strong commitment to the music—despite the difficulties he encountered—that helped inspire Wynton to a life as a jazz musician and educator.

Wynton's personal experiences with racial prejudice could not help but influence his attitude toward the society he has lived in and the music he has played, both classical and jazz. There were times when he had to search his soul to rise above his own prejudices and naivete. Anyone who lives in the United States has had to address and overcome prejudices rooted in racial, religious, ethnic, and sexual stereotypes. The jazz world has historically been the most integrated part of American society. But even there, racial complications have arisen, sometimes simply out of miscommunication. The history of jazz has largely been told by white musicologists, and most major institutions have been run by their allies. Marsalis has felt a special opportunity and responsibility to represent fully the African-American contributions to jazz as an art form. At times, his approach may have seemed to some people to border on the chauvinistic, but he has always been motivated by his sincere belief in his special mission.

Once Wynton as a teenager decided to play the trumpet, he had striking successes with European classical music, and then jazz. When he became a star quickly in the jazz world, some people envied his early fame and financial successes. Furthermore, fame gave him a forum to air his views about what was important in jazz history; with great certainty, he expounded upon the value of the tradition from the early days of the century to about 1965. He positioned himself against pop, electronic music, and much avant-garde music. Naturally, controversies arose. For a variety of reasons, some people even criticized his playing. When he became artistic director of Jazz at Lincoln Center, many people had their own firm ideas about what he should do there: whom he should hire, what race they should belong to, how old they should be, and what music he should ask them to play.

His critics had no qualms at all about asserting their opinions. But some of them objected vociferously if he had any opinions of his own about anything, including *their* opinions.

One thing is guaranteed in jazz circles: Mention Wynton Marsalis's name, and the conversation becomes impassioned. Some people adore everything he does; others detest it, and still others have mixed feelings. Nearly everybody agrees, however, that he should be given credit for his efforts and achievements as a great teacher.

Without question, Wynton's career has inspired many people, including jazz musicians, to discuss the future of jazz as an art form and the ideas they hold dearest. Most of the participants in these exchanges take their positions out of a sincere love and passionate concern for jazz. Wynton is similarly motivated, and his independent spirit, resolve, and occasional excitability have added to the general emotionalism. Some truly controversial issues that have arisen in Wynton's life and career remain unresolved, but he has come to be so highly regarded as a musician that he has managed to achieve the goals he has set for himself, to inspire other musicians and to attract large audiences for jazz music. Wynton has sailed above the controversies.

One of Wynton's most controversial beliefs is the need for the great jazz of the past to be codified and put into the repertoire. The charge has been leveled at this goal—which is not Wynton's alone—that it stultifies musicians' improvisatory instincts, a basic tenet of jazz. Of course, putting jazz music from the past into the repertoire doesn't really mean that jazz becomes static. To the contrary, after nearly a century of innovation and progress, it is wise to pause and put the achievements of the great jazz innovators and virtuosi into perspective. Neither does the repertoire prohibit anyone from experimenting on the contemporary jazz scene. Unfortunately, the experimenters don't have the same forum to work in as Wynton Marsalis does at Lincoln Center. It has been his prerogative to run Jazz at Lincoln Center as he sees fit.

There's an amusing tale that underscores the controversy about establishing a classical jazz repertoire. Someone was listening to a young musician playing tenor saxophone in the style of Lester "Prez" Young in a club. (Young, dubbed "President of the Tenor Saxophone," became prominent in the 1930s in Count Basie's band.) The listener kept saying that the saxophonist wasn't doing anything new; why did he keep playing just like Lester? The critic Stanley Crouch, Wynton's very close friend, who was standing nearby, turned and said, "Because he *can*."

Wynton Marsalis has spearheaded the latest, most successful movement to introduce classic jazz into jazz education programs in the schools, on TV and radio, and in concert halls. He wants to make sure young Americans learn about the roots of jazz and the names of its legendary masters, such as Louis Armstrong and Duke Ellington. He wants to learn from them himself.

In the last two decades—the period of Wynton's ascendance—jazz's long overdue prestige has been established in large part because of Wynton's personal charm, seemingly endless capacity for work, and great musical gifts. The existence of Jazz at Lincoln Center, which he worked hard to establish, is in itself emblematic of jazz's heretofore unprecedented prestige.

Had Wynton not helped to bring jazz before a wider American public, he would never have attained his political power, and jazz probably would not have acquired its current cultural prestige. Wynton also would not have served as a virtual lightning rod for some of society's ills. (When questions of racial discrimination arise, it's not surprising that they're electrifying, because race is probably the hottest topic in the country.)

To be sure, there is much wrong with American society, and therefore the jazz world. Jazz at Lincoln Center has its shortcomings, functioning in the context of the larger society with all its complexities. The program could and should present more varied styles of jazz composed and played by a greater mix of musicians—musicians of all ages and both sexes, representing a greater range of racial, religious, ethnic, and national backgrounds—on a consistent basis. More people could be included. And there could be more emphasis on some styles of jazz that have gotten less or even no hearing so far.

Wynton and his advisors have advanced the argument that Jazz at Lincoln Center is the most comprehensive and integrated that has ever existed anywhere, and it has put on more concerts as an institution, as opposed to a private promoter, than any other. It is definitely an integrated organization. How integrated? Is it an even split between black and white? No. It has included Asians and women in only a tangential way. But the program is still more reflective of American society than many other jazz groups—and certainly more integrated than most classical orchestras.

Wynton proudly points to the variety of the center's programming. Jazz at Lincoln Center has put people on the stage ranging from excellent Cuban musicians to traditionalists Chico O'Farrill and Gerry Mulligan; from modernists Dewey Redman, Wayne Shorter, and Don Cherry to standard-bearers Doc Cheatham and Nicholas Payton. Lincoln Center also has commissioned works by pianist-composers Geri Allen and Renee Rosnes. In 1998 one concert featured the established saxophonist Wayne Shorter alongside young pianist Eric Reed. Melba Liston was commissioned to write arrangements for a concert by Randy Weston's band. Israel "Cochao" Lopez and his Cuban Mambo Orchestra played a concert. A concert of James P. Johnson's music was played by a symphony orchestra. That concert included many women. And if women were underrepresented at first, by 1999 about one third of the players in the Essentially Ellington High School Band Competition would be women. The mixture and variety of music and musicians actually have been stunning.

Wynton, however, has taken a dim view of jazz's so-called avant-garde. He does not feel that most of this music even qualifies as "jazz," although many of its players and its audience view it as part of the jazz tradition. Courageous and energetic, these players have always fared better in Europe than at home and have attracted audiences among listeners to twentieth-century classical music. But as director of the Lincoln Center program, Wynton has the right to hire musicians he feels fit in with his conception of the best jazz.

In any case, Wynton believes that Jazz at Lincoln Center is the closest thing so far to an ecumenical jazz institution. Some critics' argument—and critics have been vehement and extreme at times—that the Jazz at Lincoln Center program isn't a pan-jazz organization—may be true. However, Wynton views the criticism of his choices as "in some strange way like saying the Next Wave Festival [of avant-garde music] in Brooklyn is limited because it doesn't bring in New Orleans music. But nobody says that. Or it's like saying that because the 92nd Street Y doesn't have baroque music, its concept is limited about what music is."

Wynton's point underscores the truism that critics rarely fault program directors for favoring the white, European musical traditions. The existence of a jazz program run so boldly by an African-American musician at Lincoln Center stands out as a new idea that has forced many people to examine their prejudices.

When it was suggested to him that Jazz at Lincoln Center could simply do more of everything, if it had the facilities—enough concert halls, standing groups, and orchestras—Wynton replied, "Of course we're going to present more music as we get older. That's all we can do." And despite critical allegations to the contrary, Wynton has already shown great flexibility in guiding the organization's development. It is likely that, as new opportunities present themselves, he will continue to address the shortcomings that both he and his critics have emphasized.

Wynton has been criticized for favoring the work of Duke Ellington over other jazz composers. Questions naturally arise: How much can one person or one jazz orchestra's musicians do? How much can they do *well*? If they are expert at Ellington's music, reproducing the brilliant work that Duke's band did with mutes, for example, can they also be expert at Thelonious Monk's or Dizzy Gillespie's or John Coltrane's or Charles Mingus's sounds and trademarks? Could there be several orchestras with varied specialties within Jazz at Lincoln Center? Of course, the program is still young; it cannot help but age and expand its repertoire and scope with greater space and more financial resources.

It's also worth noting that part of the reason why controversies have raged within the jazz world is that most people involved in jazz are proud that Jazz at Lincoln Center exists at all and want it to be perfect. But it can never be all things to all people. Every artistic director has his or her own priorities. Some people, of course, may be extremely disappointed that they don't run the Lincoln Center program themselves or influence its direction.

In the meantime, jazz has enhanced Wynton musically and professionally, and Wynton, with his ambitious nature, restless curiosity, commitment to jazz, and remarkable virtuosity, has immeasurably furthered the renaissance of the public's interest in acoustic jazz since the 1980s. If he has so far omitted most of the experimentalists from Jazz at Lincoln Center, he has chosen to put music, particularly the compositions and classic performances of some of the undisputed older jazz masters from the early years of the twentieth-century, before almost everything else in his life—everything except, perhaps, his own music. This book is the story of how and why he has done so. It is also an intimate look at Marsalis, with the help of Wynton himself, his family, some of his closest friends, and many of the musicians he has played with—as well as some of his critics.

The controversies that arise from time to time in this story do not necessarily reflect the author's own opinions. As much as possible, I have striven to be a storyteller, a reporter, and a historian, as I selected from an overwhelming number of events and projects in Wynton's career. Some choices I felt impelled to make were based on common sense, moral awareness, and some degree of insider's information. Because I discovered so many opinions in the jazz world, in keeping with the upturn in activity these days, I believe this book could stir up controversies or criticisms of its own.

For example, I stand poles apart from some very influential, serious thinkers and writers about jazz. Gene Lees, author of *Cats of Any Color*, among his many fine books and his estimable jazz journal, disagrees with me about the current vitality of the jazz scene. He feels that jazz is actually in its waning days. He is not alone. There are fewer jazz clubs, Lees points out, and fewer jazz radio stations, which he believes are linked to a decline in creativity and forward momentum in the field. Although there are some great players active now, Lees feels that jazz's heyday has passed.

The death knell for jazz has been sounding for decades, and yet somehow the music survives. Cedar Walton's balanced analysis of the ups and downs of jazz in his own experience as a jazz pianist for about forty years puts the situation into perspective. Walton says that there have always been changes in clubs; one club may close while another opens. But audiences remain loyal to jazz. Walton himself has held his audiences, often seeing the same people show up repeatedly to hear him play throughout his long career, which began during the early years of rock and roll, when jazz was pronounced dead and gone. So jazz clubs are probably not dying out. Neither, however, is the struggle of clubs to survive on a profitable level anywhere near over.

Some critics even have blamed Wynton Marsalis for a decline in jazz record sales since the 1980s. Yet, at the same time, Wynton has been congratulated for helping to boost sales in the first place. There are now so many CDs on the market that there appears to be a glut. Miles Davis noticed that same phenomenon about jazz records decades ago. There were just too many of them, he said; that's why sales declined. So perhaps it's business as usual: the popularity of jazz grows and declines in the marketplace—as well as in the public perception.

Stanley Crouch, Wynton's staunch ally for nearly twenty years, takes the interesting position that criticisms of Wynton have no influence at all. This may be an extreme point of view—as chauvinistic in its own way as pronouncements to the contrary—but is much more plausible than some of the ridiculous comments by people who have said that Wynton can't play or compose.

Polarized views notwithstanding, Jazz at Lincoln Center grows more important, developing greater depth and breadth. I see the negative and positive comments about Wynton Marsalis and Jazz at Lincoln Center as an informal system of checks and balances, which may occasionally force salutary readjustments and reevaluations when they might be needed.

I believe audiences for jazz are still having a hell of a good time—both those who go to the showpiece of Lincoln Center and those who frequent other places to hear jazz in much the way they always did. But people have to go out on the jazz scene to watch and hear the action and decide for themselves. Jazz, with all its diversity, remains a rich, dynamic music in a changing world that needs it.

Leslie Gourse

ACKNOWLEDGMENTS

The author wants to thank all the people who contributed to this book, among them research assistant Esther Smith at the Institute of Jazz Studies at Rutgers University and trumpeter Johnny Parker, who offered technical advice and sweet moral support. I would also like to thank the staff of Jazz at Lincoln Center and the many people quoted in the story, including the Marsalis family, Wynton's friends, and the musicians in all his groups. Special thanks to W. Royal Stokes, who supplied me with countless articles from his private files. Thanks also to Dr. Stanley Chang, who operated to save my left retina while I was writing this book, and Dr. Edward Holtzman, along with photographer Ray Ross and my editor, Richard Carlin.

YES, YES

For young pianist Nathan Rosenberg, it was already enough of a thrill to be playing solo at a birthday party for writer Kurt Vonnegut in late January 1998. The host was Warner LeRoy, whose top-floor apartment was so high up in a West 66th Street apartment building that Nathan could see three airports from it. LeRoy was owner of Tavern on the Green, a treasure of a light-bejeweled restaurant in Central Park; someone from the restaurant, who knew the way Nathan sang and played, had called him for the gig. Not a bebop pianist, Nathan can nevertheless play jazz; he knows the chord changes and many of the jazz and American popular standard songs. Furthermore, he can sing and improvise in a caressing, smooth, easy baritone. He has always been the sort of musician who, at the end of a gig, stays seated at the piano and keeps playing, working at his music.

"I was playing away," Nathan later recounted, "already a little overwhelmed by the party, when I looked up, and in walked Wynton Marsalis. My jaw dropped. Maybe I dropped some notes. He walked by me, patted me on the back, and said, 'You sound great.' He had a knowing smile. It seemed like he was aware of the reaction he elicits from people. He probably knew he made me nervous—and he had his horn with him."

Wynton was dressed rather formally in a suit with very good lines, Nathan noticed, and looked as if he had just come from his office at Lincoln Center, where he had been artistic director of Jazz at Lincoln Center for two years. Wynton lived in the same building with LeRoy and had been called in to play "Happy Birthday" for Kurt Vonnegut. Wynton had recently won a Pulitzer Prize for his oratorio, *Blood on the Fields*, Nathan knew, and had spent his entire adult life collecting all kinds of honors: Grammys, honorary degrees, and Peabodys, to name only a few. He had been one of the few jazz musicians ever to have a cover story written about him in *Time* magazine. A banner depicting Wynton blowing his trumpet often flew in front of Lincoln Center.

Wynton seemed to know some of the crowd: for one, Moss Hart's widow, Kitty Carlisle, the singer and actress. Vonnegut's daughter, about thirteen years old, who was learning to sing, knew two songs, including "Anything Goes." Nathan played them over and over again for her and gave her some advice on singing. Then Wynton started tutoring her. Nathan observed how easy Wynton was to work with. Wynton told her, "When you sing, you should imagine you're a drum and think of everything rhythmically. Now listen to what the piano player is playing."

Nathan recounted, "I responded to what he was saying. There was a lot of give-and-take. He was a very sensitive person. We were looking at each other as if it was a very easy working relationship together. When it came time for us to perform in front of the group with this girl, I already knew that every time we got to the end of the B section, she would add a beat and a half, or some weird figure. I had figured out she would do this every time. So I added that beat and a half. Wynton looked at me and laughed, because he knew I had caught it.

"Kitty Carlisle sang a song, too—a very dramatic interpretation of Kurt Weill's 'September Song.' When she did the verse, I faked my way through it. I looked at Wynton, and he seemed to say, 'Beats me.' She is theatrical. I was playing it in a florid way, not as a jazz piece. My feeling is he was kind of aware of my thought processes. Maybe I was being sharper because he was there.

"Then it came time for him to play 'Happy Birthday.' He was in one room at a distance from me. I went to stand within earshot, because I wanted to hear him play. He put his horn to his mouth and put two fingers up in the air, which means key of B flat. I ran into the other room to the piano, and I accompanied him. He started doing something like a

Creole 'Happy Birthday,' I would call it, a very happy jazz, improvised version, and I'm playing the bass figures—New Orleans or Creole style. My fiancé would call it swampy."

When Wynton came back out, he said to Nathan, "I couldn't really hear you very well in the other room. Let's play something."

Nathan had formed some opinions about Wynton before they had met that night: "I thought he was one of the young guys on the scene who had managed to take things over. While he was a great player, he may have overstepped his bounds somewhere. And in the jazz world he's a controversial player. There are a lot of older guys who could have had that gig [at Lincoln Center]. I was curious, because he sort of has a larger than life mystique about him.

"As soon as we started to play, he was incredibly expressive, particularly in his dynamics and phrasing and his choice of the range in which he plays. He'll play a song—say we did 'Sweet Georgia Brown.' And instead of playing it in the usual way, he'll emphasize notes and phrase differently; he'll squeal a note and trail down other notes. I noticed he was one of the most responsive players I've played with, in that he would draw off what I was doing and feed me things, lines to echo and support and reiterate. There was a level of give-and-take that astonished me.

"I was concentrating on my role as an accompanist. I wasn't trying to be fancy. I was trying to accompany him simply and let him ride over the line—the whole top of the chordal base. And when he chose to give me a solo, it was clear when that was. He was very in control and a great bandleader.

"There were other things I was impressed about: He was able to assess very quickly what my strengths were and to call songs in tempos and styles that brought my strengths out, accentuated them. I've never been a great bebop player. I'm a good jazz player, but not a bebop player. And instead of calling up [the Sonny Rollins composition] 'Pentuphouse,' he would call up some other stuff: 'Stardust' or something like that. Things that, even if I didn't know them, were stylistically appropriate for me. Or a blues tune. Or a standard with complicated changes. His choices were interesting. Or maybe we have similar tastes in music.

"The last thing I noticed, which really impressed me, is he's a real gentleman. He said to me, 'You sound great, a strong player.' He told Kitty Carlisle, 'Ask for his card; he's a great piano player.' He was very gracious. I told him I enjoyed playing with him and would love to play with him again sometime. He wrote his home phone number down on a piece of paper and told me to call him sometime."

At a gig a few days later at Merlot, the Iridium jazz club's upstairs restaurant—where Nathan was playing with bassist Steve Kirby in trumpeter Johnny Parker's trio—Nathan was talking excitedly about having played with Wynton. Nathan wouldn't dare call him, he said, but the phone number was in his pocket.

"Call him," Kirby said. "If he gave you his phone number, he means for you to call him. I know how you feel. He gave me his number, too. I wasn't going to call him. But my students were calling him. Wynton heard them playing in Terence Blanchard's groups. They were going to Wynton's house to play. I figured if my students are doing it, so can I."

Nathan laughed and decided he would do it sometime—when he got his nerve up, and when Wynton was going to be in town. At that moment, Wynton was just about finished with two weeks of rehearsals with the Lincoln Center Jazz Orchestra for a tour of the United States, Canada, Asia, Australia, and Europe. The tour would start on January 30 and end on March 28.

⸺⊱●⊰⸺

Wynton stood in front of the Lincoln Center Jazz Orchestra members in a big room at the Carroll Rehearsal Studios on West 41st Street and Ninth Avenue. They would rehearse over a hundred songs, from which he would choose each night's program for the tour called "All Jazz Is Modern." Most of his audiences would never before have heard many of the songs: a Duke Ellington piece called "Flaming Sword," for example. Wynton seemed to have a magnificent obsession with breathing new life into the old works. To the alert listener, he seemed to be achieving his aims even in rehearsals. But he wasn't always quite satisfied.

"Please remember the dynamics we went over yesterday," he said in his soft voice. "Please. . . . Yes, yes."

His hair was cropped very short; just a dark suggestion of hair covered his head.

He called out, "What's next?"

"Braggin' in Brass," (another Ellington tune), someone answered.

Wynton went to take a seat in the trumpet section at the back of the orchestra. One of his current protégés, Stefon Harris—who plays vibes and other percussion instruments—assumed Wynton's place as conductor at the front of the orchestra. To give himself a chance to play his trumpet more, Wynton had begun using Stefon as an assistant conductor. Sitting down, with his jeans that crinkled slightly over the tops of his shoes, and his suspenders over a crisp shirt, Wynton began playing the tune with its boom-chang beat.

"Hold it," he called out. He wanted it played slower. "A-one two-um," he said.

The orchestra kept starting and stopping at his bidding. "Everything hinges on that note," he said, meaning a B, and he played something that growled.

He asked, "What tempo do you want to play it in?"

After playing a little more and simultaneously hearing what everyone else in the orchestra was playing, Wynton stopped the music again and said, "Another thing is we don't want to get all wild sounding on our horns." He wanted the horn parts to work well with the rhythm section, he explained.

Tall, burly Rodney Whittaker was slapping his bass. Drummer Herlin Riley, who had joined Wynton's group shortly before the Lincoln Center Jazz Orchestra became a gleam in anyone's eyes, was playing the bass drum in the New Orleans–rooted style, boom-chang, boom-chang, playing the rhythm from the bottom up.

"Listen, bruh', that's half time," Wynton said to the whole orchestra, "like that. Okay, let's go from the top again. Let's try to get the notes under our fingers. It's still too wild. Also, try to understand the arrangement. Don't just play your part. Know the whole thing, and the music will be more interesting. And you're going to sound better. . . . Let's go again, Bruh . . ." he said.

When they finished, he said, "Go again." And "again."

So it went every day for a week, from 11:00 A.M. to 6:00 P.M., with breaks for meals—or sometimes just for the fresh bagels, cheese, and coffee on a long table in the rehearsal room.

Then the setting changed to the tenth floor of the Lincoln Center building, where the Stanley Kaplan Penthouse is housed and many Jazz at Lincoln Center events, such as lectures, movies, and solo performances, take place; the rehearsals continued.

One day, the band broke up an hour early, at 5:00 P.M., so that everyone had a chance to get to a television set to watch one of the college football bowl games. Even Wynton went home to watch the game, although his overriding passion in sports is basketball. Many other nights, taking a cue from Wynton's work ethic (he seemed to be constantly playing somewhere), some of the band members took on gigs around town. They played in small groups together in little clubs, for little to moderate-sized paychecks.

On Monday night, January 26, they went to the Jazz Standard, a new, spartan club near Gramercy Park. Wynton took a group there to play a tribute to pianist and composer Walter Bishop, Jr., who had just died of lung cancer. The gig, which originally had been planned as a fundraiser for Walter, ended up as a means of collecting money to cover whatever bills he may have had left.

On a break between sets, Wynton and some of the musicians— including Wessell "Warmdaddy" Anderson, an alto saxophonist, sat together at a table, eating hamburgers and drinking Cokes. There was obvious camaraderie between the leader and sidemen, who laughed and chatted together. Wynton shared someone's drink; he has a passion for Coca-Cola.

Moving to the bar, he began to talk to Rodney Whittaker about death. Whittaker wondered what death would be like.

An older woman standing nearby said, "You might miss being here on this earth."

Wynton said, "It all depends on what you're doing here. It might be better over there."

This was a stunning thought to come from a thirty-six-year-old man so busy doing what he loves. His remark reflected a deep faith in the possibility of life after death. Even with all his accomplishments and rewards, power and wealth, he was clearly no stranger to stress and malaise.

Despite playing so late that night, on the next morning, Tuesday, January 27, Wynton went to the Stanley Kaplan Penthouse on West 65th Street at 11:00 A.M. in time for the press conference announcing the formal start of the upcoming tour. Thick press kits with the complicated itinerary were passed out.

The band faced two more days of rehearsals. On the last day, the orchestra stopped for a late lunch. Wynton ran out of the room with one of the thirty-five Jazz at Lincoln Center staffers, April Smith, trailing after him. She was trying to catch his attention so she could ask a

question. "Wait a minute, little Wynton," she said. That was what everyone called his son, Wynton, Jr. April liked to call the father the same
thing. She, among others, noticed he liked to clown around and act the
way his son did at times. Wynton liked the suggestion.

Not only was it amusing, but it underscored Wynton's youthful
appearance. He's not very tall, though quite compactly built, and he had
become trim again after a year or so of a tendency toward moonfacedness.
He slowed down to chat with her on the way to the elevators. About half
an hour later, he walked quickly back into the rehearsal room, where a
small crew of television newspeople from Australia was waiting. He
would soon be playing "down under." He sat on a high stool and greeted
them warmly, casually—the way he greets everybody—with total ease. In
response to something one reporter asked, he said, "I'm always late. Ask
the guys."

She said something off-mike.

"No, they don't mind if I'm late. They're glad when I'm late."

Everyone within earshot laughed. Wynton enjoyed the sound of
laughter around him—except when he was at work on music. For about
ten minutes, he talked about the upcoming tour and the beauties of
Ellington's music, classic jazz, New Orleans music, and Louis Armstrong.
Wynton always pronounced Armstrong's name Lew-is, not the more
casual Lou-ee, as a sign of respect to the master. He also spoke of his
own errant ways at the beginning of his career, until he realized the value
and appreciated the beauty of the foundations of "jazz music."

Suddenly he was off the stool and facing the orchestra, which was
awaiting him. The members started again, playing one of the scores of
songs they had been honing for performances around the world. One
piece was a vivacious, exciting, joyful excerpt from Wynton's original ballet score, "Sweet Release." It had not been issued yet on any commercially
available recording, though it might be among the best and certainly most
inspiring pieces of music he has ever written.

At the end of the rehearsal, Wynton told everyone to "be on time, be
on time, be on time, yes, yes," for the bus that left the next day from the
Radisson Empire Hotel across the street from Lincoln Center. Once the
musicians were released from their rehearsal seats, they seemed to bris-
tle with excitement. They talked in short sentences, moving a little stiffly,
jerkily, reluctant to stand still and chat for more than a moment. "I'm

ready to go"; "I'm all set"; "I can't wait to get going now," various musicians told anyone who asked them how they felt.

—————————

The band set out on a mind-boggling schedule—the sort that Wynton has kept up with one way or another since he was about 20 years old. Each of his musicians would earn $20,000 for the two-month tour. They were always hired on a contract-per-engagement basis. Seasons for the Lincoln Center Jazz Orchestra started in October and went to May, with concerts every year in October, then a tour from January to March. In the spring came a high school band competition, followed by a summer tour in July. Every event was on a separate contract.

Not long after he left town, Wynton flew back from Toronto to attend a press conference to celebrate the announcement that Jazz at Lincoln Center would have its own theater, on the site of the Coliseum at 59th Street, at Columbus Circle. The Coliseum would come down, and the performance space and offices would go up. It was another dream come true for the jazz program.

Without even stopping by his apartment, he flew back to Toronto to the gig there with his orchestra. It had already wended its way from Morristown, New Jersey, to West Point, New York, then to Toronto. From there, it moved on to Cleveland; Indianapolis; Springfield, Illinois; Kalamazoo, Michigan; then Chicago, for two days. Next up were Wausau, Wisconsin; Minneapolis; Storm Lake, Iowa; and Seattle, for three days (the cities with multiple performances also afforded the orchestra a little time off between trips), and then Salem, Oregon; and Arcata, Santa Rosa, Berkeley, and San Francisco, California.

Actually, Wynton had no days off, just time off the bandstand. Joe Temperley, the band's baritone saxophonist who doubled on soprano sax, noticed how Wynton, as usual, spent afternoons in the smaller Midwestern cities. When he had no music clinics scheduled in schools, Wynton would visit the schools unannounced to give music lessons to students. Temperley thought Wynton was "terrific" to do that.

While Wynton was in San Francisco, he met with his brother Branford, a saxophonist; Slide Hampton, the trombonist and arranger; tenor saxophonist and Duke University music professor Paul Jeffrey; and Joe Temperley. They gathered together in a hotel room to listen to tapes and decide which high school bands would be finalists in the band competition—named in honor of Duke Ellington—that was scheduled for mid-May at Lincoln Center. Then Wynton flew with his orchestra to Seoul, South Korea.

The buses, the trains, the limousines, the water, the towels and refreshments in the dressing rooms, the good, clean hotels—everything was well planned and arranged. Wynton alone had been in charge when his group had begun touring in the early 1980s. Now the Jazz at Lincoln Center staff, headed by Rob Gibson, kept the machine oiled. Gibson took enormous pride in the work.

The band's itinerary covered Seoul, Hong Kong, Tokyo, Manila, and Singapore, then Sydney, Melbourne, Perth, and Adelaide, Australia, followed by a long flight to Lisbon, Portugal, on March 11. The group made the trip back to the United States on March 16, for a three-day break. Then a concert, with the tour's title switched to "In Progress: The Marsalis File," took place at Alice Tully Hall on March 19 and 21.

In New York, Wynton, with a dry cough, which he told people was bronchitis, kept up a full schedule. On March 19, he had one of his media days—entire days devoted to meeting critics and reporters—in his apartment, from which he can see the Hudson River. His building's lobby near Lincoln Center has the look of an old-fashioned library, with pictures on the walls depicting views of an audience from the perspective of performers, among them ballet dancers on stage. Here is the view from the business side of the footlights.

In the back of the lobby is the elevator to Wynton's apartment. His personal publicist, Marilyn Laverty—whom he met during his first days of recording for Columbia Records in the early 1980s, when she worked as a publicist there—answered the door. He was busy with a television crew and was delayed for his next appointment, she said. The new visitor waited in a dark, wood-paneled study, with dark green, comfortable armchairs, a lone plant on the windowsill, a pair of binoculars facing inward, and a few pictures of Duke Ellington and other musicians on the walls.

On the desk were several classical scores, among them Richard Wagner's *Lohengrin*. On the coffee table was Wynton's own book, *Sweet Swing Blues on the Road*, a tale of his life with his septet before he turned his full attention to Lincoln Center; a Cole Porter collection; books on the art of Romare Bearden; and the history of men's fashion; and *Viva Picasso*.

On the floor-to-ceiling bookshelves was a diverse collection: Frank Conroy's *Body and Soul, The Norton Anthology of African American Literature,* and books of poetry by ancients and moderns, Europeans and Americans, blacks and whites. There were collections of Ovid, Goethe, Richard Wilbur, *The Poet in New York* by Federico Garcia Lorca, who wrote magnificent, vivid poems about Harlem: "And the one with his heart broken meets on the corner the incredible crocodile . . ."; and "Each day they kill in New York . . . hundreds . . . thousands." There were books of philosophy, and *The Odyssey,* and *The Greek Way,* which is a discussion of Greek writers, and three plays by Euripedes, and fiction, and a book on the development of language, and *Music Was Not Enough* by Bob Wilber, *Beyond Category: The Life and Genius of Duke Ellington,* and *Primary Colors* by Anonymous. There were also books by Jonathan Kozol, who became famous for his first book, *Death at an Early Age,* about the failures of the public school system and the shortchanging of minority-group children, and books by journalists Charles Kuralt and Carl Rowan.

To the right of this room with its dark ambience is a little room done in blue and white, seemingly filled with light, obviously for children—Wynton's sons. It has bright blue wallpaper on the ceiling flecked with white stars, stuffed toys on the windowsills, pictures on the walls, and a photograph of two smiling women and three little boys. Though Wynton has three sons, there are only two beds in this room. His eldest sons, Wynton, Jr., and Simeon, whose mother is Candace Stanley, live within easy visiting distance of Wynton, in a suburb of New York, with Candace, her husband, and their two younger children. But Wynton's youngest son, Jasper Armstrong, whose mother is actress Victoria Rowell, lives on the West Coast with Rowell and her daughter.

The room in which Wynton was sitting with the television crew, beyond the dining room with its table piled high with papers, had a light aura with a white-and-blue color scheme, too. Without coughing at all, he talked about Louis Armstrong: how Armstrong was built like a bull, not too tall; how the trumpet is a physical instrument; how Armstrong had a big scar on his mouth from the metal mouthpiece pressing on his lip and the stress of all the high notes he hit to please audiences. And how could he give himself such a scar? Wynton wanted to know, letting the obvious answer hang in the air.

The woman interviewing him asked about Armstrong's idiosyncrasies. Wynton didn't flinch and talked about Swiss Kriss, the laxative that Armstrong took every day. "Country people," Wynton said. "He had to have his laxative and his marijuana. He smoked him some weed, every day . . . . And there was a bright shining light in his horn.

"He had profound feeling plus technical mastery, that's genius. . . . He was soulful . . . down home. He would play the harmonies and improvise off King Oliver's improvisations." Wynton explained about Armstrong's first job, when he went to Chicago from New Orleans, "not just to play second trumpet and play harmonies and improvise off Oliver's lines, but off Oliver's own improvisations on his own lines. Armstrong knew Oliver's music so well that he could improvise off the improvisations."

Minutes after the TV session ended, an interview with a print journalist took place in the dark study. Coughing, Wynton refused tea. An hour and a half later, another television crew arrived, and that session began in the bright room off the dining room. Wynton knew his schedule, because it was posted by his secretary, Genevieve—"Jen" as he called her—on the back of his bathroom door and his refrigerator.

When Wynton wants to get to the office for Jazz at Lincoln Center or Alice Tully Hall quickly, he can exit his building by an escalator at the back of the lobby. The escalator brings him to the concrete walk from which he can get into Juilliard, the elevator bank to the Stanley Kaplan Penthouse, or the Walter Reade Theatre, or take another escalator that goes down to Alice Tully Hall. On bright days, when he steps off the escalator from his building, he is bathed in sunlight gleaming on the whitish stone of the arts complex. One can have the feeling of having just emerged into paradise.

———⋙•⋘———

On March 19, his bronchitis notwithstanding, Wynton kept his date at Alice Tully Hall with the orchestra—all the men dressed in elegant beige-colored jackets, black pants, and white shirts with bow ties—to play a program of his own difficult music. This included not only excerpts from his ballet score, "Sweet Release"—commissioned for the Alvin Ailey Dance Theater's production choreographed by Judith Jamison, and premiered in August 1996 as part of the Lincoln Center Festival—but an exciting, long piece called "Big Train," in which he communicated one of his early childhood, musical impressions: the sound of a train going ka nunk ka nunk, ka nunk ka nunk, along with his elder brother Branford's impression of the train whistle's woo woo woo woo.

When Wynton coughed during his opening monologue about how the orchestra had just flown into town, he said: "If I mess up [the music], the bronchitis is no excuse." And: "We had a twenty-four-hour flight from Adelaide to Lisbon. . . . Wes [Anderson, the alto saxophonist] fell asleep during one of the concerts, and Walter [Blanding, a tenor saxophonist sitting next to Wes onstage] did not wake him up." (During this concert, one critic noted that another musician fell asleep onstage.)

Wynton invited the audience to add their names to a mailing list in the lobby for material from the Jazz at Lincoln Center program. "We're not going to send something ugly," he said. (That's one of his favorite lines.) "If we send anything ugly, be sure we had a fight in the office about it."

With a tiny trace of apology in his tone, Wynton announced the orchestra would play his original music for the night. (Wynton retains the small towner's habit of deprecating his own achievements. Bragging is a New Yorker's skill.) Then, with his introduction over, trumpeter Riley Mullins played the blues-rooted, happy, brassy introduction for "Sweet Release," and the concert took off full blast instantly.

Some of the music sounded a bit derivative, a portion slightly reminiscent of, perhaps, "Cool," a Leonard Bernstein tune for *West Side Story*. But mostly the harmonies, voicings, colors, and textures were informed by Duke Ellington's music, which Wynton has studied assiduously.

The orchestra moved like greased lightning through sharp turns and quick cuts of the evocative pieces. The musicians had achieved the communion between the rhythm and horn sections that Wynton had urged them to seek in rehearsals.

Much of the music literally tells a story. But, instead of words, the musicians use the different sound textures at their command to express the many elements of the plot. The textures and colors of the music depict the love story in "Sweet Release" and paint the passion of an amorous couple. As "Sweet Release" progressed from the meeting of the hero and heroine in a section called "Church Basement Party," to a fight they had, Victor Goines—who plays all the reeds and excels with his rich sound and fluidity on the clarinet—used that instrument to play the devil's part.

Wynton explained the action: "The man plays loud but don't get rid of the devil. The woman brings the devil to a slower tempo, and the devil's afraid. Two things the devil is afraid of: anything in 5/4 time—a lot of people are afraid of that—and a slow tempo. The devil ends up in a low register—that's it for him." For the last movement, the only thing left for the couple to do, Wynton said, is run the devil away. "And that's what happens."

The audience loved it. So did the *New York Times* critic, Peter Watrous, who, although he had reservations about the organization and length of the hour-long "Big Train," summed up the evening: "Mr. Marsalis was working with the orchestra as brush and paints, and he was after something unconventional. Even without solos, the music reached all sorts of destinations, from humor to sensuality to gentleness. Finally, after the virtuosity of the conception was put aside, he came forward as an emotionalist, moved by history and by American themes."[1]

———

Watrous's review was a far cry from some of the criticisms that had been leveled at Wynton, as he evolved over the years, by a variety of other critics and musicians. They took issue with his playing, calling it technically proficient but cold, and his compositions derivative. Some critics were most disturbed by his direction away from experimental and free jazz and new music.

Marsalis had first come on the scene playing intense, hard bop music as a member of Art Blakey and the Jazz Messengers. But, as he grew older, he moved away from Blakey's concept, to bebop in small ensembles, and then to swing and New Orleans jazz. He was essentially uninterested in the "free jazz" experiments of the early 1960s. For one thing, he thought this music alienated jazz audiences, and he personally didn't like it. He was also vehemently opposed to the blending of electric and acoustic instruments that created the commercial fusion style of 1969 and thereafter, even though fusion appealed strongly to a large audience.

Wynton had slammed the door on rock or pop music in his own life, explaining that it wasn't jazz, and he had grown to emphasize an earlier, seemingly less complicated era than bebop: primarily the swing era, in which Ellington and Armstrong had thrived and reigned. Wynton sometimes even went back as far as Jelly Roll Morton's music, or forged ahead to Thelonious Monk's compositions, and even to more contemporary modernists like bassist Charles Mingus and Wynton's beloved saxophonist John Coltrane. Yet his heart and soul seemed to belong to the old masters most of all.

Wynton's own music, notably his Pulitzer Prize–winning oratorio, *Blood on the Fields*, was palpably filled with his study of Ellington's harmonies and voicings, and many of his other compositions were strongly informed by his feeling for his New Orleans roots. As Count Basie had founded a blues-based band and discovered how well it worked for him, Wynton had realized that the feeling and style of New Orleans music gave his jazz playing joyousness, strength, and universal appeal.

Although Wynton's music recalled the work of Ellington and the New Orleans masters, it would be unfair to say he merely copied it. Many of his harmonies and voicings showed his unique touch and reflected his position as a musician—and man—living in the last quarter of the twentieth century. Wynton wanted to build on the legacy of the past greats, not merely repeat their work.

Despite the many obvious influences on Wynton's music, Wynton wasn't sure of what his orchestra had sounded like. "The energy was strange," he confided to a writer after the March 19 concert, "but I don't know. I never know. I just play. You never actually know what's going on. I just play."

Between the March 19 and 21 dates at Alice Tully Hall, the orchestra went to play for a night at Constitution Hall in Washington, D.C. Richard Harrington, a writer and jazz critic for the *Washington Post*, who caught Wynton's March 20 performance, agreed with Peter Watrous's mostly happy response to Wynton's own compositions and the way Wynton and the orchestra played them.

Wynton didn't go to bed right away after the Washington concert, despite the cough that was still bothering him. No, no. A *Washington Post* gossip columnist caught his unofficial, late-night set: "The music pouring out of the small, smoky Mayflower Hotel bar late Friday night certainly sounded a lot better than your average lounge act. After his gig at Constitution Hall, trumpeter Wynton Marsalis and his rhythm section set up in the hotel's intimate space. Marsalis wailed until nearly 2:00 A.M., and his group jammed until 3, thrilling the patrons. . . . "[2] Wynton's men had met there with a band led by a drummer from New Orleans booked to play in the bar, and they couldn't resist the chance to jam with their friend.

A few more performances followed: Newark (March 22) and Princeton, New Jersey (March 23); a Jazz for Young People's concert rehearsal (March 24) led by Wynton; then University Park, Pennsylvania (March 25), Oxford, Ohio (March 26), and Mechanicsburg, Pennsylvania (March 27), with performances each night, while Wynton led educational sessions in the afternoons.

On Saturday, March 28, when the orchestra ended its tour in New York City, Wynton went to Alice Tully Hall for 11:00 A.M. and 1:00 P.M. performances of his Jazz for Young People series—sold-out concerts that have addressed, in the past, such burning topics as "What Is Swing?" and "Who Is Louis Armstrong?" and "Who Is Duke Ellington?"

Wynton opened this performance about "What Is Cool?" by introducing his group, seven members of the Lincoln Center Jazz Orchestra; he waited for a while to mention his own name. He said, "I give my own name plenty of space. That's cool." He explained how food can be cooked over a high flame or a low flame; the low flame is the cool way to cook and just as thorough and intense a method as a high flame. So the slow flame is very deceptive, he explained.

Finding himself talking into the wrong microphone, he picked up his papers from the lectern in front of it and switched to the right microphone. "Now, you don't see me rushing and hurrying to get from one mike to another," he said. "When you make a mistake, take your time," he said. "That's your first lesson in being cool today." The audience roared, or at least the adolescents and everyone on up to their parents did.

"To be cool, you have to be relaxed," Wynton said. "Don't rush from place to place." He went on to relate his ideas to music, explaining that cool music is played at slow or medium tempos, and cool musicians figure out the ways to make fast tempos sound slow. He asked baritone saxophonist Joe Temperley to play Benny Carter's ballad "When Lights Are Low." Carter is a much-revered, traditional multi-instrumentalist, arranger, and composer in the jazz world. "Now, he took his time," Wynton said about Temperley's interpretation, "and you didn't see him moving around, messin' around."

"To mess it up, turn the music up loud. That's popular music," Wynton said, taking the opportunity to beat one of his favorite whipping posts (and to stir up critics of his opinions about popular music). He asked his trombonist, Wycliffe Gordon, to blast away on a tune. Wynton mentioned that pop music "has us all deaf." He was really pulling out all the stops to slay the pop dragon.

To show the early roots of the cool style, Wynton selected the tune "I'm Coming Home, Virginia," as it had been played in the 1920s by legendary trumpeter Bix Beiderbecke and Bix's good friend, saxophonist Frankie Trumbauer. That led to a discussion of the "President of the Tenor Saxophone," Lester Young, who first became known in Count Basie's band in the 1930s. Young had started the cool school for tenor saxophone players. He in turn was an heir of Trumbauer, whom Young had heard on recordings, which started to spread the sound of the music and help young players to learn about jazz.[3]

"Lester may have been the coolest musician who ever lived," Wynton said. Lester didn't jump around. "He had soft eyes. That was important," Wynton explained. A cool person has to have soft eyes, or else his eyes might look cold and hard, and that's not cool.

Wynton continued: "Lester spoke softly and made up witty nicknames for people and invented humorous expressions." (When he liked something, he said he had "eyes" for it.) "And he played in a soft, lyrical way. The lyrical way to play is with embellishments—but without verboseness or florid decorations," Wynton explained. "It's the difference between a man handing a woman a bouquet of flowers and saying," Wynton whispered, "'I thought of you' or saying," he growled, "'Take this.'"

The audience laughed heartily, loving Wynton, learning from him, enjoying his romance with metaphors. He had long ago noticed about himself that he could, almost magically as poets do, see similarities in dissimilarities—the relationships between all types of ideas and disciplines; ever since he had been a boy in elementary school, he had known he could do that.

Wynton went on to explain the subtlety and introspection of the cool approach to jazz and showed a film clip of Lester Young, who always held his saxophone at a tipped angle. Wynton pointed out that Lester, playing an intense, soulful blues, had been holding a cigarette between two fingers and didn't get burned. "And you knew he wouldn't get burned," Wynton said, "because he was cool."

After Lester, Wynton said, bebop came along. With his own orchestra's alto saxophonist, Wessell Anderson, Wynton played a fast, hot, bebop song, a cache of sixteenth notes, suggesting the styles of the great bebop founders, Charlie "Bird" Parker and Dizzy Gillespie.

Following bebop, among other styles, came the introspective, cool musicians thinking about private matters.

Wynton said, "The embodiment of the introspective trumpeter is Miles Davis. Miles had a raspy voice. That was the first thing that made him cool. . . . He rarely spoke more than a few words at a time. If someone came up to him and said, 'I love you, and I have all your records,' Miles said," and Wynton, who has a slight catch or rasp in his own voice, imitated Miles's whispery voice, "'So? What do you want?' Or a fan might ask Miles, 'When did you record this?' And Miles would look away and not answer."

Wynton explained that Miles primarily played spare themes in the middle register of the trumpet and had an introspective approach and sound with no vibrato. "Miles let the color of his sound [without vibrato] carry the emotion of the song. . . . Cool musicians cover up, so people don't know how you feel. Miles used a Harmon mute to cover up how he felt—and held notes for a long time." Wynton affixed a little Harmon mute to the bell of his trumpet and demonstrated the eerie, haunting sound—the antithesis of happy, New Orleans music.

Wynton further explained that cool musicians like to play in odd or complex meters—5/4, or 7/4, for example, instead of 4/4—"since the music is so simplified that the meters don't clutter it up." Wynton used alto saxophonist Paul Desmond's song "Take Five" as an example of a distinctive cool sound for intense, swinging jazz music. All along, Wynton used film clips of these musicians to demonstrate the ideas.

Then he came to Latin jazz, which anybody can tell is not cool. But Stan Getz, a disciple of Lester Young, brought some Brazilian music—the bossa nova—to prominence in the United States. That relaxed, lyrical, melodic music created sparks with its rhythmic complexity.

Wynton divided the audience into three parts. One part was asked to sing "tu tum, tu tum," a bass drum part. The other side of the room sang "chi chi chi chi" quickly. Those in the middle clapped their hands. Once the audience settled into their parts, Wynton said, "So I see you all have respect for that vibe now." Vanessa Rubin came on stage to sing "The Girl from Ipanema," a well-known bossa nova tune, which ended the 11:00 A.M. performance.

Many people have been turned away from these performances for young people, because not enough seats exist in Alice Tully Hall to satisfy the demand. Critics have praised the series to the skies. Yes, yes. It

was hoped that with the acquisition of the Coliseum space, the new theater would eventually be able to accommodate the demand for tickets in
the twenty-first century. But that theater would probably have only 1,100
seats, as Alice Tully Hall does. So the solution was not on the horizon.

Chapter Notes.

1. Peter Watrous, "Big Band, Big Premiere, Big Tour, Big Marsalis." *New York Times*,
    March 21, 1998.
2. Richard Harrington, "Marsalis's 'Train': It's the Rail Thing," *Washington Post*, March
    23, 1998.
3. Although Wynton is often accused of underplaying the contribution of white musi-
    cians to the development of jazz, this lecture—and many like it—show his full
    knowledge of and respect for the interplay between black and white musicians.

THE MARSALIS
FAMILY IN KENNER

Wynton Marsalis would always recall his father's love for playing the piano and all the lessons his "daddy" had learned about life from his steadfast devotion to jazz. Ellis Louis Marsalis, Jr., would pass on his "sayings," as Wynton called Ellis's insights and priorities, the fodder that fueled the survival of his own soul, to his children.

Wynton would also remember some of his mother's lessons that had nothing to do with music. If there was one thing that Dolores Marsalis was not going to allow, he learned, it was any of her six children hanging around in the streets: not in Kenner, where the Marsalis family lived until Wynton was in junior high school, nor in the Carrollton neighborhood of New Orleans, to which the family would move when he went to high school. "That's the one thing my mama wasn't going to let you do," Wynton knew.

Once he and a buddy in Kenner had actually set a neighbor's house on fire. The house was being built, and Wynton and his buddy thought it would be fun to set it ablaze. The boys had done it with cigarettes, which hadn't been extinguished properly. As Wynton would recall, it was actually his friend's idea to leave a lit cigarette at the construction site.

Nobody was staying in the house at the time. It wasn't as if Wynton and his friend were trying to kill someone. But Dolores viewed the incident as the first step toward a criminal lifestyle for Wynton.

When Wynton went home, Dolores asked him, "Who set that fire?" though she already knew. "Why did you burn that man's house?" she demanded. She pulled Wynton out of their house and into the street, where she yanked his pants down.

"She whipped my behind out in the street. In front of all my boys. That was embarrassing," Wynton said. "She took me to my friend's house. He had three sisters. I'm standing there with my drawers on. I was like half-naked. And she made me stand up in his house. 'Who burned this man's house?' I was twelve or thirteen. I was too old for that. I really couldn't believe she was doing it. Now, if I really didn't want to go, she couldn't have *made* me."

Wynton would recall with bravado, "It was just a curious thing. I had never seen that kind of intensity come out of her. She didn't want me to be hanging in the street, living that kind of thug life, doing that kind of dumb stuff, setting fires. She was going to make sure that didn't happen."

Another time, Wynton recalled, he, Branford, and their younger brothers, Ellis III and Delfeayo, pulled a stunt together at the same house. They lit some firecrackers and threw them at the front and back of the house. Even years later Wynton enjoyed the memory of this mischief. The firecrackers had made a tremendous amount of noise, as the boys put the house "under siege," he said. "We had a battalion working. I remember I put a big M-80, a big loud firecracker, in their carport. Wham, like a shotgun going off. That was beautiful. We had a field day."

Nobody got hurt, but this time people were living in the place. Wynton didn't remember the end of the story. Some police officers may have come to the door to find out what had happened. The story never really came out, but Dolores was suspicious of her sons and told them never to do that again. Both these stories carried the same moral: Dolores Marsalis wouldn't tolerate her children running wild in the streets.

Branford recalled, "There were piles of shit like that. Most of it was just regular family stuff, sitcoms and dramas. There was a time when Wynton stepped on a nail. We were playing in the same yard [where the house frame had burned down]. My father said, 'Don't play there. Construction's going on.' So of course we went to play there. Wynton landed on a nail."

Wynton recalled jumping off a pile of bricks and landing on a nail that went clear through his foot and stuck out the top of his sneaker. Branford said, "'Shit'—no, I didn't say 'shit' in those days—I said 'Shucks, your foot, your foot!' And he was cool."

Wynton pulled his foot off the nail. "And blood came running out," Branford said. "He freaked." Branford thought he recalled Wynton crying out, "'They're crucifying me, Lord Jesus!' He had to go for treatment"—probably tetanus shots. Wynton recalled crying to Jesus when the doctors put a needle in his foot.

Both Dolores and Ellis Marsalis had their own distinct and overriding concerns. Ellis, who was born on November 14, 1934, didn't know why he had always liked music. Nobody else in his family had any musical talent. His father, who had moved from Summit, Mississippi, to New Orleans when he was thirteen years old, married a woman from New Roads, Louisiana, and had two children: Ellis (who was Ellis, Jr.) and Yvette. Ellis, Sr., had a variety of jobs: working as an electrician, building batteries, and managing an Esso Service station.

In 1944, when Ellis, Jr., was ten, the family moved to Shrewsbury, Louisiana, where Ellis, Sr., bought a "place." It wasn't really a farm, but he raised some chickens, ducks, hogs, and a couple of cows. Coming from a rural town in Mississippi, he was used to that sort of lifestyle. He kept up his usual work with the gas station, then opened a motel in Shrewsbury. After a few years it grew profitable enough so that he could devote his time to the motel as the primary source of the family's income, and he quit the gas station.

Growing up in legally segregated Louisiana, both Ellis, Jr., and Yvette studied music in school and eventually earned college degrees in music. Ellis studied cello at the University of Southwestern Louisiana in Lafayette. Yvette played piano, though not professionally.

One summer day in New Orleans, just before he joined the Marines, Ellis met a pretty young woman, Dolores Ferdinand, on Lincoln Beach, a segregated beach in those days. She had a bright, conversational style and close-set eyes. On New Year's Eve, 1958, he and Dolores, who had majored in home economics at Grambling State College, were married. Later that year, Ellis was discharged from the Marines and went home to start his family with his bride.

When anyone asked Ellis where his sons' musical talent came from, he said it came from his wife's family. In her family background were

Alphonse Picou, a well-known, old-time New Orleans clarinetist, on her mother's side, and bassist Wellman Braud, her paternal grandfather's brother. Braud had played and recorded with Duke Ellington's orchestra in the 1930s. Dolores's mother, Leona (née Learson), was also related to the New Orleans trombonists Wendell and Homer Eugene.

Dolores, who was born on April 13, 1937, has a chirpy, clear-voiced way of talking, which has never been slowed by her slight Southern drawl. From the start of her marriage, she knew that her life with Ellis, who loved to play the piano, would be full of music. Although he had a deceptively laconic, cool way of talking, Ellis was intensely committed to playing. And Dolores *did* like music.

Dolores's family roots went deep and far back into Louisiana. Her father's family came from Napoleonville, about 120 miles "going west, by the river road west of New Orleans," she said. "They had a lot of plantations; the French settled there. My great-grandmother was born on a plantation. Her mother had come with a French family from a plantation to New Orleans." And so her mother's family was from the French Quarter in New Orleans.

Both her mother and father, like Ellis's mother, spoke French patois. "They separated when I was a baby, and they never got back together, and they never divorced. My father had common-law wives, and my mother" (who had been born in 1908) "raised three of us": Dolores Ferdinand and her brothers, Delfeayo, who was still living in 1998, and Lawrence, who had died by then.

Dolores recalled, "In the days of staunch segregation, there was really no entertainment other than entertainment that blacks made for themselves. Everyone had an upright piano, and so many were home musicians. They went from house to house, playing, entertaining one another. A lot of instruments were even handmade—galvanized tubs for basses, for example. Everybody's family had musicians and musical talent." She herself had played piano as a child and had even sung in a small jazz band. "But I don't need to be validated by any of those things," she would say.

Ellis's and Dolores's first son, Branford, was born on August 26, 1960. Eighteen months later, on October 18, 1961, Wynton Learson was born, as Branford had been, in Flint Goodrich Hospital in New Orleans. At first, the family was living at 711 Farm Avenue in Hanson City, but they soon moved to Kenner, a racially mixed but segregated community just across the railroad tracks from New Orleans.

Ellis wanted to go on the road as a musician, but, as he would later reflect, "I couldn't put any of that together." In 1964, fortified by a bachelor of arts degree in music education from Dillard University in New Orleans, he went by himself to Breaux Bridge, Louisiana, to work as both the choral and band director at Carver High School, about 150 miles from New Orleans. When he found a house there, Dolores, Branford, Wynton, and Ellis III, their third child born in 1964, went to live with him. Delfeayo, their fourth child, was born in New Orleans the next year and lived in Breaux Bridge for the first year of his life.

Breaux Bridge was not only a country town, it was also a Creole area, where people spoke patois; the town was altogether a different culture for the Marsalises. Ellis and Dolores, as many people did, discouraged their kids from speaking patois. "It wasn't so much a racial bias as an attitude. Europeans discouraged their kids from speaking the old language when they came to America," Ellis explained.

His mother and grandmother, for example, spoke patois but discouraged Ellis and Yvette from learning it. "They were Creole. That just means you're not white, and it has other kinds of connotations. It's not a real ethnic term that has any biological substance. It's cultural. You can talk about octoroons and quadroons, and those terms have a cultural connotation." The intermarrying of Europeans, blacks, Indians, and other groups had created a rich array of racial distinctions in New Orleans.

Breaux Bridge was not Ellis's favorite place to live. In 1966 he moved the family to New Orleans, where he worked briefly in his father's motel. In June 1967 Ellis joined trumpeter Al Hirt's band and played in a nightclub: Hirt's own place on St. Louis and Bourbon streets. That year, Hirt made a present of a trumpet to little Wynton, who had already shown no interest in piano lessons. Wynton would later say that he didn't have much interest in the trumpet, either, although he did start to play it. When he was eight or nine years old, he played in the Fairview Baptist Church marching band led by Danny Barker, an eminent banjo and guitar player, who felt committed to teaching music to kids.

With Barker's children's band, Wynton, who at the time had little idea of the value of Barker's music history lessons, played in the first New Orleans Jazz and Heritage Festival. Not only did he think he sounded "sad" at the time, as he said (Wynton's favorite expression for an inadequate performance), but he had to ask someone else to carry his trumpet. It was too heavy for him.[1] By 1971, and possibly before that, Wynton played in the Jesuit Honor Band, an elementary school band. The next year, he met Victor Goines, another member of that band and a budding reeds player.

For three years Ellis worked with Hirt's band, until 1970, when he went out on his own and "sort of hustled," he said. He worked as a pianist for shows—for the Burds, Tim Rice, a hypnotist, and other local acts—in a theater run by actress June Havoc, and also at a repertory theater. Then he went to work in "little small restaurants somewhere. The best way to put it is I was freelancing," he reminisced.

Wynton would recall his father as scuffling in those days. To Dick Russell, author of *Black Genius and the American Experience*, Wynton would tell about the day his father was down to his last twenty dollars. "I was maybe eleven or twelve. He was trying to determine whether he wanted to drive a cab, give up trying to play music. . . . [But] when he was gonna take a day job [Dolores] said no, he should keep playing.

"That struck me. My momma has real aesthetic understanding. . . . She understood something of what this music was about, in terms of what it represents. I think I got a lot of that from her. She has an understanding of what integrity is, too."[2]

Ellis continued: "Around 1972, I started to work on Bourbon Street with the Storyville Jazz Band. That was a really important job for me musically, because during this time, I started to learn and play early, traditional New Orleans jazz. I played for a year and a half, then left and started playing at a club called Lu and Charlie's, Lu short for Lula, and Charlie Bering. I stayed there for about a year.

"And during all the time I was freelancing, I was also doing adjunct teaching at Xavier University in New Orleans, teaching one or two classes. I developed a course in African-American music; it was really jazz history, about who the early musicians were. I was using the book *The Music of Black Americans* by Eileen Southern. But I didn't have any recordings. Most of the records that I had were bebop"—recordings from his own collection, which he played at home for his children to hear, even though they were not particularly interested in that music then. And so the people whom he was teaching didn't get a chance to hear nearly as much as they should have heard, he said, because neither he nor the people in the university's library knew how to make cassette tapes.

He had started teaching at Xavier in 1967 or 1968 and stayed until 1974. He hadn't been able to get a full-time job teaching in the music department there, because he didn't have a master's degree. So he went to Loyola University to get that crucial degree. He would always be grateful to Joe Butram, who was dean of the music school at Loyola, because Butram allowed Ellis to write his master's thesis on the development of a rhythm section.

Ellis recalled, "It was a great risk on his part, because I couldn't really put together the kind of committee that was needed [to judge] for a subject matter like that. It wasn't as if I was putting together a study on Debussy or Wagner; there were experts on those composers already in the university." Ellis got great assistance, he said, from the classical music experts at Loyola. Later Joe Butram also sponsored Ellis for an honorary degree from Ball State University in Indiana.

In August 1974 Ellis had an interview for a job at a new art school about to open: the New Orleans Center for Creative Arts (NOCCA). The Marsalis family's fortunes now took a turn for the better. Ellis had never really adored teaching until then; he had wanted to play the piano and regarded his teaching simply as a way to help support his family. He commented, "Teaching in my time meant a few things; it was a low-paying job, but it meant avoiding the mop and broom, or a job at the post office, or preaching, the only things available to me in those days. So I could teach and get my side hustle." Ellis didn't think he was going to be a great teacher, not with his way of talking or his attitudes, he said. He believed he was rather unorthodox—a jazz musician at heart.

NOCCA hired him to begin working in 1974, and he soon discovered his passion for teaching music to high school students. They attended their regular public schools in the mornings and in the afternoons went to NOCCA for music lessons. Many very talented musicians began passing through Ellis's courses in sight-singing and ear training and also in his jazz ensemble. Years later alto saxophonist Jesse Davis would say that Ellis's teaching and guidance saved his life, when he was wildly upset after his mother's death. Ellis gave him focus and encouraged him to have the self-confidence and commitment to go to Chicago to study music in college. Pianist Harry Connick, Jr., the son of the district attorney of New Orleans, would say that Ellis brought about his metamorphosis from a "screw-up into a serious student of music."

Ellis discovered that he had a flair for teaching when he got to NOCCA. "I never knew I had a great gift for teaching," Ellis would reflect. "If you're in the heat of battle, and someone tells you you're a great soldier, who the hell knew? Who the hell knew? I was learning along with the students. Jazz had no history in academe. Everything you did was based essentially on what you thought needed to be done."

It was Ellis's job to help students discover if they wanted to play music for a career or to make a move in another direction, perhaps to theater, dance, creative writing, or the visual arts. NOCCA's teachers prepared students to decide if they wanted to become professionals. That was the philosophy of the school.

———❦———

Wynton knew that he had been named for pianist Wynton Kelly, a great, blues-oriented, bebop musician, who was playing in a Miles Davis quintet between 1959 and 1963. But the name "Wynton," virtually an honorific title to Ellis, didn't particularly excite his son. He and Branford gravitated instead toward rock, rhythm and blues, and funk—pop music was more enticing than jazz.

Wynton made no move to practice the trumpet assiduously. Music was not his main thing. He preferred playing sports. And it was fun to try to pattern himself after his brother Branford. When Wynton was very young, he particularly looked up to his elder brother.

"I heard Branford talking, and so I started talking. I learned to talk from Branford . . . I liked hanging with Branford. So it wasn't like I had to be with him. I liked to be with him. We did a lot of stuff together. You know, we rode our bikes together, all over the city. We lived in the same room. We both played music."

Branford would reflect, "The thing I remember most about being a child was being a child. I did not sit down as a twelve-year-old or four-teen-year-old the way I do as a thirty-eight-year-old [in 1998] and intel-lectually dissect my relationship with my brother and others around me. Children have a tendency to be very, very forgiving and accepting, which is why it's so easy to abuse them, because they don't have any standards by which to judge that kind of shit. So there was a decided lack of intel-lectual and emotional sophistication in our relationship. That made it great, because we just did what we did without even thinking about any . . . ramifications. We did crazy things. And we always did things together."

When the Marsalis family moved back to Kenner, to 329 Webster Street, after returning from Breaux Bridge, the boys went to Our Lady of Perpetual Help Catholic elementary school. Ellis had been raised in an African Methodist Episcopalian church, but his wife was Catholic, and the children were raised as Catholics. Their yellowish brick house, Ellis would recall, wasn't a big place; it was built on concrete slabs, with no cellar, after the Second World War. Later on, because of technology, houses could have cellars, but in those days, New Orleans houses didn't have them because of the high water level. Wynton's lasting memory of Kenner would be as a segregated town.

He would think of Delfeayo—and for that matter two more younger brothers to come—as his "little brother." Perhaps because Delfeayo was younger, his point of view on the family relationships may have differed from Wynton's. Delfeayo believed that Wynton had become jealous when Ellis III was born; Ellis III had the same impression. Little squabbles took place, possibly as a result of sibling rivalry.

Wynton commandeered Delfeayo, Delfeayo remembered, and they sometimes competed in sports against Branford and Ellis III. Also, Wynton and Branford teamed up and fought against Ellis III and Delfeayo: another configuration, another team. The younger boys remembered they did their share of screaming, when they got hurt by their elders. In short, there was plenty of commotion in the house among the brothers, all so close in age.

It sometimes seemed that, on principle or by instinct, each brother wanted to speak for himself about what he was like; they were individualists, Delfeayo and Ellis III said. Their mother was highly opinionated, and the brothers had no qualms about having their own opinions and asserting them. Delfeayo and Ellis III thought Wynton was a lot like their mother, even left-handed as she was. He might have looked more like his father with his open, calm, round face and direct way of regarding people, but there were times when traces of his mother's more intense expressions flitted across his face.

From the vantage point of maturity, Wynton explains: "Everybody has viewpoints. Everybody comes to his or her understanding of the world through a different system. There's a certain skill of observation. It requires you to remove yourself so you can clearly see and understand what's going on. That's what hurts a lot of our observations. Too much of our own aspirations get caught up in what we observe, and so we can't observe clearly. We're too caught up in what we're trying or striving to do."

Dolores recalled that she had brought Wynton and Branford to New Orleans often to listen to their father playing piano in the French Quarter on Sunday nights. "We would hang out," she said. "And I brought them to a lot of concerts, because their daddy always played concerts. And of course, they studied. Wynton started studying music at five, Branford at six, in a junior school of music at Xavier University. And I would bring Branford and Wynton there for two classes a week. One was with the regular teacher, the other was in composition or something like that. So they would understand the intricacies of music.

"By the time he was in the third grade, Wynton joined the school band, and he played in a lot of competitions. Every three months, the boys had to play in front of audiences, and that experience helped them develop poise and stage presence. I loved it, I was crazy about it," she recalled, though she didn't push them to do it, she said. "And I would do little things. I would sew covers for the pianos and make myself useful, do whatever the nuns asked me to do. So then I felt a part of everything."

Wynton recollected that his mother absolutely emphasized education, and neither she nor Ellis tried to push the children to play music or aim for greatness. "They went to Catholic schools," Dolores said. "We went to church every Sunday, and they were in the Boy Scouts, and in the little neighborhood group, the CYO group, a church group, for which they had to participate in the community to make it better in some way. I was very community oriented. The Boy Scouts did certain things to help out; they would do things for the elderly; they would visit the nursing homes around the holidays."

But Wynton, unlike his three brothers, refused to become an altar boy. His parents didn't really know why. Dolores didn't force him, she recalled; she just accepted his decision. Wynton later explained that he refused because, even though it wasn't done by law, the church was segregated. He recalled, "All the black people sat on the left side. And I wasn't into the philosophy of the religion. I thought it was too much anti-'other' people. I was only about eight or nine, and I felt that way then. I didn't feel that way for philosophical reasons. It's just that I felt it. I wasn't too much on going to church anyway, just for that reason. So I didn't really get indoctrinated into that. My mom and others weren't anti-other people. I don't remember it being that much of an issue. I just really didn't believe in a lot of it.

"I believed in Jesus. I believe in Jesus. But I believe that what was being taught about what Jesus said was inaccurate. I didn't have a reason to believe that. It was just that I believed that. So I didn't really follow religion too much, even though I liked the Bible readings and the teachings of Jesus. I can remember even when I was little, I categorized them. Some of them seemed like an advertisement for the religion. Those were the ones I didn't listen to. Others seemed like the truth, like something that was about humanity and about people. And I would kind of gravitate toward them.

"I liked the stories of the New Testament. Of course, in the Old Testament, the stories were much richer. But I liked the whole story of the New Testament—the idea of the sacrificial hero and of all these people working together. They don't really believe in it, but Jesus believes in it, and they sold him out. And he ends up getting killed. But he didn't really die.

"I was fascinated with the whole story, and all the people just scamming him, and he was really innocent. But they made him guilty, and then they persecuted him. And the man who persecuted him knew it was wrong to do it. But then he just washed his hands of it. Just the whole story was fascinating, the whole story of Judas. And Peter. Jesus tells Peter he's going to deny him. Peter says, 'I'm not going to deny you.' 'But you're going to deny me,' Jesus says. And then Peter denies him. But Jesus forgives him. There's one man out here saying all this, and nobody actually believes in it, but it's like a phenomenon. All the people lining up. He's healing now. All the people in power supposed to be in charge. They don't like him.

"The whole story itself is such a great story. It's so real, so human, you've got to believe it. It's so much what people are like. But then there are other parts of it that I couldn't really follow. Like Jesus saying you have to believe in me. What he's saying is nothing like that. He's telling people it's all about love. He's healing people. It's like he's taken aback when they say, 'You have to believe in me.'

"That's how I felt at that time, as a boy. Now I'm not really into religion like that. I'm not really into any religion as a religion," he stated. "I still believe in God, and I believe Jesus was on earth. But I believe there have been great prophets on earth. Everybody's religion is based on some truth, and there's a truth to the religion. I respect all people's religions. I think all people's religions have parts that are developmental and good, and parts that are polemic."

Branford agreed with Wynton that the church was essentially "a business," but Branford thought Wynton refused to become an altar boy because "he was a miscreant. He thought that shit was romantic. I won't say he was iconoclastic exactly, but he just loved being around . . . tough guys. I was scared of tough guys. I remember Wynton came home after baseball practice with a big black eye. The guys wanted his bike, and there was a fight. Wynton kept his bike. I would have just given them the bike. I was scared of these people."

There would be times when their mother would seem to pick on what Wynton said or did. Matters might be inconsequential, or Wynton and she might simply see things from different vantage points. One friend noticed Dolores wanted Wynton to help keep the house neater than he did. Another friend believed that Dolores was demanding of all her children.

Nevertheless, Wynton thought his mother was "real smart," with "a deep intuitive sense and feeling for basic qualities in people and in life." He knew that she was very "basic," and, although she didn't like to discuss the financial difficulties of her childhood, she never had "a hierarchical type of concept," Wynton said, meaning that she didn't think that anybody was inherently better than another person. She invested a lot of herself in her family. A tremendous amount of her time, intelligence, and effort went into raising her sons.

"She put a lot of herself into us, like women had to do in that time. Women like her would be so intelligent. Today they'd be working jobs. But at that time, they would have tremendous frustration, because their talents weren't being put in the type of environment that would showcase them and allow them to develop and stimulate their intelligence and their feeling. So they were relegated to their familiar situations, which they didn't like," Wynton said.

"None of those women liked it. That whole generation, not just her. She adjusted to it. She dealt with it, like everybody did. It's like anything you don't like but have to deal with. It's not like she didn't like it, so she fell apart. It's like any injustice, something you don't like. But that's what it is. Like, did Louis Armstrong like segregation? No, he didn't like it. But he adjusted to it. . . . You have to deal with it. Did Duke Ellington like it? No. But did he talk about it every day? No. He didn't let it ruin what life he was living. And my mother was the same way. It wasn't like every day you had to hear her talking about it. She never talked about it, really."

His mother stated absolutely that she had a job: She planned the meals; she took care of a big family. But Wynton said, "That's just a manifestation of that frustration, just how she would say that. But she didn't have that type of outlet [a job outside the house], and since she had that intelligence, she put all of that into her kids."

Not only Dolores but Ellis would say that Dolores had a big job. But that was a common view among people of their generation. In those days, women often valued the privilege of staying home and taking care of children while their husbands worked.

In any case, if Dolores had had any aspirations to work outside the house, she never mentioned them and didn't believe she had them; that was definite. She had no desire to go onstage, either. The very thought of having to go on a stage for a holiday theatrical production in her community, among her friends, made her "tremble," she said. Neither did she ever have any desire to push her children and make them feel they had to be great. She and Ellis "just wanted us to be educated. That's it. That was our family's main thing," Wynton said. "You have to be educated— and don't hang in the streets."

Dolores had a game plan for everyday life. She said, "You had to follow a schedule. You had to practice a half hour and then go out and play ball. We all ate together every morning and evening. Then you did your homework. Then you had an option to stay up and watch a TV show until maybe ten or ten-thirty." Later, she would reflect on what she had taught the boys, and how they turned out, and say to herself: "These are kids I raised? . . . Which proves that other systems have a great effect on people."

But Dolores "sort of" knew her sons would be special. "Wynton always wanted to take charge, and it had to go his way. He sort of wanted things the way he saw them. I didn't think that was very good, but there's nothing you can do about it. He did have leadership qualities. He could see how something should go, would go, and other kids would follow. . . . He was sort of like a leader. He was very good at competing. He always wanted to win." She thought that Branford was "a little more outgoing, a little more frivolous. He can go from one thing to the next, and he can enjoy himself."

In 1970 a fifth son was born, Mboya. "I was one of the first to know that something was wrong with him. But I was kind of teasing my mama," Wynton would recall. "'There's something wrong with that boy,' like a joke. But then actually something was wrong with him." At age two, Mboya was diagnosed with autism. "So it wasn't funny then. But we didn't really know what it was. We were kind of country people. He wasn't talking. He'd be walking on his tippy toes; he'd be hitting his head, banging his head into a wall. We didn't talk about it that much. He was just a trip. He'd throw his food down. We knew it affected our mother. But you couldn't really tell one way or another if it affected him."

Dolores tried to protect the other children from having to take care of Mboya with all his difficulties. She took on all the chores for the boy herself, and she decided to keep him home with her and not put him in an institution, where he surely would have been neglected, or even mistreated, and have a short life expectancy. Mboya was her child, too. She found a way to communicate with him, observed one of Wynton's friends, who visited the house. Wynton would later reflect that, though there was no way she could have protected the other children from the problem, he didn't think that Mboya's autism had any special effect on him. Wynton later stated: "Only certain kids have a certain sensitivity to really absorb something like that. Someone like me, I didn't have the sensitivity to absorb that."

But at about the time that the family learned of Mboya's autism, Wynton suddenly committed himself to practicing the trumpet. He could not remember a special event that made him devote himself body and mind to playing the trumpet. It was not that he suddenly decided to become a jazz trumpeter, although he began listening to jazz carefully, as well as to all kinds of music. He actually studied classical music, after falling in love with a recording by the great French trumpeter Maurice Andre.

In addition to classical music, Wynton listened intently to a song, probably the lyrical "Cousin Mary," played by the innovative jazz saxophonist John Coltrane on his album *Giant Steps*. Wynton played that record over and over again. He had chosen to sample that record from his father's collection because of its serious-looking, plain-spoken cover. Here was a case of being able to judge the music by its cover. Coltrane's music communicated an especially marked spirituality, a yearning, an upward, high-minded striving. Wynton, enamored of Coltrane's power, learned many of Coltrane's songs by ear from his recordings. He was swept along by Coltrane's emotionally engulfing music.

It was about this time that Wynton heard his father suggest to his mother that perhaps he should take a day job and give up his musical pursuits. It was Delores who urged her husband to continue to play. This level of commitment, despite the financial hardship it brought to the family, made a deep impression on the young trumpeter.

Wynton's friend, Victor Goines, suggests another reason that Wynton began to concentrate on the trumpet so intensely in his eighth-grade year. There was another trumpet player in the Catholic school De La Salle, with whom Wynton had "a lot of encounters musically. Perhaps just the competitiveness of music," Goines opined, "and wanting to be the best . . . made him totally serious about the trumpet.

"Maybe having to be in the company of someone always playing the trumpet with him—it probably was a battle or something similar to that—the old cutting contest mentality, a battle between two eighth-grade students. Wynton began to practice seriously. He would wake up in the mornings and practice before he went to school and many times afterward. I went by the house, and he was practicing. He put his time in—long hours as a teenager—at the time it was necessary. And that's what gives him the virtuosity."

For Wynton, there was no deep change that brought about his sudden musical interest. It "was just what I wanted to do. It was just something I could relate to," Wynton said. "It was fun. I mean, I would be dedicated to whatever I was doing. If I was playing ball, I wanted to be able to play well. Whatever it was, I wanted to do well; I didn't want to be sad. So if I had to practice to do it, I didn't mind doing it. I would practice. But it wasn't like I wanted to do it. I just liked to be able to do it. The deeper I got into it, the more I liked it.

"It wasn't like that with ball. It was fun, but at a certain point, it was boring. You could only get so deep into it. You could get deep into it, but not like into music. I mean, I am still trying to get into music. You can work on your game. It's always based on what other people are doing. You're competing against them. In music you're not competing against anybody. You're just playing."

Wynton's intense concentration on the trumpet did take him away from the nightmare of Mboya's affliction. Mboya's illness had to divert Dolores's attention from her other children to a degree. In a way, Mboya's problem might have created a window of opportunity for Wynton to pass through to start making his own way in the world, to have more autonomy over himself and play music, while his mother was occupied with the responsibility of her youngest son.

As a young teenager, Wynton began a lifelong habit of rarely taking the trumpet out of his mouth for long. When he did, he would miss the trumpet. "I always liked to practice," he reflected years later in an interview with a journalist. "So many things bother me. When I play, I'm relieved."[3]

Just when he fell in love with his trumpet, he discovered Melanie Marchand, his first girlfriend, who was about four months younger than he. Melanie's best friend, Dona Wright, knew Wynton because Dona's mother was friendly with Wynton's mother. Dona wanted Melanie to meet him. Somehow, Dona arranged for Melanie and Wynton to meet first by telephone. Melanie had many phone conversations with Wynton before they met face to face. She thought he was very intelligent and intense; he talked about jazz all the time, she recalled years later, and she believed he was already talking about Louis Armstrong, Thelonious Monk, even Clifford Brown and Art Blakey in those days. It's unlikely that he did mention those musicians at that time, because he barely knew anything about them. But for Melanie perhaps memory blended with hindsight. She herself had heard only of Armstrong. Sometimes in the middle of one of their telephone conversations, Wynton played his trumpet for her and asked her how she liked it.

Finally they met; he was probably still living in Kenner but visiting his grandfather in Carrollton. "He was walking down the street with a trumpet in his hand, and he was playing the trumpet," she recalled. "What I remember most is how he was dressed. He had on green jeans, flare leg and high water," she said about his short pants, "and cowboy boots. He was very thin. He came to my girlfriend Dona's house. We must have been outside playing. He had come to meet me. Branford was with him.

"We went to get some food at a fast food, hamburger place and then ice cream at a Baskin Robbins on Carrollton Avenue. We walked and talked and went back to Dona's house. I was so impressed with him that day." To Melanie, who wouldn't remember exactly what he said, he seemed, she would later say, "mature, intelligent, deep, disciplined, and intense."

Melanie had no experience with boys at that time. But she and Wynton went into Dona's backyard, where they decided they would kiss. Somehow they got their tongues involved. "And he had the audacity to say to me, 'You're going to have to learn to roll when you kiss because I roll when I kiss.' I was astounded. That was nothing I had ever experienced or thought about. I was taken completely off guard," she recalled. Later she thought it might have actually been his first kiss, too, because he didn't seem to know what he was doing, either. He scared her a bit with his dictate about kissing. "That was Wynton," she would reflect years later. "He is just going to tell you what is on his mind."

Melanie didn't speak to him much on the phone after that. She went to St. Mary's, an all-girls', all-black, Catholic high school, and Wynton went to De La Salle and then Ben Franklin high schools. She graduated second in her class. Wynton began making a mark for himself in music. She saw him playing in his funk band at various activities, including events at St. Mary's. But she didn't call him on the telephone again until they were sixteen years old, when she felt impelled to congratulate him for an award he had won.

As soon as it became clear that Wynton was in love with the instrument, Ellis found well-known New Orleans teachers for him, including John Longo, whom Wynton loved and appreciated, and John Hernandez. Longo played recordings for Wynton by the Chicago Symphony Orchestra and jazz trumpeter Clifford Brown. Fernandez advised Wynton to work on his triple tonguing.

Years later, when Gil Noble, host of ABC's *Like It Is*, asked Wynton, what made him decide to tackle music seriously, Wynton replied, "Well, first, I respected my father. . . . He always seemed like the coolest person in the world, because then, during that time, my father, he wasn't working that much, and he was having a hard time raising [the family with all the children].

". . . It was hard for him, because he's a very intellectually oriented person. He likes to talk about a lot of different subjects. He was very frustrated, because there wasn't that many people around who were interested in what he was talking about. . . . He was really in isolation. So he would talk to us."

At first Wynton didn't understand what Ellis was saying. But "I respected him. I didn't like that music necessarily, but he was cool . . . [and] he's one of the greatest teachers, because he doesn't judge you. He lets you know when you sound sad, but he . . . doesn't discourage you because you're sad. And he also doesn't give you the impression that you're doing something great while you sound terrible. So I looked up to him. . . . He just knew a lot about the world. . . . And he had a lot of books."[4]

When Ellis went to hear Wynton and Branford playing their pop music gigs, he supported them. Wynton recalled that he said, "'Yeah, man, you all sound nice.' . . . You know, he didn't complain [about their not playing jazz]."

Wynton's memories of his Catholic school days were less happy. Racial tensions bothered him. He and his friend, Gregory Carroll, were the only black kids in their class there. Although Wynton's mother would never understand why Wynton said the school was segregated, because technically it was integrated, Wynton understood the underlying reality of his situation. He always did well in classes, getting A's for marks. He noticed one of his great strengths was his talent for seeing how ideas and subjects related to one another. But the lingering atmosphere, if not the legality anymore, of racial segregation aggravated him.

One of Wynton's teachers, trying to make him "feel comfortable with an uncomfortable situation," Wynton recalled, made an allusion to race, thinking it was a friendly remark. But it actually served only to emphasize their racial difference. Wynton detested allusions to race and their implications. He found himself constantly having to defend himself in verbal and physical fights about race. Wynton said, "That's just what it was. That's just what it was. It couldn't have been nothing else. It was the South, 1970. People started integrating. This is how it was."

One very bad thing did happen in that school, he recalled. "I was cheated out of a type of academic award that I was supposed to have. The teacher didn't want a black person to have the top honor. They lowered my grade by a few points, whatever it took for me not to be first." He discovered the situation one day when he was in school after hours and looked at the ledger sheet that contained everyone's marks. His mark was the first. "Oh, now I shouldn't have been doing that, but I did do it," he said. He didn't suspect what he was going to find. Then he got the hurtful, angering shock.

"I told the teacher I knew, and that didn't make a difference," he recalled. "The teacher said the decision was based on more than just the grade. What are they going to say? That's just how stuff was. Then my other teachers—it depends on what you want to look at—a lot of my other teachers didn't want to do that. It always depends upon what you want to look at. All kinds of stuff happen to you, the bad and the good, when you're young and when you're old. That's just life.

"Just like on the block where I lived, all that crazy shit that was happening. A woman killed her husband. A man impregnated his daughter. Dudes were selling dope. A cat was drunk out in the street, beating his wife every day. Another house had eight brothers, and seven of them got killed . . . by different people along the way. That's just life. We didn't live in no fairy tale. . . . You just did what you could do. You just had to defend yourself.

"Now, if you didn't defend yourself, you would just get walked over. That's something you had to learn early. There would always come a time when you had to say no, I'm not taking this shit. But it wasn't a big deal. . . . It isn't even that you have to be strong. That's just life. That's just how you live. You know it's not good . . . but that's just a part of what goes on . . . that's just how it was."

<hr>

When they were young teens, Wynton recalled that he and Branford were already playing little gigs in New Orleans—not jazz gigs, but pop, rock, and funk gigs, top 40 gigs—"stuff the girls liked." The music was so loud that after he finished playing at night, his ears rang until the gig the next night.[5]

In 1998 Branford recalled: "I made my father force Wynton to join this funk band I was in [The Creators]. Wynton didn't want to join. I didn't give a shit why. We needed the best trumpet player in the South in the band. He didn't want to join for the same reason he wouldn't join a funk band now. He thought it was bullshit then.

"I think a lot of times people hear Wynton talk and [think] that he arrives at [his] conclusions [because he's] looking for an angle, like a lot of politicians do. They come out and say, 'Okay, where is there an opening? Oh, populism is in? So let me be a raving lunatic conservative.' No. Wynton was always the way he is now. He thought pop music was bullshit then, and it was less bullshit then than it is now. He joined the band, but he actually had a good time [with the dance steps and horn parts] and met a lot of girls."

Their father was playing mainstream, modern jazz for audiences consisting of maybe 200 people, compared with 2,000 people in the audiences for Wynton and Branford.[6] It was not a great time to be a jazz musician. Wynton felt bad for his father and other jazz musicians who, he knew, had so much to give, but not many people wanted it. It was probably around this time that Wynton began to think about ways to shine more light on jazz.

Wynton and Branford brought home about $100 a night, more money from their packed clubs and well-attended gigs than Ellis did.

Wynton guessed their father might have earned $35 or $40 a night from a jazz gig. The brothers played together a lot in New Orleans, sometimes in garage bands, which were so called because the musicians, who played for dances, practiced in a garage.

"There was a bus that you had to take from New Orleans to Kenner," Wynton recalled. "If you missed the Kenner local bus, now that was a walk. It was through Metairie, redneck territory, and if you missed that bus, that was a long, long walk. Branford used to be saying to me, 'Do *not* miss the bus. Do *not* miss the bus.'"

CHAPTER NOTES

1. Howard Mandel, "The Wynton Marsalis Interview." *Down Beat*, July 1984.
2. Dick Russell, *Black Genius and the American Experience*. New York: Carroll & Graf, 1998.
3. Leslie Gourse, "Portrait of a Young Jazz Master." *Pulse!*, June 1985.
4. *Like It Is*, interview with Gil Noble, ABC-TV, New York, November 15, 1992.
5. *Piano Jazz*, interview with Marian McPartland, recorded on January 11, 1995, broadcast for the first time on January 6, 1996.
6. *60 Minutes*, interview with Ed Bradley, CBS-TV, broadcast on November 26, 1995.

IN NEW ORLEANS

W hen Wynton finished seventh grade and Branford the eighth in Kenner, their mother decided the two of them would travel together to De La Salle Catholic High School in New Orleans. Wynton was unaware of his mother's plan; he just thought that it was natural for Branford and him to attend the same school. But Dolores recalled taking deliberate action. "Branford and Wynton were always together, and later Delfeayo and Ellis were always together. They had to go together, for safety reasons, when I couldn't be there. You can't be everywhere your children are. We were raised that you were a family and part of your family. I was raised that way. They were close, and they loved one another."[1]

At first they commuted to school from Kenner. But by their second year in high school, the family moved to a modest house that Ellis's father owned and put up for sale, at 8318 Hickory Street in Carrollton, an essentially African-American neighborhood in uptown New Orleans. That year, Branford and Wynton switched together to Benjamin Franklin High School, a public school, so that they could attend NOCCA, where their father taught, in the afternoons. The Catholic high school frowned upon NOCCA or anything else offered in public school, Ellis recalled. The Marsalis brothers wanted to go to NOCCA very much.

In his sophomore year, Wynton was one of the winners of a concerto competition. It was the second time that an African American had been a winner in that competition. (Flutist Kent Jordan had been the first.) It led to Wynton's performing one movement of the Haydn Trumpet Concerto with the New Orleans Philharmonic. At the time he was studying with Norman Smith, who played trumpet with that orchestra. Smith also played in the Mostly Mozart concerts in New York.

When Wynton was going into his junior year, he met the man who would become his principal trumpet teacher in New Orleans, George Jansen. Victor Goines recalled that Jansen taught Wynton a great deal about the beauties and capacities of the trumpet and the discipline for playing it. "Jansen was a military man and a great disciplinarian," Victor said. "By the time he taught Wynton, Jansen was paralyzed, and he wasn't playing his horn. Not only did Wynton study with him, but later so did Kent Jordan's younger brother, Marlon Jordan, and Terence Blanchard," two more excellent trumpet players developing in New Orleans.

While in his senior year in high school, Wynton began playing with the New Orleans Philharmonic Symphony brass quintet as well as in the New Orleans Civic Orchestra. Terence Blanchard followed Wynton into that orchestra.

Wynton was playing a lot, doing a lot of gigs, and probably getting different recommendations and suggestions about how to improve his performance of classical music, Victor Goines recalled. "But he played all kinds of music, for example brass band gigs with Doc Pauline. And Wynton played with Willie Metcalfe, who had a little forum at the YMCA once a week. Wynton and Branford told me about it. Any time at all Wynton could play his horn, he took advantage of it." By the time he was sixteen, he had performed the "Brandenburg" Concerto No. 2 in F Major with the New Orleans Philharmonic Orchestra.

Wynton would later tell how difficult it was for him to immerse himself in European classical music. He recalled that he didn't like classical music when he first heard it: "Because I thought it was something white people did. So my level of understanding of what it was in relation to me was skewed by prejudice. Now, once I sat in the orchestra and had to listen to it every night, I still was prejudiced against it. But just—I had to succumb to the greatness of the music. I didn't want to. I wanted to remain ignorant of it. Because you know everybody I hung with, 'That's classical music, that's corny.'"[2]

Wynton was the only black person in the New Orleans Civic Orchestra. So he recruited a friend, Larry Dillon, another trumpet player—"because I didn't want to be in the orchestra alone," Wynton recalled.

Larry, about three years older than Wynton, became an especially close friend once they began to attend NOCCA together. Larry signed up for the jazz curriculum, and Wynton studied in the European classical section—not in his father's jazz section. "Because he said he could learn jazz at home," Larry recalled, "so why take it from his dad at school?"

Wynton convinced Larry to switch to the classical section. Larry eventually did, in part to please Wynton and also because he wanted a strong theoretical base in European classical music. "Then we hung all the time, day in and day out. We played in the civic orchestra at the Jewish Community Center. We'd get to NOCCA early and practice, sight-reading or whatever we were were working on, and hang out. We played together."

They simply liked each other, Larry reflected: "I'm laid back, easy-going, sensitive, and he's not so laid back. We had a lot of things in common, sports and music. I can't remember us really having a serious argument other than talking trash. He didn't really brag about his horn, but he might say: 'I can talk to women better, I can play basketball better than you, I know more about this or that.' Anything that came up, he would have something to say about it. And he's still like that," Larry said with a little laugh many years later. "We just always got along."

They got along so well with each other's families that Wynton's mother said Larry and Wynton seemed like brothers. Eventually Larry's brother Matt, who also played music, would become Wynton's road manager for four years. He then became involved with the Wynton Marsalis Foundation set up by Wynton to promote music and education for kids in New Orleans.

Larry recalled a telling incident at NOCCA. One professor told the class that they had a problem with sight-reading because they didn't know all their scales. On a Friday, he threatened the whole class with expulsion if the budding musicians didn't learn them—"all twelve scales in the major scales, minor, and harmonic minor and melodic minor, at least two octaves"—by the following Monday.

"Of course, everybody knew them on Monday. But Wynton played them as though he *always* knew them. When we got to class, the teacher didn't ask us to play the scales. I was so bored and tired of practicing. I asked Wynton, 'Aren't you tired?' He said, 'Yeah.' I said, 'What do you do?' He said, 'I just keep practicing.' He loved what he was doing. He had made up his mind to start practicing constantly during the summer after his eighth-grade year," Larry recalled.

Wynton made money by playing gigs and spent it on horns, different kinds of horns costing several hundred dollars apiece: a fluegelhorn, a piccolo trumpet, and many others. He didn't spend money on clothes. "He would be the only one in the whole Civic Orchestra with a blue shirt on," Larry remembered. Wynton played first trumpet in that orchestra, and Larry played second trumpet. "I think it was his only shirt. Everyone else had on a white shirt. He wore brown earth shoes, while everyone else wore polished black shoes. He put all his money toward trumpets and music," Larry said.

Through hard work and dedication, Wynton came to have his own understanding of classical music. And he came to admire the composers who created the music. Just as certain Bible stories had inspired him, the stories of the lives of classical musicians and how they created their work clearly influenced his continued dedication to playing classical music: "Mozart went into . . . the Vatican, and there were these . . . sacred pieces that you couldn't even take a copy of the music home, pieces for six voices . . . moving in counterpoint. . . . And Mozart went into the Vatican once and heard this piece and went home and wrote the whole thing out and went back, because he made one or two mistakes from memory. And, you know, to have to deal with six voices moving in a big, echoing cathedral, I mean . . . those are great achievements in music, man."[3]

Besides learning these stories, Wynton learned a lot about classical music theory, which would also stand him in good stead when he began composing himself. In the early 1980s, he described the evolution of classical composition to a radio interviewer: "Bach is the foundation of the modern systems of harmony, up to Schoenberg. Even in music like Debussy's and . . . Wagner's, where they use a lot of diminished chords and they're always moving sounds, modernistic type of sounds, you can find all of that in Bach. . . . Bach's music has a certain harmonic balance."

Nobody can beat Bach for "really, truly addressing the fundamental propositions of the craft of composition. . . . [T]hat means the ability to write the counterpoint, fugue, have command of different moods, write for different instruments, deal with the voice and the ensemble and an antiphonal conception, conception of orchestral writing, how to space the orchestra and deal with the actual sounds of the various instruments, and also his conception of form. Something like the Mass in B Minor, [these] big, humongous pieces that he would write, they're just so well balanced and so well constructed and composed. . . . You know, like, the bigger a piece you deal with, the harder it is to balance it."

Typically, Wynton thinks of a metaphor—constructing a building—to describe Bach's achievement. "So, I mean, he's just a master of construction. The more you're dealing with, the bigger the bridge, the more complex the problems are going to be, because you have to deal with putting a gigantic building up. You have to go way into the ground, and you have structural problems that you don't have with a smaller building. . . ."[4]

Wynton then selected a typical New Orleans activity—cooking gumbo, with all the different spices and ingredients that can go into it—to use as a second metaphor for Bach's achievement. "Composition is the same way. You have certain elements that you deal with—melody, harmony, rhythm, and texture—and you take those four elements and you manipulate them. Sometimes it's the melody, sometimes it's the harmony. And you change them around and you play with them. And you organize those elements in different ways. It's like playing; it's like a game."

Wynton went on to demonstrate, by playing simple melodies on his trumpet and adding voices to them, how Bach wrote simple four-part chorale music and was a master of writing fugues—four separate lines moving at the same time. "And all the composers after him bowed to him."[5]

By playing classical music, Wynton went against the musical tastes of many of his friends. Everybody in his neighborhood, he said, liked popular music, "which was really cool for what we were doing. But we just weren't really curious about that other stuff. . . . You'd say you play classical music, man, and they'd laugh in your face. Classical music, man, give me a dollar."

Wynton would grow up to try to battle narrowmindedness of any kind that kept people "away from education and away from absorbing information," he said. Sometimes he had to broaden his own horizons. He didn't believe that ignorance was a valid form of protest, and he became outspoken against insularity.

———⟫●⟪———

In the summers after his sophomore and junior years, when he was fifteen and sixteen, Wynton auditioned and went on scholarships to the Eastern Music Festival, a classical festival, in North Carolina. Ellis thought that a flutist named Richard Harrison in New Orleans may have been responsible for Wynton's getting the opportunity to audition for the festival, esentially a professional training camp.

"I always got scholarships. We didn't have a lot of money, so I got scholarships to everything," Wynton recalled. "I was basically good in everything in school. I would do homework, but it depended upon what my attention span was at that time. If I really wanted to do good, I did. My main strength was integrating the material, seeing how things related to everything else. I always liked the way math, language, and science relate to each other.

"It was a very positive experience to go to the Eastern Music Festival," Wynton would reflect years later. "I learned a lot and had a chance to be around other students. We were just playing mainly classical music. Also there were some teachers who played jazz, and I would play with them. Joe Thayer, dean of the school, now dean of a school in Los Angeles, was just a positive influence. I try to go back there every summer, and I set up scholarships there myself."

At the Eastern Music Festival, about half of the attendees were students, the rest professional musicians, Ellis said. The students sat next to the professionals and really learned. He didn't notice Wynton's progress every day, but he did notice it over a long period of time.

Ellis had only one criticism of his devoted, gifted son. Wynton could be very bossy. In the brass quartet at NOCCA—which Ellis called Wynton's brass quartet, because Wynton was its leader—"he was jumping on these kids. One of my colleagues didn't think [it was a problem]." Wynton was just trying to make the music as good as it could possibly be. That bossiness other people would call self-confidence. Beginning at this time and continuing throughout his life, this trait—whether people called it bossiness or self-confidence—became marked. Some people loved it and could benefit and be inspired by it; others found it annoying and fought it.

Donald Harrison, an alto saxophonist whose path would cross Wynton's repeatedly both in New Orleans and later in New York, met Wynton first in the jazz ensemble at NOCCA, where Donald played with Ellis, Branford, Wynton, bassist Anthony Hamilton, and a drummer. Harrison recalled, "Wynton and I always seemed to be doing the opposite things, or think that the opposite things were important. I never felt that Wynton accepted me, even in those high school years. I guess I had a mind to do what was important for me and to play the way I wanted to play. And Wynton always had an idea of what he should be doing and what everyone else should be doing. He felt he had the inside track on other people's lives. It was past bossiness. What he thought was important was the only thing."

There wasn't a feeling of tension between them, Donald said, but "I always felt he didn't accept me. If I said this is what I think is important, he would say, 'No, it is not important, and this is important,' and 'This is the way and that's it.' I think he has always been that way."

With hindsight, years later in New York, Harrison would also say, "Musically, we're on different ends of the spectrum; we're like two religions, two different ways of doing it. His way of doing it I applaud. I think that jazz is about that. One guy does it this way, and another guy does it that way. The only problem I've had with Wynton is he doesn't realize that his opinion isn't the only opinion, but once you get past that, everything is hunky-dory. He has to realize that one person can't do it all. It takes all of us. He's very important, too. Sometimes when record companies give you so much, you don't have to think about those things, being fair, and that everybody is important."

It is probably true that most creative people, particularly those who can focus their energies and marshal their talents and abilities into successful careers, block out elements that do not serve their own artistic purposes directly. The more renowned an artist becomes, the more his or her drive and methods of operating are scrutinized. Gifted people are always criticized. Nobody clamors for attention from starving artists, who are sometimes dismissed as simply selfish. But everyone wants the acknowledgment of a successful artist. Harrison would have a lot of company in his view of Wynton as opinionated as time went by.

Harrison, however, thought Wynton was "on target" in certain ways. "He was very studious. He worked very hard and diligently. I think his work ethic is something other people can really learn from."

Everyone who knew Wynton agreed on his indisputable focus and capacity for hard work.

Victor Goines had no objections to Wynton's leadership qualities. Both Wynton and Branford influenced Victor. When he played in the public high school jazz ensemble with the brothers, they introduced Victor to John Coltrane's music. Coltrane became Victor's saxophone inspiration. "Wynton had in the fake book the written solo to 'Countdown,' and Wynton could play that on his trumpet when he was fifteen," Victor recalled. "For him to be technically able to do that was just phenomenal. I had never heard anyone play sax like Coltrane. And then Wynton could articulate the sax solo on trumpet. I hadn't heard anyone do that. So he was really crucial in exposing me to the giants of jazz long before he ever thought about anything he would be dealing with later in his life."

Victor also noticed something else about Wynton: He always was attractive to girls. For some reason that Wynton never understood, girls did seem to like him. He was not the only talented musician in his high school. Adults saw him as a skinny kid. But he had plenty of girlfriends. Playing in the funk band, The Creators, between the ages of twelve and sixteen, Wynton attracted many girls.

Wynton would later try to analyze his appeal. The songs the band played had lyrics that said, "Ooh, baby, come make love to me." And that's what a funk band is for, Wynton said. "That's the job, and you do it every night. Of course I had women. You had to try to not have women, if you were playing in a funk band." He played in one nearly the entire time he was in high school. "That's the major thing we did in high school," playing at such places as the Dream Place and Caesar's East, in the sultry, sexy ambience of the New Orleans nights.

Larry Dillon, too, noticed that girls liked Wynton. "He could play the horn and get respect from a lot of people. He was asked to sit in or substitute often at the annual Jazz and Heritage Festival in town. He was invited to play on albums with local groups. He started to get a name, and that plus his good looks and personal charm and the gift of gab—when you have those things, you can talk your way into a whole lot of stuff. There were young girls and older girls around him. Some older girls in the Civic Orchestra tried to talk to him, and some college girls, too, when he was in high school."

When Larry played with Wynton in the Civic Orchestra, Wynton used to bring his homework along. "When we rehearsed, with all those string pieces, we did a lot of counting measures, playing our little pieces here and there. And he would do his school reports, big reports. I would do the counting for him while he was writing his reports. So he wouldn't miss the beat," Dillon said.

Noticing that one musician got fired from a gig, Larry thought that would never happen to Wynton, because he was such a good, articulate musician. Larry thought Wynton would say that he would never get fired because he got so much respect. But Wynton said he didn't have any problems because he always showed up on time, prepared to do whatever they wanted him to do, down to the letter of the contract. Larry learned a lesson: Just go in there and take care of business, and you'll have respect. Wynton didn't think that anybody owed him anything.

As coolly analytical and focused on music as Wynton could be, he could also shock people with his anger, his hotheadedness, some people would call it. Larry remembered a day when they got out of school early and headed to Wynton's house to practice for the Civic Orchestra. They got hungry and went to get some po'boy sandwiches. On the way back to Wynton's house, two white cops stopped them and asked what the youngsters were doing out of school during the day.

"We had the good cop, mean cop duo," Larry recalled. "Mine was cool, and the other one—I heard Wynton yelling at this other cop. I looked over at them. I thought they were going to fight. But the partner realized we were cool. The cops walked away. I had to grab Wynton. I don't know what the guy said, but Wynton wanted to go back and punch that guy."

Wynton would not have been saved, nor did he ever get special respect, because his name was Marsalis. As Ellis said, "There was no situation that I would have been aware of. The group of people with whom I was connected peer-wise, all people like me, were playing gigs on Bourbon Street." Wynton simply had uncommon nerve or courage or volatility—or all those qualities.

———————

Ellis was a well-beloved teacher, who never talked down to students. Wynton liked to wait for his father to come home at night after gigs so they could talk about music. Ellis had an unhurried and seemingly relaxed way of speaking, even though it was obvious that he had developed his ideas through rugged experiences, intense thought, and concentration.

And he was a mesmerizing speaker. Branford and Wynton would always admire the way their father talked to children.

Ellis realized that he talked to his kids as well as to students as if they were grown-ups. He didn't know how else to speak to them. He hadn't had an easy time growing up. Life was about using his head, doing his very best, and surviving, he had always thought. And survival wasn't about babbling and having good times. A black child in the South didn't have that luxury, if indeed anybody really did. And he had always been a black man in the South; even when he was a child, he had been preparing himself for survival as a black man. He had a great dignity and smouldering pride in himself and his devotion to music. There was absolutely nothing in the world that he would rather do than play. It was that ethic, character, and courage that he imparted to Wynton and that Wynton loved to hear about.

Ellis encouraged his students—and anyone else who asked him—to learn about the roots of New Orleans music and jazz. "You really want to know the best books about the history of New Orleans music?" he asked a journalist who was trying to interview Ellis about his own career. "Read *Bourbon Street Black* by Danny Barker [a great banjoist and guitarist] and *The Autobiography of George (Pops) Foster* [the bassist], and *Satchmo* by Louis Armstrong. There's another book put out by the Louisiana State University Press, written about the big race riot in New Orleans in 1900. And Cousin Joe published a book." Cousin Joe, or Pleasant Joseph, an oldtime New Orleans blues singer-pianist-lyricist, was an engaging storyteller, who wrote a book including the raw details of his tumultuous family life.

As Ellis rapped about the contents of those books, it became clear that his conversation paralleled his method of teaching. He reached out and preached to music students and turned the talented ones into high-energy super-achievers. Ellis's talents gave them direction and in some cases self-confidence in life as well as support and information about their musical performances.

Of the kids he saw in school five days a week, Ellis said, "Some had a little discipline; some had more; some were disciplined but needed direction. I needed the right approach. It was close to trial and error. Every case was individual. As time went on, I was able to do some documentation." That is, he learned by experience what to expect from new students and what they needed. "But mostly it was all experimentation.

Most times you start from scratch. And what I do depends upon how much time I have with a kid, and if the kid has interest."

As part of his resources as a musician and a teacher, Ellis had a relentless curiosity and deep respect for New Orleans, which he regarded as "a mysterious city—different from any other city in the United States." It was an analysis that any visitor could begin to guess at from the foreign patina of the French Quarter and the lushness and even a dash of eeriness in other parts of town. There is nothing more haunted-looking than a building where slaves once lived—and there are such residences in New Orleans.

"If I'm going to be objective about it," Ellis said, "New Orleans is really like a Caribbean town. The strong culture is a poor people's culture and extremely visible. At different times through the year, you see things like a Second Line, which has to do with an old black tradition." And he began teaching the journalist about the Second Line. "When the bands came back from the cemetery, when they were a respectable distance from the gravesite, they struck up a happy tune to 'rejoice when one passes,' in the true sense of Christianity." Not only did the family and friends of the dead join in, but strangers along the route did, too. Louis Armstrong did it all the time. "They were the Second Line. And there's a Second Line for all kinds of events in New Orleans now. I always tell my students about the Second Line, about history. There's even a song called 'The Second Line,' which was first called 'Joe Avery's Blues.'"

Ellis speculated that the somewhat exotic culture of New Orleans had a lot to do with its strategic location on the commercially preeminent Mississippi. "New Orleans benefited culturally; there's a lot of mystery to it," he said. Once he asked a student who had been born in St. Louis: "What's happening in St. Louis? How was it affected culturally by the river?" The student couldn't answer. He was just a kid, Ellis said.

Ellis, who realized that he wasn't an anthropologist, a historian, or an ethnomusicologist and who knew that all of the academicians asked themselves questions that led to five more questions, continued his private, intriguing speculations about the mystery of New Orleans and its music.[6]

Talent was another mystery that Ellis mulled over as part of his daily life. He concluded: "Talent is one of the biggest lies ever perpetrated. Talent is like the battery in an automobile. If you don't have a generator, you ain't going to go very far. . . . When hard work meets opportunity, that's when you get some degree of success."

Success is based only in part on the talent a person has. "There are people walking around who don't even *know* they have musical talent. Talent is mistaken for the thing that it takes for people to achieve exterior success. About those who achieve that, win awards, and get a lot of press, people always say, 'They're so talented.' But too many people are called musicians and composers when they're not, when they have little or no talent."

With such iconoclastic conclusions and fortifying principles to share, Ellis went to NOCCA to inspire his students to think about what they were doing, so that they would work seriously to become musicians—or whatever they wanted to become. At home, he treated his children to similar ruminations.

Wynton recalled that late one night, he discussed a gig with his father. "It was a sad gig. Not that many people were there. It didn't sound good," Wynton said.

"See how that is?" Ellis said. "That's how it always is. If you want to play, that's how you have to want to play. This gig here, this is every gig. This gig we just played—that's every gig, and that's really what it is. It can be a gig where the people are cheering and screaming, or it can be this gig right here."

In essence, Wynton learned from his father that if he didn't like the conditions of work, he should stop playing. "Because that's every gig, because this is exactly like the gig when you celebrate," Wynton understood from Ellis.

"My daddy gave me a tremendous amount of advice, a wealth of it. I was fortunate to be around him, because he's not emotional. . . . He talks to you like you're a man the whole time. He had these little sayings that were profound and funny, and he would drop them on you anytime. And I would laugh. My father is nonjudgmental. He don't judge people; he's not hierarchical in his thinking; he doesn't respect people because they have money; he treats everybody the same. That's just what he is. He's a jazz musician, and he loves being a jazz musician, too. Nobody loves being a jazz musician more than he does.

"He's different now. He's older," Wynton said in 1998. "When I was younger, I hung with him, and so I knew what he was like. I was with him much more than my brothers. I liked to be around him, because he was so cool. He would just tell you what something is; he wasn't going to coat it with sugar or bullshit. It was just going to be what it was."

In his own book, *Sweet Swing Blues on the Road*, written many years after his childhood ended, Wynton recounted some other words of wisdom his father tossed off naturally and constantly: "If you're going to get beat up, you might as well fight" was one of the striking maxims.[7] Victor Goines remembered that Ellis taught everyone and everything "who came through that part of town" in the 1970s.

"If you stood around Ellis and had your ears open and wanted to learn, you would learn something," Victor said. Like Wynton and many others, Victor knew that Ellis was always going to tell him the truth. He might not like it, or it might be harsh, but the teacher was a very direct person.

Ellis always made it clear that he was against the idea of a person finding something to fall back on. "He believes in doing what you want. You go for it," Goines learned. Wynton would say exactly the same thing, and so would several others who studied with Ellis. Victor knew that Ellis had gone through many hard times just because he took his own advice; he focused completely and persisted in doing what he loved to do.

Wynton would later be annoyed and amazed that people liked to say he came from some sort of jazz dynasty, with special advantages as the son of a well-known pianist. That was not the case at all. Besides doing his work around town, Ellis made a few recordings, including some for a label called A.F.O., All For One, along with other fine New Orleans musicians, and also played on a date with Nat and Cannonball Adderley. They were excellent recordings, but they certainly didn't help Ellis establish a big-time career.

Wynton may have met well-known jazz musicians who passed through town. They would visit the Marsalis family's music room in the plain Carrollton house to jam with Ellis. That was the only advantage, if anything was, that Wynton had over other young musicians.

It was true that Ellis knew many musicians and other people in and around the music world in his hometown. He knew the district attorney; the DA's son, Harry Connick, Jr., studied with Ellis. But he also knew motherless and fatherless students entrusted to his care. Ellis, by his example, won the respect of his students and their families. That was the source of his influence.

———⟶●⟵———

In Wynton's senior year in high school, Branford went off to college, first to Southern University at Baton Rouge, then to the Berklee College of

Music in Boston. Wynton missed him terribly. Branford had liked to keep the radio playing in the room they shared when he went to sleep. Wynton could never fall asleep when music was playing. With Branford gone, Wynton could sleep whenever he pleased. But he didn't enjoy the privilege and discovered he didn't really like to sleep a lot.

He and Branford had played music very well together, with a special communion, Wynton recalled: "We worked on playing together all the time. When we were in high school and when we first went to New York, we really played good together. Branford has quick reflexes and can hear real good, and we knew each other's playing. He was always in tune; he would learn music real fast. And it was always easy to play with him, because he's such a great musician."

On the other hand, Branford had felt a great deal of pressure, particularly from his mother, to be a role model for his brothers. He would later reflect on his relations with his family: "I had five brothers, and I was trying to live," he recalled. Asked if it had been difficult to be the eldest in the family, he said, "It was just difficult to be in our family. I was like my mother. She is proud, extremely opinionated, really strong-minded, and stubborn. I'm all of that, too. And she raised me to be her. . . . She raised me to be strong willed and opinionated . . . and one of the things I categorically rejected at an early age was that I was somehow responsible for the actions of my brothers. . . . I'm sorry, that's ridiculous. We are all very different and unique people.

"My brother Ellis used to sit down at the dinner table and would only eat pancakes that were white. So he would aways have to have the first ones off the griddle. Is that my fault? He would only eat bean juice. He wouldn't eat the red beans. Am I responsible for that? So everybody comes here with his own little things. I'm responsible for me, and I'm going to do what I want to do.

"So it wasn't tough being the eldest brother, because I was doing my thing. It was tough being in that family. That's the kind of family that either makes you strong or drives you to alcoholism. . . . It made us all strong."

Branford continued, drawing a distinction between his mother's toughness and those who just believed in achievement for achievement's sake: "It's a lot better than some of those traditional, strong-willed families because it wasn't the kind of family where my parents said you have to make the honor roll or you're a failure. They said you have to do the best you can do, or you're a failure. If the best you can do is a C, then you've done the best you can do. Like in history and English classes, I was goofing off. My mother was riding me. . . .

"[But] in biology I made an F, and I studied the shit two hours a day, two hours a day. She could see I was trying. I made this F. I was devastated. She said, 'Child, don't worry about it. You just can't do biology. Just go to summer school and get it over with.' That's the difference between this family and other demanding families, where other families would have said, you failed the family, you made an F. She says if I had made an F in music, she would have kicked my ass."

Branford sees the Marsalis family as strong-willed people, who understand that they have to back up their opinions either with their actions or with substantial information. "It's a very argumentative family, and one of the things that I loved the most about my family, which has basically ruined a lot of relationships I've had with other people, was that my father would not tolerate an unsubstantiated opinion. Like, he wasn't really down with the present-day interpretation of the First Amendment. The right to free speech did not mean to him that you had the right to say whatever the hell you felt like saying. You have the right to an informed opinion. So whenever you expressed an opinion, he would say, 'All right, okay, justify it.' At first you were like, 'What do you mean, justify it?' And he would say, 'You're not going to sit at this dinner table and say ridiculous things like that without some sort of thesis. What is your thesis?'

"Having grown up like that, I can have horrible relationships with people to this day who are comfortable with the passive American idea of dialogue, which is: 'Just soothe each other with the sound of our voices and not really have a dialogue at all.' . . . The most important thing is to get your point across, and the way that it works is you have your opinion, and I have my opinion, and both opinions are valid, because I may not agree with what you say, but I will defend to the death your right to say it. . . . You have a right to say things, but I will not sit and indulge this ridiculousness. You have to support this [with something] other than [your saying] this is what you believe.

"And that's just the way I grew up. It would have been tough for a lot of people. It would have been tough for me had I grown up in another household, and then moved into it. But I was lucky enough to have grown up in it. I think that has helped me and Wynton, too, as musicians, because you have to have a justification for the shit that you play. I can't just get up and play whatever I feel. Feeling without knowledge is just feeling, not music."

Wynton also had a special affinity for Delfeayo. However, Wynton didn't have a close or warm relationship with his brother Ellis III when they were living under the same roof. Ellis III remembers that Wynton demanded that things go the way he wanted them to be. Ellis toyed with the guitar a little, but for the most part he decided to stay away from music.[8] He enjoyed sports and simpler activities, and he was the only one of the Marsalis sons to stress that he liked to write poetry for his own enjoyment; he grew up to major in business and law-related subjects and ended up running his own computer business. (Wynton, too, wrote poetry but didn't talk about it much.)

Larry Dillon recalled that Wynton "was real cool with [Mboya] and would sit down with him and hold him and hug him, make him laugh, be silly. He would always do that." Then there was another baby in the house. In 1977, when Wynton was already spending summers away at music camp and much of his time during the days and nights at school and at gigs, his youngest brother, Jason, was born. He would be only two years old when Wynton left home.

Dolores didn't really want Wynton to leave at all. She wanted him to go to college in Louisiana. Southeastern Louisiana University, one of her husband's alma maters, would have suited her very well, because she felt there were too many scavengers in New York City. Wynton was, in her opinion, just a country boy who didn't really belong in New York. "But I could not stop him," she would say years later. By that time he himself would reflect that he might have been too young to be in New York. In truth he would always have a strong attachment to the South.

But he had grown up in a family that had ingrained in him respectful manners, high standards, and a fiery commitment to improving himself. As soon as he finished high school in 1979, at age seventeen, he packed a box with a few pairs of pants and tapes and a stereo recorder. He didn't have a suitcase. He headed north to New York City with the intention of auditioning for Juilliard. That seemed to him to be the right direction. The slender, usually soft-spoken youngster had a trunkful of vision.

CHAPTER NOTES

1. Their father, too, thought that the boys were sent to high school together in a buddy system. So did Victor Goines, who went to high school with Wynton and played with him in the All State Orchestra.
2. *Like It Is*, interview with Gil Noble, ABC-TV, New York, November 15, 1992.
3. Ibid.
4. Ibid.
5. Ibid.
6. Years later, during a Latin music concert at Lincoln Center, Wynton would call New Orleans a Caribbean city. The audience laughed, thinking he was kidding.
7. Wynton Marsalis, *Sweet Swing Blues on the Road*. New York: W.W. Norton, 1994.
8. He would name one of his children Django, not for his love of the guitar but because he liked that song written by pianist John Lewis of the Modern Jazz Quartet and played by Ellis Marsalis, Jr.

WYNTON COMES NORTH

The sprawling performing arts complex of Lincoln Center that graces Ninth Avenue on Manhattan's West Side is a gleaming palace of the performing arts. It is made up of several buildings—the Metropolitan Opera House, with its glass facade set in geometrical patterns like a Joan Miró painting; the New York State Theater; and Avery Fisher Hall, with its great streamers of metal mobiles—all set back from a spacious plaza and fountain.

Juilliard, the renowned music school, is also part of Lincoln Center. Wynton went to the school to audition for admission and a scholarship. Seeing an announcement for scholarship auditions for the Tanglewood Music Festival at Lenox, Massachusetts, he decided to try for that, too. He could have a summer to practice and study with fine classical musicians.

One person on the admission committee for the Tanglewood festival was Gunther Schuller. A renowned French horn player, composer, writer about jazz and European classical music, and influential educator, Schuller was, for a while, president of the New England Conservatory in Boston. He listened to Wynton's audition at the Wellington Hotel. Wynton played everything the committee put in front of him, plus one of his own compositions.

"The most spectacular thing he played was excerpts from the *Brandenburg* Concerto No. 2, a famous trumpet piece, which no one in my twenty-two years at Tanglewood ever dared to play at an audition, because it's death," recalled Schuller about the piece with its very high notes, among its other challenges. "Nobody makes it. And he did. He played it flawlessly."

Schuller would later add to the story this colorful detail: Wynton warmed up for his audition by concealing "himself behind a pillar, so I leaned over to see what he was doing. He was pumping the valves and talking to his trumpet, saying, 'Now, don't let me down.'"[1]

About twenty years later, Wynton addressed the National Press Club. He spoke of the feeling a trumpeter had when he failed miserably at playing Bach's concerto, as if he knew that feeling personally. But he didn't. Unaware that he wasn't referring to himself, the audience laughed heartily, as co-conspirators. By then Wynton had developed a mighty, often self-deprecating sense of humor that he used like a leveling wind. "It was possible," he said, that he thought along those lines, but also, he said, "It's a distinct possibility to fail to play it and be one of many who failed." Though he hadn't failed, "You never know when you're going to fail. That's just a part of succeeding—failing. And it's not that big a deal. It's something to laugh about." You can pick yourself and go on tomorrow. "That's the beauty of it. That's how you succeeed."

The Tanglewood festival wasn't supposed to accept anyone under eighteen years old. But Gunther Schuller told his administrative colleagues running the auditions with him, "We're going to take this boy."

They reminded him of the age requirement.

"Well, if he was three and a half, I would take him. My God, a beautiful, young, fresh talent," Schuller said. Then, too, an original solo piece that Wynton played for the audition was "a perfect Third Stream piece"— a mixture of classical and jazz traditions, Schuller said. He soon heard other early pieces Wynton composed "that were wonderful. They were still allusions to earlier things. You know when you're young, you're influenced, you imitate. That's how you get started." Schuller became a mentor for Wynton at this stage, regarding the young trumpeter as "one of the most precious gifts this country ever got."

Wynton played jazz, too, and "was already spectacular, Miles Davis plus," Schuller said. He had nothing to do with Wynton's audition at Juilliard and wasn't exactly sure how it went. But it was clear to him that

Wynton could have just walked into Juilliard. "I am sure it was no big deal. I'm sure they must have been as amazed and taken with him as I was," he said. Wynton won a four-year scholarship to Juilliard.

The Tanglewood festival housed its scholarship students in Miss Hall's School, a prep school empty in the summer in Pittsfield, Massachusetts. It was a short ride away from the festival, with its hundreds of musicians and composers, in a pastoral, fresh-smelling area of rolling hills and dense trees that looked black in the sunset. Eiji Oue, then a conducting student from Japan, who was spending his second year in the United States—and who spoke very little English—noticed Wynton right away. Wynton played his horn constantly and seemed to want to learn everything. He was always asking questions about music, conducting, and life.

"His eyes observed everybody. People at Tanglewood have that attitude, a good attitude, discipline, and great pride to be part of the festival," said Eiji. "They're selected over thousands of students. Wynton just wanted to be there to learn and share and have the experience. He never said he was better than the others. He didn't care. . . . Very few students from that time [stand] out . . . so clearly in my memory. He was quite an extraordinary artist then already. Wynton doesn't have any pride. . . . Music is his joy, his passion.

"I was competing in my own way. He practiced twelve hours a day, so I started to study conducting fourteen hours. I didn't tell him that. But if he can do that, I can do more, I told myself."

The students stayed in small rooms with uncomfortable beds, Eiji recalled. His room was very dark, overlooking a building next door. The students had to take a school bus, which made five or six trips a day between Pittsfield and Tanglewood. After the concert at night, if they didn't make the bus back, they had to hitchhike to Pittsfield. Often Eiji, unwilling to miss anything but the bus, went backstage and talked to conductors and musicians, then walked back to Pittsfield several times; he supposed that Wynton did, too. "Maybe he could play his trumpet on the way back," Eiji theorized. Wynton didn't remember if he ever walked; however, the hike would have been nothing like the one he had feared through Metairie—he recalled that much.

A charming storyteller, Eiji, who later became the music director of the Minnesota Orchestra, had a vivid memory of Wynton "blowing, blowing, oh my God, he made me upset, mad sometimes. He played the same thing over and over and over. One night I'm dreaming, and screaming in my dream, 'Wrong note!' I believe it was a Stravinsky piece called 'Petroushka.' He had to practice the solos, and sometimes they were difficult. He practiced at five and six A.M. I'm screaming in my dream and wake up."

But Eiji was grateful that he heard great music around him every day. He would come to believe that his standards for his trumpet sections became very high because he listened to people like Wynton.

Wynton's best friend at Tanglewood was Justin Cohen, a trumpeter from Buffalo, New York, who was getting set to return to Juilliard for his sophomore year in the fall. Justin, who had the room next to Wynton's at Miss Hall's School, knew that Wynton practiced all night. "Like most great musicians, he practiced until he got it perfect," Justin said. "Then he played a piece over and over the right way to reinforce it. One day we were going to read 'The Rite of Spring.' He practiced the piccolo trumpet part over and over." Anyone who plays the trumpet very well has worked hard at it, Justin realized. "If you hear someone play great, you know he worked hard."

Wynton would later respond, when asked if there was a wrong way to practice, "Yes, because when you're practicing you have to focus and concentrate. You have to know what your objectives are. . . . A lot of practice is very intellectual. You have to know what you want to achieve. You can't really practice your personality. You can't practice the life aspect of music. You practice the technique of music. The life of music is the life that you live, and you are developing the technique so that you can give life, in your art form, to your conception about life. . . .

"I always say that technique is the first sign of morality in a musician, or in any field. If a person lacks technique, to me it shows me that [he] . . . [is] not on the highest level of moral engagement with [his] form. Because you don't have to have technique to make a statement that's powerful. But to make a great statement, you have to have technique. That's what makes Louis Armstrong who he is, and Duke Ellington, Lester Young, Coleman Hawkins, Bud Powell, Thelonious Monk, Art Tatum, Billie Holiday. That's a long roll call. Mahalia Jackson, Art Blakey, Max Roach. These are people with that technique."[2]

At the time Wynton and Justin were at the Tanglewood Music Festival (then called the Berkshire Music Center), they had opportunities to play in an orchestra and give weekly pops and jazz concerts. The

Boston Symphony played a separate program on weekends. Scholarship students went to the concerts and studied with the musicians in the orchestra. Armando Ghitalla, then in his last year in the first trumpet seat, coached both Wynton and Justin. In their free time, Wynton talked to Justin a lot about the racial situation in America.

"He was African American, I was Jewish, and I had never met anybody before who talked a lot about race," Justin said. "We talked about the differences in what we had experienced in America. For me it was great to talk about anything with him, and besides, we could play together. And what the hell did I know, growing up in the suburbs of Buffalo, about being African American in this country? He shared with me and told me what it was like. He made me aware of it. . . . And it wasn't the legal segregation. It was the way people look at you when you're in a store. It happened. He called my attention to it in a store in the fall when we went to New York. It was great to have my eyes opened [to] the prejudice that is inherent in America.

"He was playing jazz [at Tanglewood], and he practiced jazz. . . . He put on Jamey Aebersold tapes [to learn more jazz technique].[3] And he found drummer Akira Tana at the festival."

Akira had just graduated from the New England Conservatory. He and Wynton got a few jazz gigs, after they met Chuck Israels, a bass player, who was spending his summer as usual at his house in Alford, Massachusetts, a few miles from Tanglewood.

Israels' wife, Margot, a singer, had been asked to sing a complicated, modern piece at Tanglewood to fill in for a student who became ill. Wynton played in the ensemble. That was probably how Wynton met Israels. Israels had gigs with a guitarist, Steve Brown, from Ithaca, at various clubs in Stockbridge and Great Barrington, Massachusetts, in the Berkshires on weekends. Israels asked Wynton and Akira to sit in with them.

The guitar-bass duo was earning little enough; Israels gave Wynton and Akira a bit of money out of the paycheck—"Basically peanuts," Israel recalled, "too little to be anything but insulting. So they weren't doing it for the money. My impression of Wynton then was that he was a brilliant trumpet player and a young man of enormous gifts and great personal grace—a very lovely, courteous man, I thought, brought up in a tradition of the Southern gentleman. And this goes deep. This is not something pasted on him. This is part of his character.

"He says that I told him he played badly, and someday, if he kept going, he'd get good. It isn't true. He says it jokingly, in a charming, self-deprecating way, and with deference to my situation as a person with experience. What I did tell him was that he was using up his sixteenth notes in his first choruses, playing the climactic part right in the beginning. If he would wait a while, he would have some place to go. That's the only memory I have of any conversations about his playing.

"It was an obvious observation, something any experienced improviser would say. Just good advice. Don't play everything you know in the first few minutes; that's the gist of it. And he certainly took it good-naturedly and with interest."

Chuck and his wife invited Wynton to their house for dinner and had a conversation about what would happen when he went to New York in the fall. Israels told him that "they," meaning record producers, were going to try to snap him up and make him a pop-jazz crossover star—a fusion player in jazz-rock-oriented groups. A number of "terrific" young musicians were turning to fusion to make a living, in Israels' opinion. He told Wynton, "I'm not opposed to money, and if it's the way you want to play, then everybody gains. But if you're going against your musical, artistic character, then there will be something false about it." Wynton replied, "No, it won't happen. I'm a student of this music. I'm committed. It just isn't going to happen to me."

At Tanglewood, Justin and Wynton played under the baton of conductor Leonard Bernstein, who was leading Prokofiev's Fifth Symphony one week. Wynton played second trumpet, which had a lot of low register solos. Justin played third trumpet. It was a great experience, Justin recalled.

Wynton was also listening to recordings by Woody Shaw, an imaginative, sweet-toned jazz trumpeter, who embodied traditional, mainstream jazz and freer, experimental music in his style. Woody had played with Art Blakey and the Jazz Messengers and other eminent jazz musicians and was leading his own groups. The recordings introduced Justin to jazz; he was so happy to learn about jazz from Wynton, someone he could trust and who could also start him thinking about the world in terms of philosophy, religion, and race. "We talked about everything in the world. If you talk to Ellis," said Justin, who soon met Wynton's father, "you think about these things. And we were able to help each other." Years later Justin discovered that Wynton had improved his low-register playing by using some exercises that Justin had showed him. "Low notes. You can improve in the low register. He wanted to work on that," Justin recalled.

One night they got together and played with an African-American trumpeter, Jim Tinsley, who played at times with the Boston Symphony. "It was great," Justin recalled, "three people just sitting down and making music. Tanglewood is a real trip, if you see it from our perspective— the inner workings of the Boston Symphony, an incredible resource. We had coaching and rehearsals. And they paid for us to be there." Justin deduced from conversations with Wynton that he was already thinking there should be a similar opportunity for jazz players.

———————

Justin knew that Wynton got full scholarships to many different schools, including Ivy League ones, but probably chose Juilliard because jazz musicians went to New York. Miles was there. In the fall, Justin went with Wynton to hear Clark Terry, the trumpeter and fluegelhornist, in a club in New York, where Wynton sat in. "It was exciting to hear Wynton play, because he was so exceptionally good, with amazing technique and a beautiful sound and real passion," Justin said.

Justin wasn't having a good experience at Juilliard, but Wynton was open-minded about the school, even though its resources were limited for him, as he became more convinced that he was a jazz musician.

Wynton and Akira Tana shared an apartment together on West 99th Street and Broadway for about a year. Akira believed Wynton was destined for greatness, because he was very dedicated and serious about the music, practicing both classical and jazz constantly.

They had serious discussions about race and politics, and they also joked about a lot of things—"Sushi," Wynton recalled, "and the differences between Japanese people and black people, and about women, mainly about the women Akira had." Wynton didn't have any girlfriends then, although he had had many in New Orleans. But in New York, "I was in another whole enviroment and completely unsure of where I was," he said.

He and Akira also talked a great deal about jazz and its commercialization. Wynton had strong feelings about preserving the purity of jazz. "I've been a fan of the whole gamut of jazz styles," said Akira. "He thought Herbie Hancock, Wayne Shorter, and Weather Report had sold out the music by going commercial. Wynton never liked [that kind of] fusion, though he liked fusion in relation to classical music—the Modern Jazz Quartet. He went in the other direction," away from electronic instruments.

At seventeen, Wynton didn't cook much, didn't eat sushi, and really had no experience with the sophisticated pleasures that New York could offer. Later on he would swear by them. But as a neophyte in New York, he was simply a very dedicated musician. Wynton felt that his brother Branford, who was playing the alto saxophone, was more naturally talented. Wynton told people he had to work harder. Branford didn't have to practice so much, and in any case, he didn't. He came down from Berklee College in Boston and hung out at Wynton and Akira's apartment. Trumpeter Terence Blanchard stayed at the apartment, too, when, still in high school, he was a candidate for the Presidential Scholars in the Arts Program and traveled from New Orleans to audition in New Jersey. Donald Harrison may have stayed at that apartment briefly. Akira observed them as "nice young kids who were very positive and into their music."

Wynton may have been unsure of himself at first in New York. But about music, Akira said, Wynton "knew exactly the direction he was headed in. He had a clear idea of what he wanted to do." When doors opened for him, they did so not only because of his talent but because he was at the right place at the right time, Akira believed. And that happened because Wynton was ubiquitous, always sitting in some place. There weren't many musicians in New York who didn't hear him play or at least know about him. He even sat in with experimental trumpeter Lester Bowie's group, the Hot Trumpet Repertory Company. (Later on Wynton and Bowie, who came out of the experimental group the Art Ensemble of Chicago, would be at loggerheads about music. They criticized each other's playing and emphasis in jazz or, as Bowie preferred to call it, "great black music.")

Still, Wynton didn't expect to become a star. He and Terence discussed practical plans for their futures. Terence said he would go to study with a trumpeter in the Los Angeles Philharmonic Orchestra, play in studios for a living during the week, and in jazz gigs on weekends. Wynton thought he would take the same path in New York. For one thing, it was unheard of to become a star in acoustic jazz at the time they were planning their careers.

Wilmer Wise was a neighbor on 100th Street and West End Avenue, who worked in classical and Broadway orchestras, and played first trumpet with the Brooklyn Philharmonic. He met Wynton through Jim Tinsley, who called Wise, also an African American, when Wynton was setting off from Tanglewood to New York. Tinsley told Wise: "There's a young kid coming to New York, and I'm floored by his abilities. If there's anything you can do to help him, please do."

Wynton made a date with Wise and went to play for him. "He was absolutely incredible," Wise recalled. "I hadn't heard many players of any age who played as well as Wynton." Wise heard Wynton play only classical pieces—maybe the "Brandenburg" Concerto No. 2 or a Haydn concerto. "It doesn't take much. In a couple of notes you can tell if a person has it or not," Wise said. Wise invited Wynton to substitute for him in the Broadway show *Sweeney Todd*, and for other jobs. Wynton was always first call for any job Wise couldn't take.

In 1979 Wise brought Wynton with him to Mexico City to play in two very different settings. One was with a band called The New York Gang, with Edward Corroll and Cecil Bridgewater in the trumpet section.[4] They performed on two evenings. The first night they played the Ross Lieberman Concerto for Jazz Band and Orchestra, then a straight jazz program on the second night. Wise was also responsible for Wynton's playing in the Brooklyn Philharmonic on a second trip to Mexico that same year, with Lucas Foss conducting.

Wynton, "a Coca-Cola freak," was one of the most clean-cut musicians Wise had ever met, and "just an out-and-out" classical player, as far as Wise knew. He and Wynton discussed music, the business, and its inequities. Wynton knew relatively few black musicians could find work in the symphonic field. He also knew about the politics that, technically speaking, had little to do with race. In one orchestra, for example, one of Wise's colleagues asked him if he could get Wynton to speak more clearly. Apparently his New Orleans accent and soft, blurry voice puzzled the other musician. Another musician, discovering that Wise was going to send a nineteen-year-old to substitute for him, asked, "Why?" Wise said Wynton was a great player. The other musician wanted to know, "But what can he do for you?" The availability of jobs in the music business often hinged on the favors people could do for each other and not on their abilities, Wise knew.

George Davis, a New Orleans guitarist and songwriter who had a recording studio in New York at one time and who played for the Broadway show *A Chorus Line* for years, also provided moral support for Wynton. Years later, commenting to Marian McPartland, Wynton recalled how hard it was to get started in New York. "It was rough at first, I was seventeen, and I was lucky because my home boy George Davis looked out for me . . . and I had someone just to talk to. I mean, you'll go crazy here by yourself. I was so different from everyone else here at school. I still had an Afro."[5] Wynton said he thought he might have been too young to be in New York.

Trumpeter Lew Soloff also helped Wynton. Wynton thought that Lew loved all the trumpet players and was always encouraging cats to learn how to play. Lew first heard about Wynton from Wilmer Wise, when they were working together with the Alvin Ailey Dance Company. Wise asked Lew, "Have you heard about the new whiz kid at Juilliard, Wynton Marsalis?" Lew said "No." Not long afterward, the contractor for the Brooklyn Philharmonic called Lew about a job. During the conversation, the contractor played a tape of Wynton performing the third movement of a Haydn concerto, "neatly, with no mistakes, and no bravura," Lew heard. "Wow, that sounds good," Lew said.

One day Lew was standing in line at the recording window of the American Federation of Musicians, Local 802, then on West 52nd Street in New York, when he noticed a teenager with a trumpet case. Lew had a sixth sense. He said, "Hello, what's your name?" The youngster said, "Wynton Marsalis." Lew said, "I'm Lew Soloff." Wynton said he had heard of Lew, "which pleased me, of course," Lew recalled. He told Wynton about hearing the Haydn. At first Wynton, who was half Lew's age, seemed like "a little kid" to Lew. But when Lew asked Wynton how he could play both classical and jazz, Wynton brightened for the conversation. He said, "Man, jazz is my thing." He began to talk with "incredible fluidity and a vocabulary that I wasn't capable of myself," Lew said, "and it was all of a sudden as if I was talking to a mature man." They exchanged phone numbers; Wynton went to Lew's apartment, where they played duets.

Lew heard Wynton play with trombonist Steve Turre's group in a Greenwich Village club and thought Wynton sounded very good. That night Jon Faddis had sent Wynton in as a substitute. Soon Wynton subbed for Lew at Alvin Ailey and with an excellent band called French Toast.

In 1980 at the Brass Conference in New York, Soloff introduced Wynton and had him play "Cherokee" at breakneck, bebop-proper speed. Skinny and coiffeured, with "a big Afro that bounced when he walked," recalled jazz pianist James Williams, who would soon befriend Wynton. Wynton was filmed by jazz videographer and documentary producer Burrill Crohn at that conference. It was the first time Burrill heard Wynton play. As an amateur trumpet player himself, Burrill was mightily impressed. Wynton knew the right changes and sounded fine. Wynton himself thought he had sounded "sad" on that song, but he had never seen or heard the tape, and he was wrong. It was probably the first video of Wynton, certainly the first made of him in New York.

Wynton seemed to sit in every place at that time. Paul Jeffrey, the tenor saxophonist in Thelonious Monk's last group, led a band at the Midtown Manhattan Jazz Center, in the Charles Colin Studios, where musicians, among them Wynton, went to play every Saturday. Jeffrey thought Wynton was a great player and tried to get him an endorsement from Yamaha. Although Wynton went to a trumpet clinic and astounded everyone, it took six months for Yamaha to give him a horn. By that time, Wynton had already made some inroads, Paul recalled.

David Berger, a leading transcriber and copyist of Duke Ellington's music, was playing trumpet for the Alvin Ailey Dance Company in 1980. Planning a two-week vacation, Berger called Lew Soloff, first lead trumpeter for the company, to ask for a sub. Soloff said: "There's a new guy in town. He's really good. Wynton Marsalis." So Berger called Wynton and thought he was rather cool about the job. Wynton said nonchalantly, "I guess so." Berger didn't know then that Wynton had never played anything remotely like the music they were doing. When Berger came back, he asked the other musicians in the trumpet section how the kid had done. "Okay," they said. "He's not as good as you." That was the last time it will ever happen, Berger later realized. Soloff recommended Wynton for many jobs.

Justin Cohen and Wynton maintained their friendship. Justin loved going to concerts with Wynton; they talked about the great symphonic musicians, such as the first trumpeter in the Boston Symphony, with his big sound. When Justin and Wynton went to hear *A Hero's Life* by Richard Strauss, Wynton told Justin to listen to the great difference between the sound of the trumpeter at Tanglewood and the younger man they were hearing.

With Wynton, Justin talked about how a player could impart meaning to anything: to classical or folk or jazz music. "But the great thing about jazz is you get to improvise. You have a kind of freedom that is different," Justin learned. Wynton and Justin talked about music as a way of enjoying life and telling a story. They talked about the whole creative process.

Wynton and Justin talked about their families, "private stuff," Justin said, "and he told me about the great people in New Orleans, drummer James Black and others. He talked about what a natural talent Branford had. Branford could sit down and play a tune without even knowing it. The two of them had a musical, telepathic relationship from playing together so much. They could have a conversation, playing right on top of each other, the way people do when they talk to each other and interrupt each other," Justin said, thinking that it must have been wonderful and reinforcing to have someone to play with in that way.

As time went on, and Justin began playing with the Chicago Symphony as a substitute, he heard Adolph "Bud" Herseth, the first trumpeter in that orchestra, say: "Music is the staff of life." Herseth had played there, at the top of his form, day in and day out, for decades, exerting a great influence on other musicians. Justin thought of Wynton as similar to Herseth, because Wynton was uncompromisingly musical. Like Herseth, "Wynton absolutely loved to play the trumpet and loved music. He could listen to it, play it, compose it; all those experiences were different. It was great to see Wynton make such use of his gifts. He had the discipline. . . . Discipline means remembering what you want," Justin said that he came to realize. "For some people, doing what they love is like breathing." That was Wynton, Justin thought.

Justin mused that he couldn't say what went on in Wynton's head, but his impression was that Wynton was someone who cared very deeply about people, life, and music. "It's all the same thing," Justin said. With hindsight, he would say he felt privileged to have known Wynton when he did. "We were both trumpet players. But for me—imagine, if you were in Renaisssance Italy, and you're interested in painting, and you meet this kid whose name is Leonardo. He talks about painting, sculpture, flying machines. . . . I knew he was broadening my mind and my experience from the time I met him."

Chapter Notes

1. Dick Russell, *Black Genius and the American Experience*. New York: Carroll & Graf, 1998.
2. *Like It Is*, interview with Gil Noble, ABC-TV, New York, November 15, 1992.
3. Jamey Aebersold Jazz, P.O. Box 1244 DD, New Albany, IN, 47151-1244. Aebersold is a well-known educator in the jazz field.
4. Pianist Patti Bown, bassist George Duvivier, and percussionist Warren Smith played in the band, too, along with saxophonists George Barrow and Red Press and trombonists Janice Robinson, Porter Poindexter, and Doug Purviance.
5. *Piano Jazz*, interview with Marian McPartland, recorded on January 11, 1995, broadcast for the first time on January 6, 1996.

WITH ART BLAKEY
AND THE JAZZ
MESSENGERS

In 1979 Akira Tana told Wynton that the best way he could learn to play brilliant acoustic jazz was to join Art Blakey and the Jazz Messengers. Akira said, as Wynton recalled: "Art Blakey is the only band out here that you can play with. It's your last chance, your last hope to learn how to play."

Akira knew Blakey's pianist, James Williams, and told Wynton, "I'm going to rap with James, and he'll hook it up so you can sit in." They went to Mikell's, a well-known jazz club in the neighborhood, where Akira talked to Williams. Williams went to the cellar and asked Blakey, "You mind if he sits in? He's Ellis Marsalis's son." Williams, who had met Ellis when Blakey's band played in New Orleans, knew that Ellis had some musical sons, Wynton, in New York, and Branford, who was studying saxophone at the time with Billy Pierce in Boston.

Blakey said, "You guys have to play with him, too. If you don't mind, I don't mind." Wynton went back to Akira's apartment and brought his horn to the club. In the group that night were alto saxophonist Bobby Watson, bassist Dennis Irwin, tenor saxophonist Billy Pierce, and the brilliant Russian-born trumpeter Valery Ponomarev. Bobby Watson thought it might have been Ponomarev's idea that Wynton sit in; at least

Valery had no objection to it. Furthermore, Watson noticed that Wynton was wearing a windbreaker and tennis shoes that winter night.

"He sat in for the set," James Williams recalled. "He didn't really know the music. He wasn't really a strong jazz player, but he was an excellent trumpet player. So he didn't have a real grasp of the harmonic things or the approach for jazz and even less of the conception of what the Jazz Messengers were about. But you still heard something that was special. At least, I thought it was."

Bobby Watson recalled that Valery Ponomarev was particularly moved by the way Wynton played. "I was whispering the changes in his ear while he was playing," Watson said. It was only going to be a matter of time until Wynton joined the group formally. Blakey loved strong trumpet players. Watson thought that Wynton was probably the greatest instrumentalist he had ever encountered for his control of the instrument and his technique. "He never stumbled. . . . Even when he may have been lost, he still sounded good because he had command of the trumpet."

"And so people kind of liked it," James Williams recalled. "He was playing high notes like Jon Faddis—and higher than Wynton subsequently played. He was trying to play 'Along Came Betty,' and, even if you know it, it can put a thing on your mind. So it definitely kicked his you-know-what up one side and down the other."

Afterward, Wynton spoke with Blakey, who told him that the next gig was going to be at Lulu White's in Boston. Wynton said, "I'll be there." He knew he could stay with Branford at Berklee.

"So the next day, I went to his house," James Williams recalled, "and spent about three hours. I was excited about how he could play. What he had was enthusiasm. He was very much into Freddie Hubbard at around the time Freddie [who had been a Jazz Messenger in the early 1960s] was playing 'Black Angel' and 'Red Clay'—adventurous, exciting, heart-rending protest music, far more eerie than Miles's music. Later, Hubbard changed direction toward more pop-jazz music with producer Creed Taylor at the CTI label.

"Wynton could play Freddie's solos off of 'Red Clay,' a great date, with Joe Henderson, Herbie Hancock, Lenny White, and Ron Carter. And Wynton was very much into Miles Davis, especially the *Four and More* and *ESP* albums, with [saxophonists] George Coleman and Wayne Shorter," Williams recalled about Wynton's taste in those days. Wynton was also into a little bit of Clifford Brown, Williams detected, but didn't seem very well versed in Lee Morgan, Booker Little, Blue Mitchell, Thad Jones, or Dizzy Gillespie. "Maybe he knew Lee Morgan on the 'Blue Train' date [a Jazz Messengers recording]. But I don't think Wynton was really aware of all those other great Messenger dates, not the ones with [saxophonist] Hank Mobley and Lee Morgan. But Wynton had the technique to execute most of the tunes very well. And I knew them. I used to play those tunes—'The Intrepid Fox' and 'Sweet Sue'—in college, Memphis State," Williams recalled.

Williams told Wynton, "So, hey, you've got to learn these tunes so you can come and sit in Saturday." Williams recalled going through "Along Came Betty" and four or five other tunes, "Blues March" for one, and a couple of ballads, one of them "My Funny Valentine." ("Blues March" and "Moanin'" were two songs that Blakey usually used as his signature songs, no matter what else he asked the group to play during the sets.) Wynton took a bus up to Boston to sit in with Blakey; one night the guitarist Kevin Eubanks sat in, too. "It was an exciting time, a shot in the arm, a breath of fresh air," James Williams remembered. "Other groups were playing fusion, but Wynton wanted to play the real deal."

After that, Williams said, he used to set his watch by Wynton's telephone calls. Wynton would call him at 1:30 A.M. when James was in Boston, where he lived when he played with the Jazz Messengers. Wynton would say, "Hey, bruh', what you doing?" Williams would sit up with Wynton and talk and argue.

"Wynton was opinionated even then. He and I didn't see eye to eye on a lot of things, always to do with music—well, occasionally basketball, too," Williams reminisced. "I would say: 'Bring that little weak jump shot in there, and I will block it every time.' Wynton would say, 'Why would someone be playing fusion?' He didn't want to hear Freddie Hubbard playing fusion, 'Liquid Love,' for example; Wynton wanted to hear Freddie's earlier stuff. But I was enjoying just hearing Wynton play, period."

Williams recalled that Wynton wanted to concentrate on modal playing. "Well, we all were interested in modal playing at that time," Williams said. "Yeah, playing on modes, just playing like wild types of things," Wynton recalled. Williams advised Wynton to listen to the older songs, too, but Wynton didn't take that advice until later.

Bobby Watson and Paul Jeffrey also remembered many late-night conversations with Wynton about his life and career. And so it seems as if Wynton must have been well fixed with dimes in those days.

⸺➤●◄⸺

In 1980 Blakey asked Wynton to join the Jazz Messengers. Wynton told his father that he was thinking about quitting Juilliard and going on the road with Blakey. "It wasn't like it was going to make a difference to me," Wynton recalled. "I knew myself I wanted to play. But I always talked to my daddy to see what he was thinking. I knew before I asked him that he was going to say, 'Go and play.' My daddy believes in playing. . . . Some people think you should take the safe road. He's not like that. His idea is, go out there and do it. If you fail it, you tried it. Don't stay at home. Don't be afraid. . . . You never had nothing. So you don't have to worry about losing nothing. And he used to have sayings: You can always go back to what you did. He doesn't believe in any of that ass kissing or politicking. That's not his way."

By the summer of 1980, Wynton was playing in a hard-swinging, rococo, neo-bop style with Art Blakey. Bobby Watson recalled having fun with Wynton on the road. They talked about music and played a little basketball. Watson said, "People used to try to use his classical training against him. He was able to demonstrate on his instrument that he could dispel any kind of b.s. His attitude about working toward perfection influenced me.

"He taught me that if you want to learn something, it can take a year or a minute. It depends on the limits you put on yourself. He told me that. He was young then. He always had confidence in who he is. I was very influenced by his discipline. There were times on the road when I would get up in the middle of the night to use the bathroom, and I would hear the trumpet practicing with a mute next door to me. I would get inspired and start practicing. . . . He taught me how to double tongue on the saxophone. It's unusual in the jazz sense. Sax players don't [usually] double tongue.

"And just his mindset [inspired me]. He knew what he wanted out of life. . . . He showed me the power of the mind." Watson thought that Wynton had already signed with Columbia when he joined Blakey. At least Wynton "was already doing jingles for Columbia on their industrial side," Watson recalled. "Someone asked him to do the Tom Brown thing [to become a pop music player], but he knew he wanted to [play] jazz and classical music. Columbia may take credit for it, but Wynton had the vision all along."

Watson knew that Wynton didn't have a high regard for electronic instruments: "Art Blakey did. He said they were here to stay, and they should be used." Wynton never changed his opinion on that score, but in every other way he learned from experience, "and he grew tremendously over the years," Watson would later reflect.

Wynton brought Terence Blanchard and Donald Harrison to Watson's house for a dinner cooked by Pam, Bobby's wife, a musician herself. Wynton talked about the opera, conductor Seiji Ozawa, and Beethoven, whom Wynton loved. Watson recalled that Wynton didn't like the crowd-pleasing efforts of Duke Ellington, Louis Armstrong, or the blues at that time. He recalled, "He had no respect for them. He said it was 1980, and black people shouldn't be playing the blues. That's old time stuff, Wynton thought." He also said Art Blakey was a "little haphazard about his business." Saxophonist Billy Pierce, playing with the band at that time, recalled that Wynton—and many others—realized Art should have taken the business affairs of the band more seriously.

"You know, Art wasn't the world's greatest businessman about paying us or demanding enough money for himself," Pierce recalled. "He was old school. He would let promoters pay less than they should have, and we went on the road from gig to gig, with no hard contract, and no one taking care of the contracts. The arrangement was loose. Art grew up in the Depression. Just playing music was the biggest thrill for Art. He should have gotten five times as much money as he did."

But Pierce believed that Wynton learned a great deal about how to play jazz in Art's band—how to pace himself, how to build solos and play ballads—"things that old guys always know more about than young guys do," he said. "All of us learned from Art. He was everybody's teacher and surrogate father; he could be a lot of other things I can't go into, a man for all seasons. He could be your best friend, your worst enemy, the devil's advocate if he chose to be. But just being around Art and looking at life from his perspective, I learned a lot. People who worked for Art went away with more than they left. All of us owe Art. . . ."

In horn players, Blakey looked for people "who could play and swing, and he could see star potential. A guy like Wynton was a real focal point," Pierce analyzed. "Art encouraged us to start our own bands. He had a pyramid scheme of jazz. The younger guys should play more, and there would be more bands and more people involved with the music. And the music would be taken to a wider audience. He preached that. He also preached self-reliance and manhood and how to take care of business and stand up for yourself. Don't let yourself be taken advantage of as an artist or as a person. He instilled these ideas in us because he didn't take any shit off anybody. And when he came to play, he came to play. He expected that of all the guys in the band. He told us: 'Be true to yourself. Whatever you are, you be it, and be it all the way, because nothing else is going to work anyway.'"

Bobby Watson thought Art Blakey represented "faith in action." Blakey used to tell his musicians, "Don't worry, the angels are with us." Watson said, "He had supreme faith in a power higher than he was. He wasn't a verbal person. You watched him, took what you wanted, and left the rest. He was one of the most positive people and loved young people. He pretended to be stupid or deaf at times. And he would pretend to be forgetful of people's names just to test other people and see what they knew. He taught his musicians: 'Always keep your mouth shut so people won't know how stupid you are. Once you open your mouth, everyone knows.'"

As part of the requirements for belonging to the "brotherhood"—as Billy Pierce called it—of the Jazz Messengers, Wynton had to compose music. Blakey always insisted that his sidemen write music so they could grow artistically and collect royalties; he preached that their compositions were their legacy, trust fund, and inheritance for their children. Wynton had been composing music anyway.[1]

Pierce saw Wynton only occasionally after they left Blakey. From a distance, Pierce thought Wynton remained pretty much the way he had always been: "And interestingly, Wynton was somewhat insecure when we were with Blakey. . . . He seemed genuinely concerned if he would make it and whether he had all the attributes of a top-shelf musician. Underneath, he had a sense of who he was and where he was going. But he was just like everybody else at about that age, with all his gifts, wondering if he would [be successful] and make any statement about himself and the music.

"A lot of times he was like a pesky little brother; other times he had wisdom beyond his years. I guess it was his thoroughness when it came to music. He was very demanding, even with the older guys. He couldn't tell us what to do. We ignored him. But he put a lot of [food] for thought in our minds, because he had a classical background, I guess. Some of the rigors of dealing with that music and the rigidity of that world did give him a certain discipline. And he took that, though not overtly, into the Jazz Messengers." In their rehearsals, which were open forums, people could say anything they wanted. "A lot of times he said things we listened to, and most of the time he had really good ideas, good concepts, of how to present music," said Pierce.

Pierce really appreciated Wynton's contribution of youth and energy to the band: "I think a lot of what he brought was the attitude. Some of us might have been a little jaded. I was about thirty, not that old. But he brought that youthful exuberance back into what we were doing and put us on our toes because he was playing so well. And even if he didn't know [everything], he had a natural gift for getting audiences involved in his solos. . . . He picked up the trumpet and played the hell out of it.

"He was still sorting out a lot of things. He had ideas that didn't work that well and a lot of concepts even for tunes. He did ask for a certain amount of counsel from other people. . . . Sometimes guys like Bobby [Watson] and James [Williams] would really help him to get to where he was going. But he probably knew where he was going."

Billy noticed that Branford was a different sort of kid, "a little more gregarious, looser in a sense. He definitely by no means was as disciplined, but he was a guy with a lot of natural ability. Whereas Wynton was a natural as well, but he really worked very hard. Branford's musical gifts came to him pretty easily. Not that he didn't work, too, but his attitude was slightly different than Wynton's. They were brothers and very close. But Wynton was a perfectionist, trying to make things correct. Branford was not that way at all. He was very loose. Wynton was more conservatory trained; Branford wasn't. And Branford really liked pop music."

In 1981 Blakey let Wynton, who, some sources say, was the musical director of the Messengers at that time, take a leave of absence to tour with the group VSOP II in Japan and the summer music festivals. Wallace Roney took Wynton's place in Blakey's band. Then Wynton returned, bringing Branford, who was playing alto, with him, and Bobby Watson left Blakey. The brothers often played in perfect communion, the way they were accustomed to working, as other great teams in jazz had done: Cannonball Adderley, the alto player, with his brother Nat, a trumpeter, and also Dizzy Gillespie with Charlie Parker. Dizzy said that sometimes it sounded as if only one horn was playing, when he and Bird played together. That was true to a degree of Branford and Wynton.

Wynton's endless hours of practicing and thinking about his playing paid off magnificently. In a *Down Beat* magazine critics poll for 1981, he was chosen the Talent Deserving of Wider Recognition. On a tune called "A La Mode," for example, recorded with Blakey live in January 1982 at the Keystone Korner club in San Francisco, Wynton had the amazing command to add fascinating little squeals in exactly the right places to enhance the entire group's impact. And all his work was virtuosic.

An especially gifted pianist/composer named Donald Brown joined the Jazz Messengers when James Williams left. Williams had brought Brown to Blakey's attention. Born in Mississippi, raised in Memphis, Brown was a resident of Boston, then of Knoxville, Tennessee, where he taught at a university. As so many others were, Brown, then about twenty-seven years old, was immediately impressed by Wynton. "I was turned on more than anything by the way he was always studying, always trying to learn new tunes and listening to different musicians and trumpet players, and drawing from everything he heard," said Brown. "I also always saw him as a controversial person. I always thought he liked to argue, and so do I in some ways. We argued a lot. I felt like it was a great exchange.

"Once we got into an argument about affirmative action. I think it started about . . . a black coach at Georgetown University who was boycotting a rule they were passing that would make it harder for black athletes to get into college, because they were raising the level of the [tests] to let blacks get into college. I admired him for taking a stance like that. Wynton thought it was a bunch of crap, or something. He didn't dig it. I said, 'I guess you must be against affirmative action.' He said, 'Yes.' I said, "Well, I think the best person should get the job, but as long as you don't educate people equally on the lower levels, then blacks will have a tendency to come up short.' And we argued about it, kind of.

"But I felt like I learned a lot about things from him. . . . When I first joined the band, we sat down at the piano and tried to write some tunes together. We had different approaches to writing. . . . At that time he was more technical and analytical about his approach. . . . And it seemed like he thought about it instead of letting it flow naturally. I thought the more tunes he wrote, and the more he studied music, the more weapons he had—a broader repertoire of ideas to draw from.

"Each time he wrote a tune, you could hear so much growth from one to the next. By the time he left [Blakey's] band, he played me tapes from his own band rehearsing, and I could hear his own sound starting to evolve—something somewhat similar to what he was playing with Art, but Wynton was starting to take off in his own direction. The musicians he had in that [first band] helped a lot with the possibilities. There's a big difference between Art Blakey and Jeff Watts [Wynton's first drummer], Jeff being a modern player [with] the colors he brought to Wynton's music. Art being up in age, he wouldn't hear or have the facility to do certain things that Jeff could," Brown said. "And the chemistry between Wynton, Branford, and the pianist in the band, Kenny Kirkland, provided Wynton with inspiration."

In the Jazz Messengers, Donald hung out with Branford more for entertainment, "but most of the time if the conversations were about music, I'd be hanging with Wynton," Brown recalled. He loved having a man in the band he could "always sit around with to talk to about the music."

Among the Blakey band members, bassist Charles Fambrough became Wynton's closest friend. Fambrough thought that Wynton "was amazing from the first note" he played with the Messengers. The two bonded rapidly, Fambrough said, "because Wynton was very personable, energetic, and always wanted to make the music sound as good as it could possibly sound. I was with that program." Wynton and Fambrough became roommates, listened to music, and hung out together all the time.

About ten years older than Wynton, Fambrough, who was particularly fascinated with clothes, tried to make Wynton conscious of style. When Fambrough looked at clothes in expensive men's shops, he took Wynton along. "He caught the bug and started buying a lot of clothes," Fambrough noticed. In San Francisco, shopping with Fambrough, Wynton bought a very expensive suit that he later wore for a photo for the cover of his first album as leader. "In Blakey's band, we were wearing our overalls and cowboy hats," Fambrough said. He didn't really like that. Recalling how Blakey's men had worn suits in the 1960s, Fambrough had begun to dress up. "Then Art took over and bought us tuxedos, each one a different color. Pierce had a blue or grey, Branford blue, I had burgundy, and someone had a brown one. Wynton had a black one."

Fambrough thought Wynton was actually a little "overconfident," as he described his friend. When Fambrough dated women, Wynton was often attracted to them and didn't hesitate to let them know it. "Of course, that would humor them to some extent," Fambrough recalled, "and he was always threatening to take my girlfriends away from me." They joked about it between themselves. It wasn't a major issue.

"Wynton was sort of like my little brother," Fambrough said, "and he was a terrorist in Art Blakey's band," even "antagonistic" to certain members of the band. "If you did anything wrong, he'd wear you out with it. If you fell into his trap, you were in trouble. His trap was to antagonize folks in a positive way, not in a negative way. There are people who need that, people who slough through things. Just because you're a musician doesn't mean that you're well rounded. There are parts of your life that you could overlook. So if there's a part of your life you should pay more attention to, he would make you aware of it. Most of it was none of his business, but he was on a mission to make music and the environment of music better. He was sort of a social policeman."

Fambrough knew Wynton's sometimes annoying, sometimes endearing capabilities as a "social policeman" well, because the two roomed together on tours. "Let's just say, as a hypothetical example, that I didn't brush my hair every morning when I got up. He might be the first person to tell me, 'Hey, yo, man, how come you don't brush your hair?' I would tell him to shut up. He would tell me that he thinks I'm out there representing the music, and I should brush my hair. He was right.

"That's what made him a pain in the ass. He was like a why person. Why is this? Why is that? He would ask questions about why is it that you do this when you should actually be doing that. He was trying to put your attention on what you should actually be doing. He didn't tell you what you should be doing. Art and I really found him amusing. He didn't mess with Art and me. We were immune. We really didn't care what he thought. But even when he was a pain in the ass, he was enlightening. Some people can be a pain in the ass and that's all. But he had good intentions. That's what I liked about him the most."

One time when they were in Copenhagen, Wynton asked Art why he got high. Art said: "I get high in front of God, and who are you to ask me?" But Fambrough thought that Wynton was right to ask, because Art was slowing down the tempo. "And that was fucking Wynton. He got this frown on his face. I knew he was going to do something wrong. He was right, because indirectly that was affecting him. And we were playing, by the way; we were on the bandstand. And it worked. It pissed Art off. He woke up," Fambrough recalled.

"We used to play jokes on each other. One time I stuck a bow up Branford's behind, while he was playing a solo. Art nearly died." That was just one of many practical jokes the band mates played on each other. "We always were playing vicious tricks on each other, because we were young and dumb. But it was cool. It kept energy happening."

Not only did Fambrough and Wynton become very close friends, but Fambrough also liked Branford. In retrospect, Fambrough thought he liked Branford because he was "carefree, kind of," and "really spontaneous" and "not predictable. You never know what he's going to play."

About Wynton, Fambrough reflected, "Wynton has had so many periods. When he was in Art's band, he was still developing his sound and ideas. He was listening to a lot of musicians. And if someone influenced him, he would really get into him."

Fambrough thought the musicians in the Jazz Messengers at that time weren't really close friends. Although they played together very well, they didn't stay in touch when they left the band. Branford and Wynton were close—"sort of," Fambrough recalled. Although Wynton was younger than Branford, "Wynton was the big brother, and Branford didn't like that. Branford was very cool. He didn't need anyone telling him what to do. I saw that Branford would do the opposite of what Wynton told him to do. 'You should be doing this,' Wynton would say. That kind of meant that Branford was not going to to be doing it." Fambrough thought that was normal behavior for siblings. He would later notice that his own younger children liked to tell the older ones what to do, and the bigger ones never listened. It wasn't anything serious between Wynton and Branford, Fambrough thought, taking a calmly measured view of their complex relationship.

"They were brothers and seemed very close," he recalled. "One time, they jumped me, because I was getting to them, saying New Orleans musicians weren't 'all that.' They punched me a little. I punched them back. It wasn't really a big thing. It was kind of like, 'Look, shut up. You ain't gonna talk about us.' Actually, it was amusing to me. I thought that was good. I love New Orleans musicians. I think they bond together more than any others. They look out for each other. Wynton looked out for Terence [Blanchard]. Wynton looks out for his home boys. Actually,

Wynton and Branford were friendly and not arrogant—but a little, a wee bit, overopinionated, Wynton was."

Traveling with the Blakey band, Wynton began to forge friendships with people outside the music world. Tony Parker, a police officer, was working as a security guard at the Chicago Jazz Festival in Grant Park, probably in 1980, when he overheard Wynton and the Blakey band members talking about basketball. Wynton was bragging so much about his prowess that Parker, who had just gotten through playing a league game that day, couldn't resist the challenge. He led Wynton to a sports club on Michigan Avenue, where they staged an impromptu game. Parker, who is 6 feet 1 inches tall and weighs 230 pounds, thought he would easily beat Wynton, "who was only about 5 feet 9 with his stacked gym shoes on," Parker said.

"Wynton swished in a couple of jump shots. I said to myself: 'It's got to be luck.' He hit about two more. I said to myself: 'I better get on this cat.' He was giving me a look. He hit a couple more jumps. I realized this guy was a ringer; he could play for real. So he didn't say too much on the court. He just kept looking. He had Bethany Pickens, a girl pianist, and another fellow. Bethany could play basketball, too. We were playing two on two, and we wound up losing about three games. I walked away. I came up with an excuse; I was sore, I said. We played one on one. He beat me so bad, I had to go and hide from myself. I've never been so humiliated. He is usually quick, dissing people, playing the dozens. And he beat me about four games. So this is the never-ending competitive saga between Wynton and myself. He is competitive about anything he does."

The relationship begun that day deepened into a friendship, as Wynton and Tony met every time that Wynton passed through Chicago. Tony often did favors for Wynton and the others in his band, once Wynton was working on his own. Wynton would come to regard Tony as one of his closest friends.

———————————>●●<———————————

Wynton would meet many, many women on the road, where he spent about 300 days a year on the average for most of his life. Of all the women, one of his closest friends turned out to be Melanie Marchand, whom he had always regarded as his first girlfriend. They met again when she was twenty years old in 1982 and a chemical engineering major at Tulane University, vacationing in New York City with her friend Dona.

They had free rooms because Dona was working for the New Orleans Intercontinental Hotel, which had reciprocal relations with the New York Intercontinental. The girls got in touch with Wynton, who met them to have a meal. A dancer came along, too—Greg White, who was also a hair stylist and makeup artist. "Wynton was very rebellious and radical at that time. He was just pissed off at the world," Melanie recalled. "He didn't like the state of things. He gets deeply passionate. It may have been the situation of black people. He was just bitter and rebellious. I can't tell you why, but I think that part of it was his compassion for his race and what he had experienced as a black man. He had always been affectionate with me. We never lost that feeling. It was kind of cute. He was sitting real close to me and hugging me, acting like he liked me. We had an old bond. We didn't have to warm up.

"After we ate, Wynton drove us to the hotel. He couldn't drive worth a damn. We thought we were going to run over people. He dropped off Dona and Greg and drove me around. We talked for a while. That day he just wasn't happy. He was complaining. I can't remember his focus. It was more like the state of things—how a black man couldn't get a break; how black people were constantly being fucked over." Melanie thought that he was far more intense and emotional than other people. "Then I left," she recalled.

After that, she occasionally saw him when he traveled to New Orleans. "He was friendly, but he was completely focused on the music. He was a little distant at that time. He was so deeply involved in building a career. When he focuses on something, it doesn't matter what's going on around him. Music was everything, his priority; everything else can become completely obliterated."

During his early days in New York, Wynton sent his little brother Delfeayo a birthday card. It was the first and only birthday card that Wynton ever sent Delfeayo, and it made a big impression on the budding trombonist in his early teens in New Orleans. The card had a picture of Aladdin's lamp and said that Delfeayo could have a wish, or perhaps all his wishes, come true. But when Delfeayo opened the card, it said, "Okay, nosy, the catch is: If you open this card, you get nothing." Delfeayo thought it was a funny, bizarre card. He didn't really understand it.

Wynton himself thought he had sent it just because it made him laugh. But if it had any subliminal message, it was: "There's no magic genie, bruh', no magic lantern. It's a do-it-yourself world; you have to do everything for yourself"—words of wisdom from Wynton to his little brother, and a little joke about how difficult life could be.

CHAPTER NOTES

1. Another of the myriad lessons Blakey taught Wynton was: "Stay until you digest the information. Digested information is knowledge. Knowledge is power." "I didn't know much until I worked with Art Blakey," Wynton reflected. Wynton Marsalis and Frank Stewart, *Sweet Swing Blues on the Road*. New York: W.W. Norton, 1994.

SIX

ON HIS OWN

George Butler, an executive in charge of jazz and new music at Columbia Records, had heard Wynton play and had become very interested in the young trumpeter. George also had his eye on another trumpeter from New Orleans and mentioned him along with Wynton to Bruce Lundvall, then president of Columbia Records. Butler had it in mind that Wynton should play popular jazz—not an idea that appealed to Wynton, he recalled.

By chance, Bruce Lundvall heard Wynton play one night at Fat Tuesday's, a club on Third Avenue at 17th Street in Manhattan, when Wynton sat in with trumpeter Woody Shaw's group. Wynton was sitting in quite a bit with Woody in clubs in those days and had even played on a double bill featuring Art Blakey's and Woody's groups at the Keystone Korner in San Francisco.

There's a tale, which could be apocryphal, but is most likely at least partly true, that Wynton met Woody Shaw for the first time at the Keystone Korner. He introduced himself and extended his hand to shake Woody's. Woody, himself an important former Jazz Messenger and part of that brotherhood, didn't take Wynton's hand. Wynton stayed calm.

Then Woody, perhaps indoctrinating Wynton into the more usual style of greeting between jazz players, said, "Don't shake my hand. Hug me, motherfucker."[1]

Lundvall, who had signed Woody Shaw to Columbia, was very impressed by Wynton's performance. After the set, Lundvall introduced himself and said, "Aren't you the guy that George Butler has been telling me about?"

Wynton said, "Yuh."

Lundvall said, "Well, I'd like to sign you to Columbia Records."

The next day, Lundvall and a lawyer at Sony met with Wynton and his lawyer. "And we signed him," Lundvall said.

Lundvall called George Butler and said: "I've just signed the trumpet player you've been telling me about."

Butler said, "What? What?"

Lundvall said, "Yeah, I just saw him last night. He's amazing. George, it's your signing, because you were there, you found him."[2]

So suddenly Wynton had the chance, beginning at age twenty, to lead his own group and record for a major record label, which planned to promote him. Columbia signed Wynton first to record only jazz, Wynton said. Then someone heard him playing in a concert broadcast on WQXR and gave it to Columbia executives, who decided to sign him to record classical music, too. There were people who objected to Columbia's enchantment with Wynton's ability to play classical music as well as jazz. This double signing alienated people in both the jazz and the classical worlds. But Columbia had made its decision. Wynton's versatility enticed the label.

Wynton had nothing to learn about playing the trumpet per se by staying with the Jazz Messengers, but he still had a great deal to learn about jazz and jazz history. Gunther Schuller regarded Wynton as the world's greatest trumpet player, although not necessarily the greatest jazz player. Wynton, recognizing the deficiencies in his education in the jazz tradition, would spend many years learning, as most people connected profoundly with the jazz world did. But he had been given an opportunity that no other player on any instrument in his generation was offered. Naturally, he had to leave Blakey and sink or swim on his own. Blakey worked so much, particularly in Europe and Japan, that Wynton couldn't play in that group and lead his own at the same time.

Wynton called Terence Blanchard to audition as the trumpeter replacement in the Jazz Messengers in 1982, and Terence, who had studied with Ellis Marsalis, got the job. Donald Harrison followed Branford into the group. (Trumpeter Wallace Roney would later play with Blakey again, too.) For a while, Blakey kept both Wynton and Terence in the band. It was Blakey's habit to have the outgoing and incoming players work together during the transition period.

When they traveled to Japan, Wynton and Terence were often mistaken for each other, perhaps because both were African-American trumpeters of a similar height and both wore glasses. At one press conference, to be playful, Wynton and Terence exchanged name tags. Then Shorty Rogers, a trumpeter who was at the conference, walked up to Terence and said how much he liked Ellis. The young trumpeters were embarrassed; they didn't try tricks like that again!

Instead, Terence toyed with the idea of wearing contact lenses, but he couldn't adjust to them. Wynton, however, began wearing them at times years later, when he was about twenty-five years old. Terence wondered mischievously if Wynton had done it because he didn't want to be confused with Terence.

Branford helped Wynton organize a group to begin recording. A very talented young pianist named Kenny Kirkland, born in 1955, had a Manhattan loft at 251 West 30th Street that served as a virtual jazz salon for gifted young players in Manhattan. Among them were saxophonists Michael Brecker and David Sanborn, guitarist Hiram Bullock, and Tracy Wormworth, the beautiful daughter of bebop drummer Jimmy Wormworth. She went with one of her sisters and some friends to listen to the music, and she soon surprised Kenny when she began playing the electric bass seriously. Their mutual love for music formed part of the basis for a long-lasting, personal relationship.

Branford, who had heard Kenny play, went to the loft and introduced himself. At this time, Kenny was clearly under the influence of Herbie Hancock's style begun in the mid-sixties, when Hancock was playing with Miles Davis's group. Kenny had studied at the Manhattan School of Music for three and a half years. Branford immediately asked him to record with Wynton. Kenny met Wynton for the first time when the new group recorded its first tune, "We Three Kings of Orient Are," for a long-playing record called *God Rest Ye, Merry Jazzmen*, in June 1981, in New York City.

Drummer Jeff Watts, too, entered the band through an introduction by Branford to Wynton. Born in January 1960, Watts had come from Pittsburgh and met Branford at the Berklee College of Music, where they had become friends. Watts probably met Wynton for the first time when he sat in, alongside Valery Pomonarev, with Blakey in a Boston club. Watts had first been a classical player, then gone on to rhythm and blues, to fusion, and was trying to make himself even more versatile when he started to learn more about jazz.

In the December 1982 issue of *Down Beat* magazine, Branford and Wynton, in a joint interview, entitled "A Common Understanding," described the members of Wynton's first group, a quintet. Branford recalled how Jeff Watts's playing had confused people, when Branford first heard the drummer in Boston. "They couldn't tell where 'one' was when Jeff played," Branford told the interviewer. That made Branford love Watts's playing from the start. Wynton said, "He knows a lot of shit, man. He has a concept about music."[3]

But Watts would recall it took Wynton a while to warm up to him and love his drumming. "I don't think he felt open with me at first," said Watts, who would develop into one of the most creative and admired drummers in jazz. "He kind of told me that he had a strange initial impression of me. I don't know why. But I thought he was okay. I like most people. But he was always cool."

It was in Wynton's group that Jeff acquired his nickname, "Tain." Wynton's nickname became "Skain" at that time, and he sometimes answered the phone by saying, "Skain," from then on. Everyone in the band had to have an "ain" type of nickname, Wynton recalled. Although people called Wynton "Skain" only in private, "Tain" actually became a part of Jeff Watts's professional name.

Also in Wynton's first group was Charles Fambrough on bass, along with Clarence Seay on some tracks. It isn't clear exactly why sometimes Seay and other times Fambrough showed up for gigs as part of Wynton's group during this period. They may have shared the bass seat. Fambrough left Blakey's group and joined Wynton's soon after Wynton left Blakey. And, of course, Branford was a member of the group, although Wynton asked him to switch from alto to tenor saxophone.

Around this time, Lew Soloff found a little gig at a restaurant called the Possible Twenty in New York, and he needed a rhythm section to play with him. The job paid only $200 for a weekend. He told Wynton, "I'm thinking of hiring some name musicians, my contemporaries."

Wynton, mindful of how much his fledgling group was struggling, said, "Why don't you give some kids a chance, some kids that you can really direct?"

Lew asked, "Do you know anybody?"

Wynton said, "Yeah, meet me down at the Village Vanguard."

At the appointed time, Wynton and Lew showed up. Along came Kenny Kirkland, and Jeff Watts who lived in Boston, and Clarence Seay from Washington, D.C., and Branford. Lew knew it was Wynton's band. He not only hired the youngsters—who were eager to play even though they would earn only $50 a person—he also hired Branford, which brought everyone's pay down to $40.

The band members decided to go to the gig "decked out," as they said, in suits and ties. When one said he would simply wear a sports shirt, Branford ordered him to wear a suit. The gig went so well, especially on Friday night, that people advised Lew to record with them. He decided not even to dream of it, however, because he knew Wynton had loaned him his band. That was generous enough.

In August 1981 Wynton was in the studio both to record his first solo album and to join the VSOP group for their second album.[4] VSOP was made up of members of Miles Davis's famous sixties-era bands; at this time VSOP included bassist Ron Carter, pianist Herbie Hancock, and drummer Tony Williams.

At this time, Wynton was still touring and playing with the Jazz Messengers. Nonetheless, he began focusing on his own group. They played in New York and on the road, and Wynton began to meet people around the country, fans and budding musicians among them.

"People really accepted [the group]," Kenny Kirkland recalled. "The work was strong." Looking back years later, he realized how it helped promote a resurgence of interest in jazz. Wynton was playing bebop and looking for logical extensions as a way to develop, both he and Kenny said. Thanks to the group's tours and the album, "young people began getting into the music," Kenny reflected.

Nominated for a Grammy award—which it didn't win—*Wynton Marsalis* nevertheless caught the attention of the public. The nomination was a milestone that made Wynton aware of what a Grammy was. Fairly quickly, jazz critics began scrutinizing him more. There were critics who thought Wynton was an exceptionally talented musician, a wunderkind. Others maintained that Wynton had a cold sound and attributed it to his background as a classically trained musician. Still others said he was too young and inexperienced for all the acclaim he was getting. The controversies were beginning to heat up quickly.

On the bright side, New Orleans mayor Ernest Morial proclaimed a Wynton Marsalis Day in February 1982. The young reeds player, Victor Goines, who had gone to school with Wynton, heard Wynton's group playing the songs "Father Time" and "Sister Cheryl" at the New Orleans Jazz and Heritage Festival that year. At that time, Wynton had no thought of trying to be politically correct or savvy at all. He simply wanted to promote his own thing, he told Goines. Goines, who had already heard Wynton play in Jacksonville, Florida, the year before, felt very happy "just to hear them play that kind of music."

Among the positive critics were some of the best-known names in jazz writing. Chris Albertson, author of a classic book about the great blues singer Bessie Smith, praised Wynton's first album to the skies in the magazine *Stereo Review*: "There is not a blemish on it."[5] And in "Baby Miles and Baby Wayne," an article published in the *Village Voice*, Gregory "Ironman" Tate remarked that Wynton's group members were "heraldic" for reasons other than "just their fast young chops." They "represent the first new generation of black musicians to take impetus from Miles Davis's seminal quintet of the '60s. . . ." While recognizing Wynton's youth, Tate still praised his incredible skill: "Wynton's inexperience and bluster [don't] detract from [his] chiming tone and unerringly fleet articulation. . . . "[6]

With an energetic sendoff from Columbia Records' publicity department, Wynton's first album sold around 100,000 copies. In the 1982 *Down Beat* poll, Wynton won both the Musician of the Year award and the Best Trumpeter award, placing over both Miles Davis and Dizzy Gillespie. Miles made no public comment about being replaced in the number one position, in truth, more often a measurement of a publicity coup rather than an indicator of a musician's ever-abiding worth.

Exactly how aware Miles was of the poll at that time isn't clear. He may have been sick in 1981, at the beginning of a long string of illnesses. But Miles said he became aware of Wynton and Branford in 1981 and at first liked Wynton. It's definite that, if he did, he and Wynton soon became embroiled in a bitter competition between the generations.

Miles was a very competitive man, who took seriously his title as the greatest trumpet player in jazz, something he had earned from years of playing. He ascended to the throne, on which he had sat throughout the 1950s and 1960s, until he converted the coin of his realm from acoustic music to jazz-rock fusion with electronic instruments in 1969. It was Miles's acoustic music, with his eerie, peerless tone, that had instructed and influenced Wynton. But, Wynton would come to publicly decry fusion and its founding genius, Miles.

Who threw the first stone? Wynton thought it was Miles, who began criticizing Wynton to jazz writers. When Miles and Wynton first met, Miles greeted him by saying, "So here's the police." Or Wynton might have gotten the ball rolling by voicing to anyone who would listen, including jazz writers, his aversion to jazz-rock fusion. Once the feud got started, it would become a matter of no importance who started it. Wynton and Miles would always have an edge, and a sharp one, about each other. Such feuds dotted the entire history of jazz, although most were carried out behind the scenes. Miles and Wynton garnered a lot of publicity through their criticisms of each other's musical styles and even their playing abilities.

In a way, it could be viewed as a classic battle for the heart and soul of jazz. Miles wanted the public to believe that he was pushing jazz forward to new frontiers of instrumentation, composition, and style. Whether he believed that himself is a good question. Wynton would later say that Miles confided in him and said that his post-sixties music was essentially unimportant. Miles stated publicly that Wynton was hopelessly reactionary by playing the bop-influenced acoustic jazz styles of the 1960s. But theirs was also a classic intergenerational struggle: Would a young turk be able to replace the now aging trumpet legend?

Wynton continued to win warm reviews from critics for his live performances. On March 5, 1982, Richard M. Sudhalter, himself a professional cornetist, an authority on Bix Beiderbecke and early jazz, and a writer, called Wynton's group "a tonic" when it appeared at Fat Tuesday's jazz club: "Wynton is classically trained, disciplined, with a large, warm tone and a sense of phrase shape and placement rare these days in one his age. He is also open, engaging, widely knowedgeable across a broad musical range. In one night's opening set he and Branford barged happily through a blues full of fun—phrase displacements, surprise figures, can-you-top-this variations. They enlivened 'Mack the Knife' with key shifts, melodic interpolations. . . . [Bassist Ron Carter] threw chord substitutions at them—only to have the brothers field them and throw them right back. . . .

"Wynton and Branford . . . seem to be at the center of a circle of young, highly skilled players determined to find their inspiration across the entire history of their music . . . the music is delicious."[7]

In 1982 Wynton and Branford recorded one side of an album called *Fathers and Sons* with their father for Columbia. On the other side were tenor saxophonists Chico Freeman and his father, Von, from Chicago. On May 16, 1982, in an article featuring both the Marsalis and Freeman families, Robert Palmer analyzed Wynton and his father's influence on his playing. He noted that "[Ellis] inspired his sons to learn the fundamentals of be-bop, probably the most difficult of all improvisational styles to master because of its whiplash rhythmic displacements and harmonic complexity. Wynton Marsalis learned be-bop so well that he actually sounds more comfortable playing a standard jazz repertory (pop standards, blues and 1980's modal tunes) than he does in freer improvisations."[8]

Wynton worked hard at making his quintet's tours go smoothly. The hotels weren't first class at the outset. The group wasn't always met on time at the airports and wasn't paid enough. The water and towels in dressing rooms weren't looked after well by the clubs. Insisting on better treatment, Wynton got results. The rough times didn't matter, Kenny Kirkland said, because "we were all very dedicated. But the conditions got better quickly. For a jazz gig it was a blessing." The hard times lasted just long enough to give the musicians a taste of the difficulties of life on the road. Kenny admired Wynton for his major efforts on behalf of the group.

Wynton liked to stay up late at night as long as the musicians were listening to music or talking about it. Branford and Wynton had a close relationship, Kenny observed then and through his long association to come with the brothers.

At Columbia Records, a young publicist named Marilyn Laverty was assigned to work with Wynton. Seven years older than he, she was born in New Jersey and attended Cornell University. She flunked out of the music program as a composition major, so she went for a degree in philosophy instead. After graduation, Laverty took a job with Columbia in the publicity department to support herself while she tried to launch a career in music journalism. She soon discovered that she excelled as a publicist and a guide for other writers.

In 1980 George Butler had begun telling everyone how excited he was about signing Wynton and how important Wynton would be for the establishment of a roster of young jazz artists. Against the background of the great, corporate enthusiasm about Wynton, Marilyn had eventually been sent backstage to meet him at Lincoln Center, where he was playing with Herbie Hancock in VSOP II. "It was just a brief meeting," she recalled. "My impression of him was that he was very polite, very intense, and dressed great.

"Everybody thought there was tremendous potential, not only because he was such an incredibly talented player in both classical music and jazz but also because he was so thoughtful, attractive, and articulate. He had a real point of view. He was talking about things, like preserving the history of the music at that time when other people weren't saying anything about it." Actually, throughout the jazz world, musicians, fans, and businesspeople had been worried for years about the future of jazz. They constantly asked each other: How was jazz going to survive the onslaught of pop music and the deaths of the great masters? But Wynton had the will and the way to make the subject more public.

In the publicity department, Marilyn wrote press releases, got albums reviewed, and arranged interviews with the print media and television. "I was given a lot of time to spend on Wynton and the mandate to publicize him as widely as possible," she remembered. "The message was traditional: Send his music out to people, let them know what his ideas were, and keep people informed about how his career was taking off. It didn't really involve a lot of expenditure of money. We weren't flying journalists all over the world to see him. But he was playing in New York pretty frequently. Of course, most of the jazz press is centered in New York. And within a short period of time people talked about him. He was extremely hard working and willing to do interviews and photo sessions."

For his cooperative spirit and personal affability, Marilyn thought she had a dream artist to work with. She felt gratified by the many remarkably favorable reviews and long feature stories written about him, and she didn't pay much attention to "a few that seemed skeptical and somewhat jealous," as she recalled. She was glad he was speaking his mind and exhibiting a strong sense of himself and what he wanted to accomplish. Even though he didn't particularly like photo shoots, he kept his dates for them. Other artists were prone to sit around and complain about the amount of publicity that other people were getting. "Yet if you set up an interview for them, sometimes they don't show up," she said. "Wynton was like a ray of light, a fireball."

But one of Wynton's greatest strengths—his outspokenness—would soon present itself as a double-edged sword within the jazz world.

Sometimes, the young jazz player would say things that he would later regret, even small things said to other musicians. A budding jazz piano star, Renee Rosnes, who was playing in an after-hours club, Basin Street, in Toronto, went to hear Wynton's group at a club in North Toronto and invited the musicians to her club—probably in late 1981 or early 1982. Branford, Kenny, Jeff, and Charles Fambrough showed up there. Afterward one of Wynton's sidemen told Wynton about her. When she went back to hear his group again, he told her to get up and play something. Then nineteen, she was shy. "I'm not into that. I didn't feel like I had to prove anything," she recalled. So she didn't do it.

She was supposed to have a lesson with Kenny Kirkland at a hotel, which was either connected to or near the club where Wynton's band was playing. Kenny, who was detained, sent Wynton instead. He could always be depended upon to keep dates with young musicians. "Wynton played and got me to play," Renee recalled. "We became friends. And it was okay. It turned into a jam session. . . .

"That same week, Wynton and I had a talk. I told him my aspirations to go to New York. I had either applied for a Canadian Arts Council grant, or maybe I was just thinking about it, because later I did apply and get it. I wanted to go to New York to become a better player. He said to me, 'Why do you want to go to New York? You'll never make it there.'"

At the time, Renee simply wanted to go to New York to study and then return to Canada. "I didn't have stars in my eyes. But a lot of my favorite musicians played there, and it was a healthy environment for music. He may have assumed I had aspirations. I didn't care what he said. But it stuck in my mind because I respected him as a musician. I think he said it because I'm white and a girl. But I'm assuming things. . . ."

The conversation stuck in Wynton's mind, too, and bothered him, she would discover years later, after she had achieved great success on her own in New York. He invited her to work with him there, and he apologized to her for his early awkwardness.

—————

Wynton was in and out of New York constantly, working with and for his group. One night, James Williams went with Wynton to hear a Jazz Messengers gig at Mikell's. Wynton told James that Terence Blanchard, who had replaced Wynton in the group, sounded good.

Williams responded, "Yes, you ought to like Terence, he's playing all your solos."

Wynton thought that was hilarious.

Wynton's first group was never really popular, he believed. "People always came to hear us play," he said. "We could fill up clubs. But the first summer was rough. After that we worked all the time." Wynton hired booking agents; he knew that Columbia helped with publicity to launch his first album beyond what the company usually did for jazz artists. "But you have to pay for that assistance," he noted Columbia deducted publicity expenses from his royalties. And though "they did more than they had done for any jazz musician," Wynton recalled, it was "not a lot. And the contract was so stupid. I didn't know nothing about that kind of stuff.

"It would kill me. Cats would be all mad and jealous. CBS paying me all that money, the cats thought, and CBS wasn't paying me shit. I'd just laugh. It was so little money that it was actually funny. Just the perception of it was something: 'Hey, they got him out here, pushing him.' And they were trying to push me to play pop music. Maybe it was $10,000 a year."

That contract was signed before Ed Arrendell, who would stay with him for most of his career, became Wynton's manager. Until Arrendell took charge of Wynton's affairs in 1983, Wynton earned very little and had no idea how to manage what he was earning. "Suffice it to say it wasn't no money. It was nothing," Wynton summed up about his initial contract with Columbia.

Wynton later praised Arrendell as "a major part of what we were doing; the success was in large part due to him. It was providential when I met Ed. The Lord was looking out for me. I didn't have a conception of money except for—don't spend it. I was naive about contracts."

The two men met when Arrendell went to a Seattle gig featuring Wynton's quintet. They talked, then met later in New York City, where Arrendell, a financial consultant with a master's in business administration from Harvard University, decided to become Wynton's manager. He made all the connections for the business end of Wynton's career. "It would have been inconceivable for me to stay out here and do what I did without his management and friendship, which he gave me constantly and totally," Wynton reflected.

"The quality of all we were doing went up. The hotels, contracts, everything; he took care of it all—the way we were treated and the intelligence of the bookings. He conducted all of it and made sure we were paid, and that I paid all the taxes." Wynton would just have put the tax form away someplace and forgotten about it, he said about himself. "Ed straightened me out." He used to give Wynton little tests to see what he was learning about the business end of his career. "Ed said, 'Man, you're going to return to slavery like that.'" Wynton loved the education. "We've been close the whole time."

Trumpeter Jon Faddis, Dizzy Gillespie's protégé, went to hear Wynton and Branford playing with Wynton's quintet one night at a club called Seventh Avenue South in Greenwich Village. Faddis thought Wynton sounded a great deal like Miles. Or perhaps Wynton reminded Jon of Miles, Faddis would later say, because Wynton didn't talk at all, nor did he introduce the members of his group. Jon mentioned this impression to Wynton and said he should announce the musicians' names. Wynton was furious about the comparison to Miles, Faddis said. But a little later on, he heard Wynton lead his group again. Wynton talked to the audience in his soft-voiced, charming way and announced the musicians. ("When he wanted to, Wynton could charm the bark off of trees," Bobby Watson has said.)

Jon Faddis had taken an interest in Wynton's career beginning in 1979. Wynton regarded himself as "country" at that time, he said—just a country hick in the big city. One time, Faddis, who loves health food and naturual remedies, went to the apartment the Marsalis brothers were sharing on Bleecker Street, near the Village Gate jazz club, and found them eating big bowls of Count Chocula, a breakfast cereal "full of sugar, like fruit loops," he recalled with horror. "Garbage," he told them, taking an interest in their welfare. "You shouldn't eat this stuff." They said, "Man, this is good, man," Faddis recalled.

The brothers had truly been kids when Faddis first met them. Lew Soloff may have been the one who introduced him to Wynton. "I remember laying some Dizzy Gillespie records on Wynton," Faddis said. "He didn't know Dizzy much or at all at that time. I guess he took them home and listened to them." Faddis also got Wynton some studio gigs, where Wynton played background music on pop-oriented sides. "He did pretty well," Faddis recalled, "because he could read and play, and he could play in a section."

Faddis called Wynton to substitute for him from time to time, and then heard Wynton with Blakey on a few gigs. "At that time I guess part of his 'country-ness' came out in a lot of things he was saying about established players. That turned a lot of older musicians off," Faddis said, recalling that Wynton criticized Blakey and Miles. "And he said that Dizzy had no tone." That comment particularly upset Faddis.

Faddis noted, "Wynton later put that off on his youth. When Wynton first came to town, he was very, very opinionated, and sometimes I felt that a lot of the things he was saying were the types of things that musicians said but didn't make public. Wynton made them public. When musicians ride in a band bus, they might say something, but on the q.t. . . . But I continued to hear him and his brother play."

Wynton still wasn't paying much attention to either Louis Armstrong or Dizzy Gillespie. Terence Blanchard had been mostly familiar with Armstrong's singing. Wynton still didn't know enough about the jazz heritage to understand what revolutionaries and geniuses both Louis and Dizzy were. The full impact of their styles, innovations, and contributions would dawn on him slowly, and eventually he would be completely carried away by them.

Although Wynton admired Blakey and learned from him, Wynton couldn't maintain his interest playing in Blakey's style. Every song was the same: the group played the head; then the soloists played; then the group returned to the head, led by the bombastic drummer. Wynton was quoted as saying that, after a few nights of that routine, he felt bored. Actually, he meant that he was simply ready to do something else. Blakey had no objections to having Wynton do something else, and Blakey enjoyed Wynton's ideas.

Tickets for the Wynton Marsalis quintet jazz concerts did sell, too. Young women stood in front of posters advertising him and said of his picture, "Isn't he cute?" People showed up for his club dates, willing to pay high prices to hear a neophyte.

By that time, Wynton had become an adorable-looking fellow, very well groomed, purposefully wearing suits and ties to his gigs. His Afro was trimmed; his sideburns were gone. His eyeglasses with heavy-looking frames had been exchanged for little round spectacles. The metamorphosis was stunning. Some critics would begin to focus on Wynton's wardrobe, and a few people even sniped at him for it, referring to him and his quintet as "the young men in suits." But most people loved Wynton's high standards for the appearance of his jazz groups. Wynton later told Ed Bradley during an interview for *60 Minutes* that he liked to be well-dressed on stage and happily pressed his suits for concerts, because he wanted to be considerate of his audiences. They had worked hard all week and were paying money to hear him; if it turned out that he wasn't playing well enough, they could say, "Well, at least he was clean."[9]

It was not just that Wynton could be a thrilling player. In the late 1970s, jazz had begun to experience a renaissance in the public perception. Rock concerts weren't as popular as they had been, partly because they had become too dangerous, with too many fights breaking out. Parents didn't want their kids to attend. People were looking for entertainment to replace rock concerts. Video games became popular with teenagers. Older people searched for more sophisticated diversions.

So at record companies, people decided to take a risk. Executives went into the company vaults and took out old, acoustic jazz albums from the 1950s and 1960s—Miles Davis albums, for example—and reissued them. Much to the surprise and delight of the executives, the LPs began to sell, some perhaps better than they had ever sold. The time had been ripe for another risk when Columbia signed Wynton, a young, virtually unknown artist, and gambled on his acceptance by the public. The gamble began paying off so well for Columbia that other jazz labels went scurrying in search of more "little Wyntons."

Terence Blanchard observed that Wynton's success had an enormous impact on the prospects and plans of young musicians, who suddenly set their sights on stardom in jazz. "Who else became so popular so fast and showed how someone can be successful in a short period of time? We hadn't seen that before in jazz," he said.

To one journalist around that time, Wynton summed up his real concerns: "You have to think of something to play all the time. That's pres-

L to r: Wynton Marsalis, unknown, and Wilmer Wise in San Miguel de Allende, Mexico, 1979.
Photo courtesy Wilmer Wise

The New York Jazz Gang in Mexico; Wynton is second from left, top row.
Photo courtesy Wilmer Wise

With Walter Booker, Jr., at the
Jazz Forum, July 30, 1982.
Photo by Raymond Ross

Wynton Marsalis in
New York, 1982.
Photo by Raymond Ross

Wynton in one of
his first publicity
pictures for
Sony/Columbia
Records, 1982.
Photo by David Gahr

Jeff "Tain" Watts, undated photograph.
Photo by David Gahr

Stanley Crouch in his early days as
a jazz drummer.
Photo by Raymond Ross

Kenny Kirkland at Zinno's in New York City, c. 1998.
Photo by Leslie Gourse

Wessell Anderson, undated photograph.
Photo by David Gahr

Branford when he was playing with
Wynton's original group, c. 1983.
Photo by David Gahr

Bob Hurst, undated
photograph.
Photo by David Gahr

Wycliffe Gordon, undated photograph.
Photo by David Gahr

The Septet in performance, 1994: Wycliffe Gordon, Wynton,
Victor Goines, Wessell Anderson.
Photo by Jack Vartoogian

Wynton enjoys playing counterpoint with Gerry Mulligan,
JVC Jazz Festival, 1993.
Photo by Jack Vartoogian

Wynton with friend
Tony Parker, a
policeman in Chicago.
Photo by Haroon Rajee

Marcus Roberts, Wynton,
McCoy Tyner, Louis Hayes,
c. 1985.
Photo by David Gahr

L to r, standing:
Greg Stafford,
Wynton, Dr. Michael
White; unidentified
child in front.
*Photo courtesy
Dr. Michael White*

Stanley Crouch,
Alina Bloomgarden,
Wynton at Lincoln
Center, c. 1989.
Photo by Suzanne
Faulkner Stevens

Peabody award winners Murray Horwitz of National Public Radio and Wynton.
Courtesy Murray Horwitz

sure. You get assigned a personality by the media that's not yours. There's the business aspect. Everyone's trying to make as much money off you as possible. And you have to try to play jazz and go on the road with a group, with all the responsibility. That's hard."[10]

—>•<—

A key early article on Wynton and his brother Branford appeared in a double interview in the December 1982 issue of *Down Beat* magazine. Although both brothers were pictured on the cover, the story focused on Wynton's leadership. The groundwork was being laid for a temporary rift between Wynton and Branford. A strong personality in his own right, Branford would soon meander, it seemed, onto a different path; it would, abetted by his talent, intelligence, charm, and name, bring him independent fame and fortune.

Wynton, who was twenty-one at the time, was leading his quintet around the world, while Branford, then twenty-two, had just signed a contract with Columbia. The brothers made it plain in *Down Beat* that Branford's group, which was yet to be formed, wouldn't include Wynton, because Branford didn't want to be overshadowed by his brother's personality. The brothers were very candid; most interesting of all about the article were revelations the brothers made about their individual principles and plans for their futures.

The story tried to explore the brothers' personal relationship and approaches to the music business. As innocent as they may have been simply because of their youth, they asserted themselves as very strong characters with vivacity, nerve, and attitudes.

Wynton stated absolutely that he didn't favor a cooperative band, because a group needed a leader. However, he also thought a leader shouldn't tell his sidemen exactly what to do. He said, "What you do is hire the cats who can play well enough to tell you what to do. But you have to make it seem like you're telling them. It's psychological. You have to be in charge of it, but you don't want to be in charge of it. . . . What I'm saying is that the direction of the band is formed by the band, but it goes through one person: the leader. If you're a leader, you lead naturally, automatically."[11]

Neither brother thought that all-star bands worked anywhere near as well as a band that played together all the time, because in all-star bands, everyone was a chief; there were no Indians, Branford said. Wynton also mentioned that he had learned from Art Blakey about how to regard sidemen. Although Blakey was the leader, he understood that his sidemen knew their instruments and what they could play. Wynton sometimes had to ask his sidemen to tell him what they were playing. "The hardest thing about being a leader is that you have to lead a group of cats who might know more than you know," he said.

On the other hand, Branford characterized himself as a great follower and believed that great leaders developed from great followers. In Wynton's band, Branford said, he had the luxury of observing what Wynton was learning about the music business. "He's setting the path for me, and I'm not going to have to make the same mistakes and go through the same crap that he's going through. While he's going through it, I'm sitting back observing, watching everything that they're trying to do to him.

"Record companies, agents, managers, the whole works. The hassles with the music, the gigs, riders in addition to contracts."

Branford said he was often asked how it felt to have an eminent brother. He truly felt he would rather have Wynton in the hot seat. Branford said, "[Wynton] thrives better under pressure than I do. If I had to deal with it, I'd deal with it. But he functions best under pressure. I function best when people leave me the hell alone and I don't have to deal with a lot of crap. . . .

"I'll admit I'm the classic lazy cat. I didn't want to be bothered. I didn't want to practice. I just wanted to exist. So I didn't practice. I played in a funk band and had a great time. When it was time to go to college, I went to the easiest one I could go to with the best teacher for music. But I really wasn't serious about music.

"Wynton played classical music because someone told him black cats couldn't play classical music. The first time he went out there, every one of the oboe players played the notes kind of out of tune, just to throw him off. He thrives best under that kind of stuff. If it were all relaxed and they said, 'Anything you want, man,' I think he'd be kind of shaky. When people tell him 'No,' that's when he's at his best. So all the pressure's on him. Good. When I come round and get my band, there shouldn't be that kind of pressure."

Wynton tried to explain how brothers who were so close could be so different. "My mother," Wynton said. "My mother's a great woman. She treats everybody the same, so we're all different. When you treat everybody the same way and don't tamper with the way you treat them in accordance to their personalities, then they act differently. They develop into their own people." In other words, his mother didn't cater to, or interfere with, the separate personalities of her sons, and so they could make many of their own decisions and go their own ways. She helped make them independent.

The piece then focused on their competitive friendship. While they seemed very close, it was clear that they often disagreed on major issues. Wynton agreed, saying, "Anything I would say, [Branford]'d say just the opposite." The interviewer asked if Branford did that to be obstinate. Wynton said, "Just to say it."

Branford quickly contradicted Wynton. "It wasn't just to say it. It was because I didn't agree."

"Nothing I say he agrees with," Wynton said.

Branford retorted, "Some things I agree with."

They didn't agree musically, either, Branford said. But he was very illuminating about their basic understanding: "I think we agree on the final objective. I think the common goal is there, but the route to achieve the common goal is totally different."

Branford said that it was easy for him to work for Wynton, because Wynton was the leader of the quintet. Wynton said Branford was in Wynton's band because Wynton couldn't find anybody who played better than Branford did. "Shit is very cut and dried with me," Wynton noted philosophically. Branford said they got along well playing music because they worked in the Wynton Marsalis Quintet, and when they were at home, they were brothers.

Wynton said the most difficult part of keeping his group together was to find gigs for it. He discovered he couldn't make money playing in clubs. In May 1982, he had found only three gigs for his band, and each of the jobs had lasted only an hour. The concert hall situation was better, because the type of music the group played was suited to concert halls. That is, it wasn't contemporary pop music.

In the 1950s and 1960s, Wynton said, pop music played in jazz settings could sound hip. But pop music in the 1980s didn't have any allure for jazz musicians in his opinion. "All of the popular tunes are sad pieces of one-chord shit. Today's pop tunes are sad . . . the melodies are static; the chord changes are just the same senseless stuff repeated over and over again." *Down Beat* readers would undoubtedly recognize this as a critique of Miles Davis.

Wynton made the fascinating observation that the pop tunes of the old days—the standards—hadn't lost their meaning, "but they're old. You've heard them played so many times by great performers that you don't want to play them again." One of his insights was that nobody wanted to do somebody's else's song. "Everybody thinks that they can write great tunes, and all the public wants is that it sounds different. Music has to be played before it gets old. The music that Ornette Coleman played, that Miles and Trane [John Coltrane] played in the '60s, some of the stuff that [Charles] Mingus and Booker Little and Charlie Rouse and these cats were starting to do . . . that music isn't old because nobody else has ever played it." It was an insight that would seem to guide Wynton throughout his career and influence some of his choices of music to play.

Wynton recognized that some listeners and critics said he was derivative of the 1960s masters for playing their tunes. "People say, 'Man, you sound like you're imitating Miles in the '60s.' Or else, 'He sounds like he's imitating Elvin Jones.' So what? You just don't come up with something new. You have to play through something. The problem with some of the stuff that all the critics think is innovative is that it sounds like European music. European, avant-garde, classical, twentieth century, static rhythm music with blues licks in it. And all these cats can say for themselves is, 'We don't sound like anybody else.' That doesn't mean shit.

"The key is to sound like somebody else, to take what is already there and sound like an extension of that. It's not to sound like that. Music has a tradition that you have to understand before you can move to the next step. But that doesn't mean you have to be a historian." He would repeat the same message to other interviewers in the future, even as he began to reject the post-bop repertoire that he at first admired.

Although Wynton said he had nothing against funk, he didn't think this music should be called "jazz." This led to a lengthy critique of Miles Davis, another example of Wynton's tendency to express his opinions bluntly, no matter what the consequences. "They call Miles's stuff jazz. That stuff is not jazz, man. Just because somebody played jazz at one time, that doesn't mean they're still playing it. Branford would agree with me." Dependably, Branford laughed and said, "No, I don't agree," staying off Miles's toes.

Wynton went on: "The thing is, we all get together, and we know that this shit is sad, but we're gonna say it's good, then everybody agrees.

Nobody is strong enough to stand up and say, 'Wait, this stuff is bullshit.' Everybody is afraid to peek out from behind the door and say, 'C'mon, man.' Everybody wants to say everything is cool."

Branford went on to say he didn't feel he was more open than Wynton, but Wynton was "kind of set in his ways." He then echoed Wynton's general critique of some of the more popular jazz-fusion bands of the day: "Everything has become Los Angeles—everything is great and everything is beautiful. It's kind of tired. Cats come up to me and say, 'What do you think of Spyro Gyra?' And I say, 'I don't.' That's not an insult to Spyro Gyra. I just don't like it when people call it jazz when it's not."

The brothers then were encouraged to discuss their views of practicing and how young players should learn to play jazz. In this discussion, they showed remarkable agreement, often finishing each other's thoughts and generally reflecting the influence of their father's teaching on them.

As advice to young players, Branford emphasized the importance of the bass player in particular and the whole rhythm section of a group. Wynton wanted people to listen to the music; he wished that high schools would have programs and records for students to listen to—and not just "Buddy Rich and Maynard Ferguson," he said, but "[Charlie] Parker and Coltrane and some of the more creative cats. That should be a required thing." By mentioning the latter, he was talking about inclusion of the great African-American innovators.

Both brothers felt that young players should learn the classic solos by other jazz musicians. However, youngsters shouldn't learn them note for note, but try to re-create them in order to gain proficiency on their instruments. Listening to what other musicians were doing was equally important, not just playing a solo as a set piece to be repeated night after night.

Wynton summed up his advice to young players by stating, "Music goes forward. Music doesn't go backwards. Whatever the cats couldn't play before you, you're supposed to play."

Branford added, "There's a huge movement for the perpetuation of ignorance in jazz. Play. That's all."

Reflecting on this interview years later, Branford said, "The ironic thing about it, if you study our careers carefully, it pretty much holds true to that article." Branford also recalled, "Wynton was pretty pissed about it. He thought I was trying to undermine him. I told him: 'The whole idea of [my] doing a dual interview is not to just sit around and agree with you. If I agree with you, yes, but I just didn't happen to agree with you on those issues.' But he was very, very angered."

Characteristically Wynton disagreed with Branford's memory of how he reacted to the interview. He was not angry about Branford's differing opinions but leery of the way the press would handle them. He felt that writers tended to look for opportunities to poke fun at him in the interests of producing entertaining stories. And so he wished Branford had offered a little better protection.

The brothers had a very complex relationship fraught with sibling rivalry, although based on a profound and enduring love and loyalty on both sides. Never would they be free of their bond, despite their occasional private biting criticisms of each other. The bond overrode many maelstroms—those between them, and those between them and the rest of the world.

Branford would often take the side of his brother, "if there was a crisis," Wynton believed, and he would do the same for Branford. "Whatever quarrels I have with Branford," Wynton said, "that's my brother. That's my attitude."

Chapter Notes

1. That meeting happened in 1980 or 1981, before Wynton recorded with Blakey at the Keystone Korner in 1982. Blakey played there about four times a year.
2. When Bruce Lundvall left Columbia and became the head of the Blue Note record label, he tried to sign Wynton to Blue Note when Wynton's Columbia contract was up. Lundvall was sure that Warner Brothers and everyone else tried to sign him, too, but Sony wasn't letting him go. Within just a few years, it would become apparent that Wynton was more than just a great trumpet player; he was becoming "a spokesman for the music and an extraordinary man," in Lundvall's opinion.
3. A. James Liska, "Interview with Wynton and Branford Marsalis: A Common Understanding." *Down Beat*, December 1982.
4. It was eventually issued under the title *Quartet* as a Herbie Hancock album.
5. From an article by Chris Albertson in *Stereo Review*, May 1982, as quoted in *Current Biography Yearbook*, 1984, p. 257.
6. Gregory "Ironman" Tate, "Baby Miles and Baby Wayne." *Village Voice*, June 8, 1982.
7. Richard M. Sudhalter, "Jazz a Piece of Pie to Marsalis." *New York Post*, May 5, 1982.
8. Robert Palmer, "Jazz Families Bridge the Generation Gap." *New York Times*, May 16, 1982.
9. *60 Minutes*, interview with Ed Bradley, CBS-TV, broadcast on November 26, 1995.
10. "Wynton Marsalis: Portrait of a Young Master," by Leslie Gourse, *Pulse*, West Sacramento, June 1985.
11. A. James Liska, "Interview with Wynton and Branford Marsalis: A Common Understanding." *Down Beat*, December 1982. All of the following quotes come from this article.

GURUS AND GUIDEPOSTS

Stanley Crouch and Albert Murray

When Stanley Crouch, a jazz critic for the *Village Voice*, first met Wynton, the trumpeter was barely mentioned in newspapers, jazz periodicals, or other magazines. Wynton was still playing with Art Blakey. Crouch, who had formerly booked the music for a popular club called the Tin Palace, on the Bowery, had played drums with a variety of musicians, particularly some avant-gardists such as saxophonist David Murray. But Crouch had left his playing behind when he began his career as a journalist. He often invited young musicians to his house to talk about music, and he especially liked Wynton because he was "smarter than most jazz musicians," Crouch would later reflect.

"Most jazz musicians aren't interested in much," he said. "Wynton was a guy who was interested in a lot of different things, sciences, history, technology." Crouch thought that Wynton had "some good education" in the first place, and his father was an intellectual, "not just another guy who plays the piano." Crouch said that Dizzy Gillespie and other great jazz musicians were intellectuals, too. But they weren't emblematic of jazz musicians in general.

Crouch never got the impression that Wynton had ever been the "barefoot country boy" in New York City. By the time they met, Wynton had enjoyed quite a bit of playing experience in town. And, Crouch recalled, "I didn't see any initial resentment toward him. He wasn't a big star then. He was just a flashy young trumpet player with Art Blakey's band. There was no big deal about that. Nobody would care. He was just another guy. Freddie Hubbard was still out there playing; Woody Shaw was around, playing great. So there was a lot going on.

"Dizzy was alive and still capable of playing extremely well. Wynton knew of Dizzy. It didn't appeal to Wynton, that way of playing; I think Wynton thought [the style] was too much like playing a saxophone. I think Wynton has probably rethought that since," Crouch reflected.

Crouch would become a mentor to the young trumpeter, furthering his musical—and intellectual—education. From the beginning, he delighted in sharing his opinions with Wynton. Crouch advised Wynton to read *Joseph and His Brothers* by Thomas Mann, all four volumes by the great German novelist. Perhaps it was actually another intellectual, Albert Murray, Crouch's own mentor, who recommended those books. Certainly Murray had first advised Crouch to read them. "Wynton used to call me from the road, when he was reading," Crouch remembered about his discussions of the Mann books with Wynton.

Crouch was also important in Wynton's education about the history of jazz. For one thing, not only did he play Ornette Coleman records for Wynton, he educated Wynton to realize that some people who played avant-garde music could really play well.

Crouch recalled, "Ornette Coleman turned him around. [Wynton] didn't really know much about Louis Armstrong. So I started loaning him Armstrong and Ellington records. He didn't really know that much about Thelonious Monk. We talked about Monk. What he actually knew at that time was John Coltrane, Clifford Brown, Miles Davis. I'm sure he knew Freddie Hubbard, those kinds of people.

"But in terms of the background, where those people came from, he didn't really know. And so we spent a lot of time going over recordings and different things."

Crouch was in many ways a perfect mentor for Wynton. Highly intelligent and very opinionated, he was unafraid to express what he felt was right—and willing to go to the wall for his convictions.

Like Wynton, Crouch was greatly influenced by his family life. His father was a heroin addict who spent time in jail for a drug-connected conviction. Off and on for a few years after his release, he and Stanley had some contact, but that connection petered out. However, Stanley's mother, who worked as a maid in Los Angeles to support her eldest child (a daughter), Stanley, and a younger brother, had vision. She exposed her children to the classics, encouraging them to watch films of Shakespeare's plays on television. "My mother was Little Miss Perfect Lower Class," Crouch told an interviewer many years later. "She was an aristocrat in that strange American way that has nothing to do with money."[1]

Sickly with asthma, Crouch spent his childhood reading books; by the time he finished high school in 1963, he had read many of the great American novelists. He became involved in the intellectual activities and sociopolitical ferment of Watts: the poetry readings, the dramatic presentations, even black nationalism. The nonviolent civil rights movement and the riots in Watts in 1965 made a deep impression on him.

Reading his own poetry in Studio Watts, a local repertory theater, Crouch impressed another local poet named Garrett Hongo. Hongo recalled, "He had these chantlike lines that resembled [Walt] Whitman, but they were in a black street vernacular that was eloquent and pissed off. He'd run this rap, with quotations from Shakespeare and [Herman] Melville, riff on Langston Hughes and Cecil Taylor, and then relate it all to that day's news."[2] Crouch also began turning himself into an expert on jazz and with friends listened to records by Charlie Parker, Dizzy Gillespie, Thelonious Monk, Miles Davis, Sonny Rollins, and the great, innovative reeds player Eric Dolphy.

In 1967, in a poetry workshop at Watts Happening, a local coffeehouse that served as an intellectual center, Crouch was distressed when the workshop leader, Budd Schulberg, was loathe to criticize the "awful" poetry—as Crouch described it—written by one of the African-American members. Crouch didn't want to excuse "third-rate work," as he deemed it, by anybody.[3] Crouch would later be a critic of affirmative action for the same reason, feeling that blacks had to earn their place in society, even though they had faced segregation in the past.

Crouch went on to become the poet-in-residence at Pitzer College in Claremont, California, then the first full-time faculty member of the Claremont Colleges Black Studies Center. From that base, Crouch, although he had no college degree, propelled himself into a teaching position in Pomona College within Claremont Colleges, where the majority of the students and teachers were white. He did it by visiting members of the English department and impressing them with his knowledge of

James Joyce, Herman Melville, and others. And he had the talent to become a charismatic, outspoken, even gutsy teacher.

As one of his side ventures, Crouch taught himself to play drums in the avant garde style of spontaneous improvisation. He didn't think he played very well, but, instead of giving up drums, he founded a band called Black Music Infinity, including David Murray on tenor saxophone, Arthur Blythe on alto sax, James Newton on flute, Mark Dresser on bass, and Bobby Bradford on trumpet. All of them built notable careers. Bradford gave Crouch lessons in jazz history, particularly about Louis Armstrong. The insights would stand Crouch in very good stead.

For seven years, Crouch taught at Claremont. He became particularly involved in theatrical productions and wrote plays that shocked his audiences. In an adaptation of a Melville story, he had a ship's captain murdered by slaves. David Flaten, the director of the production, recalled years later: "Everyone was shocked and horrified, because at the time this was everyone's worst nightmare. White liberals found it racist, and blacks were offended. Crouch always wanted to make the audience feel threatened."[4]

Relocating to New York in 1975, Crouch immersed himself in the bohemian lifestyle of the Lower East Side. He moved into a loft with avant-garde saxophonist David Murray. Crouch began promoting jazz performances, then booked one of the leading jazz clubs of the period, the Tin Palace, on the Bowery. But he lost his taste for bohemia, if indeed he had ever really liked anything about it except that he could afford it.

Crouch began writing critical articles about black nationalists. Soon after meeting Albert Murray, Crouch entered the American Establishment through a back door, by writing for a well-accepted bastion of left-leaning liberalism, the *Village Voice*. Joining its staff in 1980, he developed a reputation as a sometimes brilliant writer about jazz and social and political issues.

Crouch also became known as a tough, extremely volatile man who was unafraid and actually fairly happy to challenge people to verbal and occasionally physical fights. Sometimes he threw out gratuitous and faulty insults, seemingly convinced of their righteousnesss. Though not tall, he was sturdily built. On the other hand, he also could effect a tender, endearing open-mindedness and liked to encourage, teach, and mentor some people. In the early 1980s, he was one of the very few male writers about jazz who would even talk to a woman beginning to establish herself as a jazz writer.

Without knowing it at the time, with his quixotic combination of assets and shortcomings, he was the right man in the right place. Neither he nor Wynton Marsalis had any idea what the near future held for them in their careers, but they befriended each other and, in a way, provided a safe haven for each other. Both driven, they could appreciate each other without any hint of competition in their relationship.

Wynton remembered he was about eighteen when he first met Stanley Crouch. Years later, as a guest on Marian McPartland's *Piano Jazz* show on National Public Radio, Wynton reminisced about how important Crouch was to his musical education. "I thought I knew all about jazz, I'm from New Orleans," he told McPartland, "and my daddy is a jazz musician.

"Over the years, we had a real good friendship," Wynton said about Crouch, "and he turned me on to a lot of records, and just a perspective on the history of the music that I didn't really have."[5]

Wynton was impressed by Crouch's love for jazz. "At that point, I wasn't knowing anything," Wynton recalled. When he went to Crouch's house, "Stanley's girlfriend would cook some good food, and I could eat. I'd be starving. I was so used to eating that food I was cooking." Wynton said he "really, truly was grateful for those meals."[6]

Perhaps most important of all, Crouch, as Wynton's mentor, started to feel loyal to the gifted trumpeter. Highly opinionated and argumentative in his own right, he had qualities that may have reminded Wynton of his family life, with its emphases on discussions and the necessity for backing up opinions with facts.

Crouch was astounded at how great Wynton's prowess on the trumpet was and how little Wynton knew about the jazz tradition, while Crouch's thirst for knowledge dazzled Wynton. "That was a very abstract concept for somebody like me," Wynton recalled. "You didn't think about people knowing anything outside of school, not in the circles I was in."[7]

Wynton commented years later, "[Stanley's] one of the first people who made me understand the value of the historical perspective in jazz music and the fact that there's a philosophy that goes behind any type of aesthetic achievement. I used to think that people just could play.

[Thelonious] Monk, he was just a genius, he had talent. It was Crouch who made me understand that Monk's music was hard because [Monk] made it hard. It's not just hard because he woke up one day and some hard music came out. . . ."

About jazz in general, Wynton quickly learned, "You have to seek it out, figure out what it's about. You have to make sure you learn how to play. A lot of times you have to teach yourself. But there's a lot of musicians who will help you. But it's not like in classical music where there's all kinds of camps and you know very clearly what you have to do. . . ."[8]

Crouch began his role as Wynton's cheerleader-in-chief on the liner notes for Wynton's first album in 1982. The notes introduced Wynton and his group with the proper praises of the young trumpeter's obvious virtuosity. Crouch may have also put words in Wynton's mouth, when he quoted the young trumpeter as saying: "What I'm trying to do is come up to the standards all of these trumpet greats have set—Armstrong, Gillespie, Navarro, Brown, Miles, Freddie Hubbard and Don Cherry."

Despite Wynton's dislike for Miles Davis's repertoire at the time, the elder trumpeter's influence was particularly obvious in 1981 on Wynton's first and second albums, recorded in 1983. Wynton admired Davis's acoustic work from the early to mid-1960s, when Davis was playing with such gifted young sidemen as Herbie Hancock, Ron Carter, and Tony Williams. Davis's influence is particularly apparent in Wynton's playing on "R.J.," written by Ron Carter. The bent notes in his solo on "Who Can I Turn to When Nobody Needs Me?" clearly evoked Davis's style and made Wynton's interpretation very poignant.

In addition to individual tracks, the overall virility and facility of Wynton's playing came directly from Miles at his peak in the 1960s. Critic Larry Kart in the *Chicago Tribune* immediately recognized this debt: "Marsalis obviously feels that the innovations of [Davis's sixties-era group have] yet to be superseded," he wrote, "because almost every performance on [the first two albums] he has made under his own name pays homage to the style of the 1960s Davis Quintet."[9]

* * *

In 1982 Crouch introduced Wynton to Albert Murray, a blues and jazz historian, biographer, novelist, and social commentator, among other things, for more education. Wynton made repeated visits to Murray's apartment on 132nd Street in Harlem, to ask for information and to build upon previous lessons. Murray thought Wynton's brilliance resided, at least in part, in his recognition of what he didn't know. Wynton remembered sitting through conversations that he didn't understand between Murray and Crouch. But then Wynton began to understand.

Murray was born in Mobile, Alabama, and adopted by a family there. Distinguishing himself as a student and an athlete, he loved listening to blues musicians while he was in high school. Years before he turned to teaching in colleges and then writing books, he went on a scholarship in 1935 to the Tuskegee Institute, the school founded by Booker T. Washington, then served in the Air Force during World War II and the Korean War. By the time he retired from the Air Force in 1962, he had attained the rank of major and had trained many young airmen.

Murray lived through the glory days of the music of the Swing Era, and his personal friends included luminaries such as Duke Ellington and Count Basie. The contemporary and protégé of many great intellectuals and musicians in African-American culture, counting the distinguished writer Ralph Ellison, author of the classic novel *The Invisible Man*, as his special friend, Murray received Crouch's unabashed affection and reverence. Murray immersed himself proudly in the riches of African-American achievements as well as in world literature, philosophy, and music. Naturally, Crouch wanted to expose Wynton Marsalis to Murray's influence.

Wynton always visited Murray in his Harlem apartment; Murray didn't visit Wynton. Wynton's first peek at Murray's universe revealed a collection of hundreds of books by great American and European writers, including Ernest Hemingway, William Faulkner, Thomas Mann, and André Malraux in first editions, and large photographs of Duke Ellington composing and Louis Armstrong blowing his trumpet.[10] Murray also owned a collection of paintings by artist Romare Bearden and would eventually give one work as a gift to Wynton. Wynton gave lovely gifts to Murray, too, as the years went on—a fine, inscribed watch, for one thing.

Dick Russell described a meeting between Murray and Wynton. "The older man beckoned Marsalis to a couch and invited him to examine his photo albums. There were many pictures of Murray's close friend Ralph Ellison. . . . Here was the pianist/bandleader Count Basie, who had Murray put together his autobiography [in the 1980s]. There stood a handsome crew of the Tuskegee Airmen, the remarkable all-black World

War II squadron which Murray helped to train. Here were the Spanish Steps in Rome, and the entryway to Jefferson's Monticello."[11] Marsalis would say years later, "From Albert Murray, I learned to envision things on a grand scale."

Some people would come to believe that Albert Murray, who published his first book when he was fifty-four, developed into a writer of the stature of Ralph Ellison, despite the marked differences in their writing styles. In 1997 Murray was inducted into the American Academy of Arts and Letters and received a lifetime achievement award from the National Book Critics Circle. At a gathering to celebrate the publication of the *Norton Anthology of African American Literature*—a truly remarkable collection of centuries of varied writings—he was introduced as "the dean of African-American letters."[12]

Murray was special among jazz writers because, like Crouch, he wrote on both music and culture. His first book, *The Omni Americans*, published in 1970, was an important look at black-white relations and American culture in general. In it he argued that American culture came out of the rich interplay of both black and white elements. At the same time, he thought that blacks were the most authentic Americans because they arrived with "the least baggage," and that slavery and oppression had made African Americans heroic and their culture life-enhancing.

In the realm of music criticism, Murray is probably best known for his 1978 book *Stomping the Blues*. Although written in a somewhat convoluted style, the book—a sociophilosophical and educational work—revealed the importance of the blues as one of the most eloquent of all African-American musical forms.

Murray introduced Marsalis to a world of culture that both transcended race and honored the greatness of the African-American culture. When Crouch introduced Wynton to Murray, Wynton had already heard about Murray from a young woman in New Orleans who had taken a creative writing class with Murray at Barnard College. In turn, Wynton recommended that other young musicians visit Murray and ask for reading lists.

Many of Murray's recommendations centered on literature, particularly the classic literature of the South. Murray told Wynton that William Faulkner was a Southern writer "steeped in the folklore and wisdom of Uncle Remus" who nonetheless gave his black characters "a greater humanity. . . ."[13] There is no doubt that Faulkner, in his most famous novel, *The Sound and the Fury*, a quintessentially Southern story, portrayed Dilsey, the black maid, as a heroine representative of high moral values.

Wynton related how Murray's literary recommendations influenced his musical growth: "You've got to come through Faulkner. . . . You've got to do something so that if you're in a jam session with Faulkner, he would say, 'Hey, that was a good solo.' From Faulkner, I got the challenge of dealing with time. But the economy I got from Hemingway. See, [Faulkner] was the master of epic style. Hemingway's a genius for simplicity. Faulkner's a genius of convolution."[14]

Murray also read the poetry of W.H. Auden to Wynton. And from the novels by Mann that Murray loaned to Wynton, "I got the idea that you could find an aesthetic model in your [own] idiom for literature," Wynton said. "So when he started talking about a dialectic orchestration and leit motifs and things like that, I started thinking about riffs, breaks. . . ."[15] Clearly, Wynton perceived principles and standards of other artists in ways that inspired him and served the purposes of his own music.

Murray spoke to Marsalis of a belief "in a kind of Whitmanesque nationalism that Bessie Smith and Fats Waller are a part of." He showed Wynton dozens of books on the Civil War, asking, "How could you be a colored guy in the U.S. and talk about your position and not know anything about the Civil War?" Murray offered historical perspectives: "You don't have a better prototytpe for the self-created American than Harriet Tubman, Frederick Douglass, or Louis Armstrong picking up that horn."[16]

Wynton was intrigued by Crouch's reverence for Albert Murray and by the unorthodox education they provided for him at museums, with books, and during dinner table conversations that touched on the Greek classics, history, science, drama, fiction, and poetry. Not only Wynton but also other musicians, saxophonist and conductor Loren Schoenberg for one, had similar experiences with Crouch and Murray. Asked what books and writers Murray recommended for him, Wynton replied easily, in addition to Mann, Faulkner, and Ernest Hemingway's lesser known *In Our Time*, *The Coming Victory of Democracy*, *Doctor Faustus*, Heinrich Zimmer's *The King and the Corpse*, and Joseph Campbell's books.

Wynton attended a university without walls for an eclectic, unofficial degree in world culture offered by Murray and Crouch. Their intellectual heroes would become Wynton's intellectual heroes. He would often cite them as guideposts.

———————

Around the time Wynton met Crouch, perhaps because Wynton started to feel curious about the old New Orleans trumpeter, Wynton's father sent Wynton a tape of Louis Armstrong playing "Jubilee." Wynton recalled, "Pops plays a solo on it, and I tried to learn the solo, and I didn't have the endurance to make it through the solo. So then I really had to deal with his tone and what he was playing a different way, because I had never really tried to learn any of his music. I was only dealing with the media image of Louis Armstrong. He was smiling.

"And then when you pick that trumpet up, that's when you really knew. It slaps that respect into you. You know, 'Bap, oh, oh, I see.' That was like, if you're in hysteria, and someone just slaps you into something else. And I could just hear the phrasing and the timing, and it sounds so natural and perfect that it seems easy.

"He was just a great, tremendous musician, and he refined his style to such a high degree before he died. . . . [I]n the '50s and '60s, it's unthinkable—just the level of majesty . . . the nuance and control . . . so when you listen to it, it doesn't sound like what it actually is. . . . [T]hat's the sound that has been imitated so much. . . .

"Plus he addresses the central meaning of the music from a humanity standpoint, and he is the representative of the New Orleans tradition."[17]

In addition to introducing him to great literature, Crouch and Murray were responsible for giving Wynton new insights into jazz history. Because of Murray and Crouch, Wynton came to realize the importance of Louis Armstrong and Duke Ellington, among other early great jazz musicians, bandleaders, players, and composers. Although Wynton had grown up in the birthplace of jazz, he had virtually taken its riches for granted and never explored them.

Tutored by Crouch and Murray, Wynton, who had once thought of Louis Armstrong as an Uncle Tom playing such commercial hits as "Hello, Dolly," came to respect Armstrong and liken him to Merlin the magician. Other musicians before Wynton had noticed the similarity even between the words "magician" and "musician" and felt that musicians were magicians. Wynton spoke enthusiastically about his new discovery. "[Armstrong] brought back a real joy to music. [He] loosens up everybody's phrasing, their concept of where to place the beat. You get bass players trying to sound like him, and trombone and saxophone sections, and arrangers writing Louis Armstrong licks. Because more than any other musician's, his sound carries the feeling and the meaning of jazz. Anything you want, he has it—warmth and intelligence, worldly and provincial, spiritual and tawdry, down home but sophisticated. The most complex player there's ever been, yet he can still sound like a country boy," said Wynton.[18]

From Crouch and Murray, it seemed, Wynton was beginning to appreciate older, classical jazz music—the music of the early titans of jazz. Actually, Wynton was getting support for his own inclinations about music since his childhood days. While he was leading his first group from 1981 to 1985, composing fresh music that would fascinate even some staunch avant-gardists, Wynton kept immersing himself in the music of the jazz founders. His growing familiarity and reverence for early jazz, however, seemed like a secret in those days (even though he did engage in some performances with groups that had a touch of the traditional Second Line New Orleans music ambiance in their presentations) when he lived on the fast track of young modernists.

CHAPTER NOTES

1. Robert S. Boynton, "The Professor of Connection." *The New Yorker*, November 6, 1995.
2. Ibid.
3. Ibid.
4. Ibid.
5. *Piano Jazz*, interview with Wynton Marsalis, by Marian McPartland, National Public Radio, 6 January, 1996.
6. Ibid.
7. Ibid.
8. Ibid.
9. Larry Hart, quoted in the profile of Wynton Marsalis in *Current Biography Yearbook*, 1984.
10. Dick Russell, *Black Genius*. New York: Carroll & Graf, 1998.
11. Ibid.
12. Ibid.
13. Ibid.
14. Ibid.
15. Ibid.
16. Ibid.
17. *Piano Jazz*, interview with Wynton Marsalis, by Marian McPartland, National Public Radio, 6 January, 1996.
18. Russell, *Black Genius*.

CANDACE STANLEY

B y 1983 Wynton had met another very important person in his life: Candace Stanley, a young woman whom he encountered by chance in Brooklyn. Born on January 18, 1962, only a few months younger than Wynton, she quickly became his girlfriend.

Dr. William Kenneth Mask, a radiologist who grew up in Hamlet, North Carolina, and whom everyone called "K," introduced Wynton to Candace Stanley. Some members of K's family and Candace's father Barry and mother Marilyn, both architects, were friendly. Visiting relatives in Sag Harbor on Long Island one summer, K met Candace, whose grandparents had a summer house there. Candace, who had loved to go there as a child, was beginning to find it too quiet, when she was fifteen, the age at which she met K.

In 1982 or 1983, Ed Arrendell, Wynton's manager, went to meet the budding basketball star Michael Jordan at Chapel Hill, where K was attending Duke University. Arrendell, who knew that K and Michael Jordan were friends, wanted an introduction. Wynton, devoted to basketball himself, went to Chapel Hill that weekend with Arrendell and met both K and Jordan. "We just hit it off," K remembered about his first meeting with Wynton.

When K was on spring break from college in 1983, Wynton invited him to come to New York. "Come and hang out with me," he said. K had that quality of calmness that Wynton, who was so intense, seemed to like in people. All his closest friends, except for Stanley Crouch, could be called laid back and flexible. Wynton and Branford were living in an apartment in Brooklyn at that time. So K went.

"One night we went out to eat at Two Steps Down, a restaurant in the neighborhood," K said. "We were on our way out, when Barry [Stanley] and his daughter Candace, who lived in Brooklyn, were coming in. Candace and I were buddies. We doubled back and sat with them for a while."

As K recalled, the following day, she went to Wynton's apartment to visit, at K's invitation. Candace remembered that she and a friend went there the same night she met Wynton. The month was April, and it had just snowed. Candace had recently seen the Grammy Awards show on which Wynton had won his first two Grammys for jazz and classical recordings. She and some friends watching the show had been very impressed because "he was young and black," she said, "with these little rimless glasses, and a conservative haircut . . . no shag. . . . He was kind of conservative looking back in those days."

Candace was very impressed by how well he played his horn, first on a classical piece, then on a jazz song. "Then he turned around and got on the mike, and everyone in the room was 'Wow, he talks like a brother.' The expectation was that someone who played classical music, and was proficient at it, steeped in classical music, would . . . talk like white people. . . . He was an anomaly to me."

At Tufts University in Boston, where she had graduated with a degree in general engineering and computer science, Candace had met many African Americans who had spoken in the way she was accustomed to hearing white people talk.

Soon after seeing the Grammys, she recognized Wynton in the restaurant Two Steps Down; if she hadn't seen the show, she would have had no idea who he was. In the restaurant, "he was his normal, charming self," she recalled. "Wynton likes to engage people, to find out what's happening with you. Initially, I was just thrilled to talk to him." He seemed very interested in getting to know her better. K said, "Why don't you come by the house?"

When Candace and her friend went to the apartment to visit Wynton and K, they were looking to "party" with the young men. "I was a native New Yorker in that way," Candace said. "I was into a heavy party scene. You go to a club and you dance for hours. We used to come down from Boston on a Friday night, and we would go to the Garage, a club. We would get there at midnight and leave the next day at 11:00 A.M."

Candace loved to dance. "I took dance classes my whole life." She didn't know it at that time, but Wynton wasn't into the "party" scene, she said. Had she known, she wouldn't have insisted on their going to dance in a private house. Wynton later recalled that he had no problem with the scene, because he had spent so much time playing for dances in New Orleans. In any case, he had a good time, Candace thought, because there were new people and new experiences. And of course there was Candace.

"We didn't stay long," she recalled. "We were just talking a lot, talk talk talk. That was our favorite thing to do, for hours, anywhere, on the phone." It would always remain a favorite pastime for both of them.

Wynton began calling K and asking, "You think she likes me, man?" The next thing K knew, Candace and Wynton were dating.

"When we got together, it was dynamite," Candace said. "I was very attracted to him intellectually and every other way. I was living with my parents right around the corner from him, and I was going for my mas-ter's in computer science at Brooklyn Polytechnic. And I was around. It was definitely deep attraction at first sight. I also felt it was for him, too."

Candace was impressed by his intellect. "He's very clear, extremely clear. In fact, that is one of the things about him that is most enlighten-ing and intriguing. Things that you take completely for granted—he has thought about them and clarified them. When I first met him, we had a long discussion about the black consciousness-raising movement. In our generation, we had struggling black nationalists who were very well versed in the Black Panther movement, and the political black writers of the 1960s and early 1970s."

Candace's was the only African-American family in her Brooklyn Heights neighborhood for the first eight years she lived there, after the Stanleys moved from Washington, D.C., when she was three. She wore clothes and a hairstyle to symbolize who she was: "That was a big thing for me. I guess it was engendered by my parents. I had an Afro and an Afro puff hairstyle and the garbs, the dashiki."

But while Candace was talking about black power on the one hand, she saw black people portrayed in a negative way in society. She dis-cussed the situation with Wynton; she was acting proud of herself while surrounded by "imagery that says we are less than. . . ." Wynton told her about his similar experiences as a child. He explained to her that "what the movement missed . . . was any kind of conversation or integration of the rich history of black people in this country," she said.

"Slavery was the only history we had. Now they're trying to be politically correct, but when I was in school, black Americans, who did anything meritorious, were not mentioned. So they didn't use our rich history. But Wynton was clear about it, because [he had the perspective of music], the contribution of black folks and their evolution in this country. That was powerful. He hipped me to it. That made 'Black is beautiful' seem genuine to me."

There was no glamour in the early days of their relationship. "He was unglamorous," Candace said. He was unimpressed by the glamour of his situation as a star, she noticed. He would eventually live in "a posh apartment and have beautiful clothes. But he has no emotional relationship to any material wealth at all. That's one of the most admirable things about him . . . there was no glitz in his makeup."

At first she thought Wynton was making a statement: "'Everyone else is impressed, but I'm going to show you I'm not.' But he has no emotional relationship to anything material. It's the most incredible thing. I don't know anyone like that. I am certainly not like that. So when he was living around the corner from me in Brooklyn, his shoes were lined up in the living room, and [parts of the apartment were] funky, and there was no lifestyle stuff that would indicate to you that this was glitz at all. There was never any food in the refrigerator. Then he would get dressed up and go on stage and do his thing."

Candace recalled the first time he took her to the White House, where she met President Ronald Reagan. "And it was so cool to go with Wynton, because he was super-grounded. A lot of people would have been . . . bubbling over about being invited. He had a cynical relationship to what was going on. And he made it fun. Because pomp and circumstance is not him. He would just as soon be in a room with a piano. That's all he needs. He's totally entertained. So his attitude made it fun . . . it was like being on the inside of an inside joke.

"Life with him was like that in general. He was into work, and pomp and circumstance was around him. Therefore I didn't feel in any way compelled to create any. I didn't have any traditional homemaker role, because he wasn't into having dinner parties, not even company coming by unless musicians were coming by to jam . . . and in the early years there was no glitz to be swept away by. But I was cerebrally swept away by his supreme intelligence. That was the huge attraction.

"I had no idea how great he was or would be," she reflected years later. "I knew he would be popular just because he was unique. . . . Nobody else was doing what he was doing. But I had no clue about his contribution to our lives, to humanity. And I was extremely naive about the whole music industry. . . .

"I came from a technical world. So the people I hung out with were not musicians certainly, although in college I was very attracted to those kinds of people. [But] I was naive. I never even [understood] the interview thing. From my perspective it was such an intrusion. [It was] what he needed to do for the public and to get his message across. I didn't know what he was doing, and that you were supposed to do this in order to get that. So it was quite a learning experience. . . .

"And what I loved about that life was just being around Wynton [and] the creative process. He was the kind of person who would call anybody up and say, 'Listen to this.' I didn't know what I was hearing, and he could explain it to me."

Their relationship was up and down, on and off, for quite a while. It would seem that because Wynton was on the road so much, his absences strained the relationship. But Wynton said it was the nature of their relationship itself that made it unstable. He would never divulge much about his personal life with Candace, whom he called a very private person. He said: "She was into computers at Morgan Stanley." Later she went back to school for education courses and began teaching in elementary school. He would only describe her in a general way: "She likes music. She has good rhythm, and she's smart, honest, and has integrity. She's beautiful and sweet."

Many of Wynton's friends and professional associates thought Candace was an especially attractive woman. Alabama-born Carol Clarke, an electrical engineer, who developed a friendship first with Wynton, then with Candace, described Candace as "stylish, not one to wear conventional styles; she could be very plain, not flashy; she wasn't trying to prove anything. She was very secure within herself. She was dark complected, and her hair was not processed; it was naturally curly-wavy and long enough for her to pull back straight into a ponytail or a bun; sometimes she wore it loose and down. She had a long, thin face, and she was slender. But she was shapely, with curves in all the right places. She had an enviable body. Maybe she wouldn't turn every head, but she had beauty in another way; she had essence."

Candace could have considered Carol a threat—as a female friend of Wynton's, to begin with—but didn't have that attitude at all. "She was not intimidated or threatened. I admired her a great deal for being smart, independent, natural, and friendly," Carol said.

Stanley Crouch met Candace at a mixing session for one of Wynton's recordings. Afterward, Crouch recalled dimly that he, Wynton, and Candace were driven by a chauffeur to a restaurant. Crouch liked her instinctively: "She was kidding. I just remember how much I enjoyed her independence, the combination of affection and independence" in her personality. He had the impression that, if there was something going on that she didn't like, "she would stand firm and tell Wynton," whether it was about something affecting his welfare alone or their relationship. If she didn't like someone or something, she would say so, Crouch deduced.

Crouch said he never was around the couple when they were having a disagreement. "I guess I lucked out on that one," he commented. "When I was around them, everything was swinging. They were joking. And what I liked about her when I first met her, she treated him like another guy. She made fun of him, made jokes. He might say something, declaim something, and she would make fun of it. I thought that was what a guy like Wynton needs, along with her levity and sense of humor.

"Usually when a guy is that great, it's difficult for a woman not to be overwhelmed by him. She very obviously had a great affection for him. But she dealt with him the way a woman deals with a man that she likes, not like a woman dealing with an image she is overwhelmed by."

Yet other people were surprised at how little Candace seemed to know about Wynton's music. She didn't seem to sit around and discuss it with him. One of their friends thought Candace "was not so interested in his work, which is his life." Wynton would later reflect that neither of them had been sufficiently interested in what the other was doing.

However, another of the couple's friends thought that Candace and Wynton had problems because Wynton met so many women on the road and didn't make a calm, constant commitment to Candace.

Naturally, other young women flocked around him. If there was one thing that never changed since the first jazz musicians began playing, it was that fans wanted to get close to the cats under the spotlights. No matter who besieged him and wanted to occupy his time, Wynton managed to make himself available and still keep working hard at music. "I made time," he said succinctly.

Some of the women who met him in the early 1980s, when Candace was new in his life, found him rather aloof; he didn't encourage any romantic involvements at first. At least two of the women whom he counted among his close friends noticed that. Others among Wynton's friends—even Wynton himself—disagreed. K claimed that Wynton always had a virtual harem of women on the road, while another male friend, Skip Norris in Detroit, said that Wynton flirted backstage but went to his hotel rooms alone. Yet another friend—a woman who would eventually become a girlfriend—said that, on at least one night that she knew of, Wynton went to his hotel room alone because he had previously slipped her the key to the room and met her there. But that would not happen until after his relationship with Candace had deteriorated to a serious degree.

Skip Norris, by the late 1990s a senior buyer in worldwide purchasing of truck components for General Motors, began his friendship with Wynton when the trumpeter was playing in a Detroit club with Art Blakey's band. Skip said that Candace occasionally went on the road with Wynton to a specific place such as Blues Alley, but not on tours for the one-nighters.

"He lives a hermit's type of existence on the road. This is bullshit about his running around," said Skip, reciting a litany of Wynton's usual activities on the road—the master classes, clinics, sound checks, concerts, last autographs, buses, cars, and planes, especially the buses.[1] "Very rarely does he sleep overnight in a hotel," Skip said, "and if he says different, he knows that's a lie." More important than the talk promulgated by Wynton or others about any harem, Skip said, was the direction that Wynton began finding for himself in music in the 1980s. He concentrated primarily on music, not sexual escapades.

Wynton would take mini-vacations from his stresses and responsibilities; one of them was his brief love affair with an Astin Martin, a dark blue car with pale upholstery—a very expensive, beautiful car that cost somewhere between $100,000 and $125,000. Wynton called his manager, Ed Arrendell, one day and said he wanted "a bad ride." So they came up with the Astin Martin, actually buying it. Wynton loved racing it full blast on the New Jersey turnpike late at night. He didn't worry about the danger, he said. But he got tired of people staring at it and asking him questions when he parked it on the street. "Is that a Sting Ray, man?" many people asked. It attracted women, of course.

Essentially, Wynton thought that having the car "was the dumbest thing I ever did. I never did nothing like that," he said. "The whole thing of purchasing a lot of stuff, going out and being seen and talking about it—that's fun, if you're really into that. There's nothing wrong with that. Somebody's got to do it." He explained his outlook on the luxurious car: "I work all the time, and I don't spend a lot of money. I don't have a boat; I don't like water and can't swim." The novelty of the car wasn't enough to hold his attention forever. He ended that love affair and got rid of the car after about a year.

The relationship with Candace Stanley, however, went on for about a decade, and it would have lasting, positive results in both their lives. Even though Wynton made no legal commitment, the couple loved each other, some friends, who observed Wynton and Candace at home, believed. One woman, who visited their house, never saw them fight over anything more serious than a bag of cookies: "Who ate the last Sausalito cookie?"—the couple's favorite. Candace later could not recall any fights with Wynton. She was sure there must have been some, but she couldn't remember them.

More important, their friend observed, echoing Wynton's assessment, both Wynton and Candace felt a certain lack of interest in each other's life's work. Candace tentatively agreed with this conclusion. Although she felt proud of him and loved his music, she might not have been interested enough in his music to adjust to him. Music was the core of his existence. In return, Candace might have thought he had less respect for her than she wanted, observers said—although Candace didn't say that.

Perhaps the problems that they couldn't solve had their roots in their strengths—their youthful energies, strong wills, and individual priori-ties—even the different rates at which they matured and set their life goals. Candace later expressed the opinion that she had been naive in her approach to the relationship. She thought she would have had to go through a maturation period, no matter whom she had been involved with at that time. Certainly, for Wynton it would have been unthinkable to put anything before his music. Yet in the early years of their romance, Wynton seemed to feel strongly committed to Candace.

————————

Carol Clarke, whose father and uncles were musicians, was taken by her father to hear Wynton play a concert in the very early 1980s in Atlanta. She had developed a secret, romantic interest in him then. After the second concert she heard him play in Atlanta, where she was studying at Georgia Tech, she contacted him by telephone at the Hotel Colony Square. Wynton was with another musician, Ricky Gordon, "a local guy," Carol said, who became her friend. Wynton spent time talking with Carol.

"I thought he was fascinating. He preached to me about jazz. I went to the hotel and talked to them both. Wynton was like this pompous, very opinionated fellow. I couldn't really refute him about anything he was talking about. But he was authoritarian, and he was talking about his taste in music. And that was just the truth. And that was absolute.

"I don't remember anything in particular, but we discussed [John] Coltrane and Bird [Charlie Parker]. That's what stands out. It may have been all I could talk about at that time, because I had been listening through the late seventies to fusion, creative improvisational music, Return to Forever, Chick Corea. I knew the others from my father. But my move to traditional jazz may have been inspired by Wynton," Carol said.

She was doing a radio program on her campus —"a jazz program.... But my knowledge and scope were limited." She learned more as a result of meeting Wynton. She also knew Rob Gibson, who was doing a world music show called "Continental Drift" at the same station, WREK. Gibson, who would later have a momentous collaboration with Wynton in New York, brought Wynton to the school to give a lecture at that time.

Carol Clarke recalled going with some friends to hear Wynton play at a concert at North Carolina A&T, probably in 1984—the third time she heard him play. She was interested enough in seeing him again to make the trip from Atlanta. Going backstage to listen, she met Wynton's brother Ellis, whom she considered witty and intellectual; she enjoyed talking with him. She also met Branford, Kenny Kirkland, Tain, and the group's bassist.

After the concert, she and Wynton went to a Taco Bell fast-food restaurant. Then they went to his hotel room, where they found Ellis and some other people. Wynton telephoned his mother. During that phone call, Wynton gave Carol the impression that he called his mother frequently, perhaps every day. Someone in the room said that Wynton was doing "his check-in routine" with his mother. "Or someone was joking when he said it," Carol said.

Wynton's mother had been in frequent contact with her son early in his career, but it became more difficult for them to talk all the time. For one thing, he was always on the move, and he couldn't possibly explain everything to her. Plus, she wouldn't even really understand all that was going on in his daily life, Wynton's mother said.

Carol didn't remember what Wynton said, but she had the impression that he and his mother had a great friendship, one in which he talked to her as if she were one of his peers. He also talked to his father that night with the same esprit. Carol was in the habit of talking to her own parents with deference, and so she was surprised by Wynton's relationship with his parents.

Afterward Wynton called Candace. It was her birthday, and she had gone out dancing. "He was disappointed," Carol noticed, learning of Candace's existence that night. "He let it be known he was in love with this girl. I said to myself: 'Forget about that.' So I was definitely standoffish. But the visit was nice."

Carol stayed in touch with him over the years. For the most part, she was the one who reached out and called him. "When I called him, a lot of our conversation was: 'Hey, check this out.' He would play something, and then he would say, 'The piano is going to do this, and the drums are going to do this.' The conversations consisted of a few words and a lot of listening." Or else, he would say, "How are you? You really okay? I got to go, I'm working on this speech."

Yet Wynton had friendly feelings for Carol, and he respected her achievements; she was getting an education. Later on in their friendship, by which time she had met Candace, she learned that Wynton and Candace had a fight one day. Candace had challenged him to name one woman whom he really respected. Wynton responded by saying that he respected Carol Clarke, although they had spent very little time together.

By then, Carol had become a computer engineer. Whenever Wynton performed in Atlanta, where she was living, they would sometimes get together to talk. He sent one of his friends, a writer with whom he had grown up in New Orleans, to see Carol when the writer went to work at the *Atlanta Journal Constitution* newspaper.

Melanie Marchand had similar experiences with Wynton. Between 1982 and 1988 she saw him primarily in New Orleans, when he went there for the jazz festival and other performances. They had friendly, brief encounters. "He was completely focused on the music," she recalled.

Carol Clarke knew that Candace and Wynton actually broke up for some reason for a year and a half in the 1980s. Finally, Wynton called Candace, and they reconciled and resumed their love affair. But they also continued their differences.

Wynton and Candace had begun living together in the late 1980s. Candace had made up her mind that she wanted a child. Although he didn't really want children at that time, Wynton agreed to have one. "When I was pregnant, he put headphones on my belly," Candace recalled. Wynton was already interested in inspiring his unborn child to experience the beauty of music.

Six months after Wynton, Jr., was born on May 18, 1988, Candace's mother became ill. She died two years later. She had been a special guide and inspiration for Candace. When Martin Luther King, Jr., was assassinated, Candace had written a letter to her white girlfriend living across the street and said they couldn't play together anymore; Candace's mother intercepted the letter. Until Candace was eleven, she had been an only child. Then her mother had twins, and she shared them with Candace. "She had one, and I had one," Candace recalled about the way her mother included her eldest daughter in the changed dynamics of the family.

"So, much of the relationship when Wynton and I were living together, I spent mourning the loss of my mother," Candace recalled. "I was consumed by that a lot. When she died, I felt like I had to make sure that my life was how she wanted it to be. I was reconciling all my mistakes or loose ends, and now I had to make them right." But nothing, no one thing, precipitated the final breakup between her and Wynton.

Candace came to realize that she had not been ready to be in a successful relationship with Wynton—nor perhaps with anyone else. "But I was really clear—I wanted to be a mom when I was twenty-six." She thought that Wynton might have been inspired to accept her idea because Branford already had a son. Wynton, too, wanted to become a parent, she believed. "And so my relationship to my child was more clear to me than my relationship to Wynton," she said.

She recalled her naive view of parenting: "You want a baby, you have one, and you take care of it. What's the problem? I think that was Wynton's attitude, too." Candace's mother had advised her not to try to do it all herself. Candace went ahead, however, and had a child. But neither she nor Wynton gave any thought to what a child could mean to their lives with one another. Two years later on April 28, 1990, their second son, Simeon, was born.

"I wasn't planning," Candace recalled. "I didn't think: What if? You think everything will work out. . . . [But] we have different ideas of what [a committed, long-term relationship] is. He thinks it's what we have together. We're committed parents, working together to raise these kids."

Originally, Candace had subscribed to the Cinderella myth, she said: "And the man comes and sweeps you off your feet and takes you to some palace. But then you have the baby, and you have to explore your life. And then you know you have divergent views. And you have to explore and [decide] how you want your life to look, and what a committed long-term relationship is. . . .

"Wynton did not want to settle down. [His idea was that] you stay in relationships with people for the rest of your life. You don't have to marry them. You don't even have to live in the same house. I have to say that I appreciated his spirit. It's probably why we never had a falling out, and why we stayed friends. I didn't take it personally. I looked at it as if it was his thing. I was pretty clear it was not what I needed, though."

One of Wynton's friends told Candace that Wynton needed to settle down, and he would do so in time, if Candace could wait. But Candace didn't think that way. "I was brought up by a liberated woman," she said. "I wasn't taught to sit around and wait for anything. If you want something, go get it." Furthermore, she didn't really believe what Wynton's friend said. "Wynton thinks he was put here to do something else. He's all about teaching and promoting the culture. He's in a relationship to something else, not a person. Music comes before everything."

Candace went on to make another life for herself. Inspired by her delight in her own children, she decided to study for a degree in education. She had begun studying even before the breakup with Wynton, going first to New York University, then continuing with a scholarship at Columbia University's Teacher's College. After the final breakup in 1991, she raised her children alone. Because Wynton had been on the road a great deal anyway, single parenting did not present any mysteries to

Candace. Wynton would have supported her, she knew, because of the great care she gave their children. But she wanted her own career.

A "new" man came into her life, Greg Pinn, a systems engineer who sells software for a New York City company. They had known each other in high school and remained friends ever since. By 1994, after years of enjoying a simple friendship, they decided to try to start a real relationship. "And the rest is history," Candace said. In 1996 they married and moved to a house in Westchester County with her two sons. Then she and Greg had two children of their own, son Cameron, age two in 1999, and Sydney, a girl, age one. Candace taught kindergarten in the public school system of a Westchester, New York suburb.

Both she and Wynton have encouraged their sons to listen to music; Simeon has gravitated to the clarinet, and Wynton, Jr., has chosen the piano. Both have approached their instruments individualistically. Simeon has an abstract relationship to music; he can be inspired by the sound of a Sidney Bechet recording. Wynton, Jr., prefers to play the background music of a TV show he likes. Wynton, Sr., thinks that both of them could become good musicians, if they would study music seriously.

"We broke up when we were young," Candace explained. After she was well settled in her marriage, she had "a really interesting conversation with Wynton about marriage and commitment," she said. Why marriage? was the question they posed to each other. Candace told him, "I believe that people were put on earth to be in a relationship with one another. It's your work. It's hard. It's easy not to be. I told him that's why it's worth it to make a relationship, and he said he didn't think that way at all."

CHAPTER NOTES

1. Wynton hated to fly after he experienced a 23,000-foot drop in a jet. "It wasn't a drop," Wynton said, "it was a dive." The plane was going to crash; miraculously, it stopped just short of a catastrophe. That brush with death scared him. After that, whenever he could drive to a job, he did, even if it meant driving cross-country.

NINE

EARLY FAME

In April 1983 Sonny Rollins, basking in the glow of his reputation as one of the greatest living tenor saxophonists in jazz, scheduled a concert at Town Hall, New York City, with the wunderkind Wynton Marsalis as guest. The group played several songs. Wynton thought that Sonny sounded wonderful, playing at the top of his form. He had no hint of any trouble. Suddenly, however Sonny's arms shot up; he fell flat on his back on the stage.

Wynton would never forget the moment. He thought Sonny might be kidding but then realized Sonny had actually fainted or collapsed. Although Wynton had no idea of the cause, he thought that Sonny would be all right. "I knew he would get up. It seemed so to me. Or I hoped so," Wynton recalled.

Sonny's blood pressure had, in some way, caused the calamity, the newspapers said. He had not even known that he had a high blood pressure problem. The concert was canceled but soon rescheduled for June at the Beacon Theater, where Rollins kept his promise to outdo himself. Wynton, too, earned high praise from the critics.

Robert Palmer in the *New York Times*, applauding both Wynton and Rollins, said that Wynton "was in superb form, playing with a singing, open-hearted lyricism and rhythmic authority that recalled the young Lee Morgan"—actually, not one of the trumpeters whom Wynton listened to the most—"but with the sort of attention to details of attack, inflection and timbre that one usually hears only in the work of trumpeters who are older and presumably more mature.

"His fondness for bebop led to some riveting exchanges with Mr. Rollins. The saxophonist's playing through the evening cruised some intriguing byways, far from the expected harmonic and rhythmic routes, often in response to a particularly daring and felicitous modulation or harmonic extension from Mr. Marsalis.

"The trumpeter also performed a service by bringing the band's volume level down to a near-whisper midway through several of his solos. The rhythm players listened more attentively to what both horn players were doing after Mr. Marsalis first took their dynamics in hand, though with two electric guitarists . . . and electric bass . . . they never managed the sort of springy, swinging lightness a more conventional jazz rhythm section would easily have achieved. . . . Still, only a curmudgeon would have complained."[1]

Such performances added to the luster of Wynton's growing reputation. The year was about to become his best to date. Critics praised his second jazz album, *Think of One*, released in June, along with his album of classical trumpet concertos by Haydn, Johann Nepomuk Hummel, and Leopold Mozart. The *New York Times* lavished praise on Wynton, as it would for virtually every recording and performance throughout his career. While mentioning Wynton's ongoing debt to the Miles Davis group of the 1960s, critic Jon Pareles praised Wynton's versatility and virtuosity on the jazz album.

Echoing some of Pareles's analyses, Eric Copage, writing for the *New York Daily News* on June 30, wrote of Wynton's "mercurial phrasing and velvety tone" on three original works, plus "Melancholia" by Ellington and the album's title tune by Thelonious Monk. Copage continued, "His jazz tone has a fullness reminiscent of Miles Davis; his improvisations display a kaleidoscope of jazz history and influences ranging from the earthy New Orleans jazz of Louis Armstrong to the stratospheric whimsy of Dizzy Gillespie or the folksy mutterings of Don Cherry."[2]

Running contrary to the general acclaim accorded Wynton, the veteran jazz critic Whitney Balliett, in his review in the *New Yorker*, panned the album. Balliett disliked the arrangements, the handling of tempos, the melodies of Wynton's originals, and the "fadeout ending."[3] Exactly why Balliett took a dim view of Wynton isn't clear. But it wasn't the first time that Balliett, ordinarily a perceptive critic, had disliked the work of an important jazz artist at the start of his career.

Other critics were divided between the Marsalis lovers and those who felt he was an overrated newcomer. Veteran jazz writer Nat Hentoff said he wasn't sure if Wynton would become a dominant personality in the jazz world. "He might be. I don't think he is yet," Hentoff was quoted as saying in the *Daily News* in August.[4]

Wynton's star kept rising anyway. Playing one night with Herbie Hancock and VSOP II at the Kool Jazz Festival in New York early that summer, Marsalis received more applause than Miles Davis and his group, who were appearing on the same bill. And Wynton had enough charisma to earn a spot in the free jazz concert in Washington Square Park to kick off the Second Annual Greenwich Village Jazz Festival. The festival always chose very popular musicians for the opening concert as a way of gaining publicity for the entire program. Dizzy Gillespie had headlined there the year before.

John F. Szwed reviewed the concert for the *Village Voice*. He noted that the discipline in Wynton's group was exceptional. If Wynton didn't equal Clifford Brown or Miles Davis, "[the] playing [of the sidemen] is nonetheless so full of sunlight and promise, so flush with their success and their sense of the rightness of what they're doing, so touched by a great understanding of the power of the jazz tradition, that it scarcely seems to matter."[5]

Perhaps the most interesting analysis of Wynton's performance style at this time in his career came from Rushworth M. Kidder, writing in the *Christian Science Monitor:* "Wynton . . . is full of promise. He simply loves notes. And he has about 40 ways of attacking them— from full-bodied clarion blasts aimed straight at the audience to soft croonings with the bell of his instrument covering the microphone like a candle snuffer, and on through *glissandi*, squeaks, and tiny pips of sound. His trumpet does everything but talk: An instrument of astonishing flexibility, it produces both hot verve and cool humor. . . . Standing old orthodoxies on their heads, he's just as happy to begin a piece with a drum solo as with a clear statement of theme—and to end by walking away (literally) from the microphone in the middle of an almost inaudible phrase. . . .

"Perhaps because Marsalis . . . also plays and records with symphony orchestras, his performances concentrate—even exhaust, at times—the intelligence of his listeners. Yet the pieces he writes and selects are often wildly centrifugal. Unlike the measured, tightly rehearsed, and centripetal compositions of some of his contemporaries, his threaten to fly apart into cacophony—and would, were it not for his presiding genius. Leaning more on mind than on soul, he holds them together."[6]

Wynton's classical performances also continued to garner praise from the critics, including one with the soprano opera star Kathleen Battle, with whom he would collaborate more in the future.

Following Charles Fambrough, bassist Lonnie Plaxico had toured with Wynton's group. Then bassist Ray Drummond had joined and recorded with the quintet for the album *Think of One* in 1983. Phil Bowler came next, and a few others followed. It took a while for the group to settle down with bassist Charnett Moffett by January 1, 1984.

One of the bassists, who worked briefly in the group in the period before Moffett, reflected on how much he had liked Wynton, but objected to the amount of authority Wynton exerted over the music. "He was a control freak," said the bassist, who had definite ideas about what he wanted to play. For the most part, Wynton specified exactly what music he wanted. The bassist longed to be in Wynton's position, but bassists have more difficulty than other instrumentalists in achieving recognition as leaders. He was not the only musician to object to the amount of authority Wynton liked to exert over the music, although in Wynton's groups the critics on that issue seemed to be in the minority.

Aware of the objections to his leadership style, Wynton explained, "I had to tell them how to play. If you're the one who leads, you have to tell them how to play. That's the job."

Drummer Jeff "Tain" Watts saw Wynton and the group go through many changes between 1982 and 1988. From Tain's vantage point, Wynton was in control of all the changes that occurred each step of the way. With each new lineup, Tain thought the combination of the musicians was better than each of the group's parts: "We were kind of like oblivious, but [we had] the desire to play. The group would become somewhat historical."

Tain was always aware of "Wynton's musicianship, his dogma, his influence on musicians that came after us in his groups. He would just lead by example and would be tough on himself. That would give you a certain amount of inspiration. He was hard on himself in every way, for whatever his criteria are for music and responsibility. I think I can honestly say," Tain reflected, "he is into maximizing potential and talent, and that's how he has been able to excel. [No matter] how you feel about his direction, you can't say that he's a slacker." The mere idea sent Tain off into a long roll of laughter. "He has a strong work ethic."

Tain thought that New Orleans music as a source material was underlying the band's work even in the first group's early days. Wynton recalled being unable in those days to figure out how to encompass all the different styles of jazz, including New Orleans music, of which he was actually always keenly aware. "But with that band," Tain said, "we would never do New Orleans music. Wynton was into bebop. The cats were into bebop . . . Trane [John Coltrane], Miles, Ornette Coleman. It wasn't so obvious at first about Ornette, but it's there."

Branford and Wynton were close, Tain also observed, "and will always be." As an example, he told a story of one time when the group was playing a gig at Blues Alley, in Washington, D.C. Tain was late for the sound check, not for the gig. He had played the club many times and for that reason didn't think the sound check was important. But Wynton told him in the dressing room that he was going to withhold some of Tain's pay because he missed the check.

Tain got angry and started screaming at Wynton. Then Tain looked in the mirror; behind him, he said, "I saw Branford was in position to physically address me if I tried anything. But I wasn't going to.

"I love all the Marsalis family. They kind of have their individual thing going, a certain amount of obligation to each other as brothers. But I think part of their family thing is: We're a family, but that's coincidental. I think they try not to feel that bad if everything doesn't line up like family things [ideally should] line up."

Tain spent time with Wynton and Branford in their one-bedroom apartment in the same building where Art Blakey lived at one time, at 77 Bleecker Street, near Broadway. Tain recalled sleeping on the bed with Wynton in the bedroom, while Branford took a pullout bed in the living room. "From time to time millions of Jazz Messengers and people who had keys and Juilliard students came there. It was a serious crash pad for a lot of musicians," Tain recalled.

Like most people who knew the brothers at that time, Tain noticed that Branford didn't take his music as seriously as Wynton did.

Branford had other interests and commitments. He was involved with Teresa Reese, whom everyone called Tess, a singer. She would become his first wife, in 1985, and they had a son, Reese Ellis, born on November 25 of that year. But Branford and Wynton exhibited superb teamwork. Tain recognized Branford's contribution to the group: "The best thing about Branford and Wynton was the way they had of playing with and off each other."

———

Wynton pulled off a major coup in 1983 when he won two Grammys in the same year—one in the jazz category for his second album, *Think of One;* another in the classical category for *Concerto for Trumpet and Orchestra in E-Flat Major.*

Wynton recalled the circumstances of recording the Mozart concerto. It had been slated for Prague, Czechoslovakia, but the arrangements for the date didn't work out. So Wynton moved to London, where the entire recording was completed in three days. "I was so nervous on the first day," Wynton recalled, "that Ray Leppard [the conductor] had to tell me, 'Look, are you going to play this, or are we going to go home?'" At the Grammy ceremony, Wynton played with both jazz and classical groups.

It wasn't the first time a jazz musician had played classical music; far from it. Many jazz musicians played some classical music on occasion; even Coleman Hawkins, the "King of the Tenor Saxophone," famed for his recording of "Body and Soul" in 1939, could play classical violin. Art Blakey, among others, had often said that jazz musicians could sit in with classical orchestras, but classical musicians couldn't sit in with jazz bands. However, no jazz musician before Wynton had tried to compete on the same level as the great classical players. Wynton was, of course, truly a great classical musician.

Wynton surprised many people with his acceptance speech at the National Academy of Recording Arts and Sciences ceremony when he won his first Grammys. He was critical of the direction jazz was headed in at the time. It may or may not have actually happened that Miles Davis, hearing Wynton's remarks, commented, "Who asked *him* a question?" The comment "Who asked *him* a question?" began to be a theme in Wynton's career. People started to become aware of the blazing intensity of his opinions.

Around that time, Marilyn Laverty set up a joint interview, which was supposed to be a dialogue between Wynton and Herbie Hancock. Marilyn thought the event would be a "nicey-nice chitchat thing, a free-flowing and pleasant conversation." It turned out to be a signal of things to come, "an eye-opener," Marilyn called it. Wynton challenged Herbie several times during the interview, which was at times more combat than conversation.

A younger musician, Wessell Anderson, an alto saxophonist, who would become one of Wynton's closest associates and greatest admirers years later, defended Wynton against the criticism engendered at the time by his remarks about other musicians. Anderson analyzed the situation: "Basically, all the musicians loved him when he was with Art Blakey, but he was getting too much publicity, and talking too much. And musicians didn't want to talk to him. . . . It got to the point that they stopped talking to him in the street when he got his first Grammys. They were shrugging their shoulders. 'He shouldn't be saying anything bad about Miles Davis,' like Miles was the Lord Jesus Christ.

"With that kind of celebrity status, a lot of envy came up," said Anderson. And in a lot of the articles, writers didn't think Wynton should be "just speaking out, period, about jazz music. Musicians shouldn't say anything. [They] should just be quiet and go along with what was written. And they were quoting him. Musicians didn't want to be spokesmen for their own music. Let other people write about them without getting the right information. Now, hold on. How are you going to write about this music unless you get information from these musicians?" Anderson said. He thought that writers wrote things that were "totally false, or nasty, or accidentally nasty, and no one corrects it, and it becomes right. If no one is there to debate it, it must be right, people think. . . . Wynton assumed the position that he knew what he was talking about."

Although Wynton was critical of Miles, the criticism was "nothing really serious," Anderson said, completely protective of Wynton (in a way that Wynton himself was not). Anderson took the position that Miles shouldn't have been "bashing this young guy who's trying to keep the frame[work] of the music alive."

Despite the waves that Wynton could make, everyone at Columbia was "jubilant" about Wynton's Grammy victories, "an early triumph," as Marilyn Laverty described it. Wynton's work was being well received by critics, and he was packing the clubs in New York. Not just the jazz press but the TV shows *Entertainment Tonight* and *Today* welcomed him, as did *People* and *Life* magazines. All of them seemed intrigued by "the young guy from a musical family who was so smartly dressed and had such clear and pressing opinions about the direction his music should go in," Marilyn said. He changed his opinions, that was true, "but whenever he had an opinion, he was always clear about it at that time. And he didn't seem to get any personal gratification out of the press's responses to him."

Marilyn recalled once reading a good review from the *New York Times* to Wynton, who basically started cursing about it. He was annoyed that the critic had liked the concert, because Wynton had thought it was horrible. "If a review of a show didn't represent the same viewpoint of the show that Wynton had, he was going to be suspicious of it," Marilyn noticed.

Wynton was learning what it felt like to be jostled in the jazz world. But a toughness and fearlessness, which he himself said he had always possessed, helped bolster him. One night, for example, in New York around this time, after a steady stream of television appearances, concerts, and media interviews over a period of a few days, he showed up for a hanging-out date to share music with Ron Carter at Knicker-bocker. "I love Ron Carter," he had told a journalist the day before. "He taught me about phrasing, about listening to everyone's part, about how to approach learning how to play." Wynton was really looking forward to seeing Ron and relaxing for an evening. But Carter, an extremely busy and pivotal modern bassist, didn't show up, for some unexplained reason. The journalist watched Wynton's feelings get hurt. A little crease furrowed Wynton's brow; he waited, then gave up, and left the club.

Wynton may have gone to Stanley Crouch's house; that was always a safe haven for Wynton, and he could complain to Stanley, lighten his burdens, and continue his education. Carol Clarke was one of the friends who often heard Wynton criticizing the state of jazz, and she knew that he and Stanley habitually gave each other an earful on the subject. Or Wynton could have called or visited a number of friends whom he was marshalling as a cadre of supporters and protectors at this time. He would collect many as the years went on.

Wynton was becoming musically venturesome, with his knowledge of jazz history broadened by Stanley Crouch and Albert Murray on the one hand, while he maintained an interest in modal music and became more familiar with some free jazz, too: Ornette Coleman's and trumpeter Don Cherry's work. But this broadened palette was not yet showing up in his music. In 1984 Wynton was getting ready to lead his third jazz quintet album, *Hot House Flowers*. He was still playing music with some of its basis in the Jazz Messengers format. But some critics noticed how his horizons were beginning to expand.

Destined to provide a special continuity in Wynton's life beginning at this time was his relationship with Steve Epstein. On staff as a recording engineer at Columbia Masterworks, Epstein had met Wynton one night in 1982 at Avery Fisher Hall, where Wynton's group was playing as the opening act for the great jazz diva, Sarah Vaughan. Epstein's boss, Christine Reed, took him backstage and introduced the two. She wanted them to work together on Wynton's album of Baroque music for trumpet in London. At this time, there was no talk of Epstein's becoming involved in Wynton's jazz recordings. Epstein's background was primarily in classical music, although he had grown up listening to jazz with his father, who had loved jazz.

Epstein had done a recording of Gershwin's music with Sarah Vaughan and Michael Tilson Thomas with the Los Angeles Philharmonic Orchestra in 1981. It went on to win won a Grammy, Sarah's first, in 1982. A gorgeous recording, it became Sarah's favorite of her own albums. She thought that people could listen to it and get the feeling of what it was like to hear her, with her exquisite voice that could actually move her audiences to tears. Wynton liked that record very much.

Just before they began working together on the classical album in London, Wynton, who was traveling with his group, and Steve Epstein met accidentally in the airport at Vienna, Austria, where Epstein was working with the Vienna Philharmonic.

"So we're talking and enjoying some Perrier," he recalled. "Wynton said he loved my recording of Sarah Vaughan and Michael Tilson Thomas."

"I want to get some of that sound for my jazz records," Wynton told Epstein. "I don't like that dead sound in the studio. What's your philosophy?"

Epstein said, "My philosophy is to have all the musicians in the same room at the same time to capture that real-time feeling. That's the only way you can do jazz anyway." He thought that Wynton's earlier jazz recordings were made that way. Other recording engineers might isolate the musicians with headphones to make a "cleaner" separation among the instruments. Epstein preferred not to do that unless absolutely necessary, so that musicians could rely on what they were hearing acoustically rather than through headphones. Thus they could have a more accurate balance and play off each other and still have the feeling of a jazz club.

Wynton asked him, "How would you like to do my next album, *Hot House Flowers?*"

"Fine," Epstein said.

They went looking for a hall in New York to record in and found the RCA studio. It was second in quality only, Epstein thought, to the old Columbia studio on 30th Street, a glorious old church, where Miles Davis recorded. Many cast albums of Broadway shows and other beautiful records had been done there, too. "Then some jerk at CBS decided to tear it down," Epstein said, "[because of] a quick buck mentality. I daresay that if Wynton had been around at that time, he and perhaps some other artists would have saved it, an old church from 1850." Nevertheless, Steve Epstein and Wynton had RCA, a good, if more complex studio than the 30th Street place. (Even the RCA studio doesn't exist anymore.) "At RCA, you had to work more at it," Epstein said.

"*Hot House Flowers* turned out to be a classic album in its genre," he said. "I must say I was a little nervous, because, when I produce classical recordings, the nature of the job is to have the musical score in front of me. A score is like a map, a reference, so you know what the notes are supposed to be, the balances. But for a jazz recording, you're working with charts. The music isn't really printed out for the most part; just the chord progressions are. And it's not really a producer keeping track of right or wrong notes. It's more vague. You have to go with your feeling and your taste about a take. An artist might think what I like is terrible. It's not as clear-cut as it is for classical performances.

"So for jazz, I guide the sound and the microphone technique and offer suggestions. And, of course, Wynton has been such a great learning experience for me. I have learned a lot about good jazz and taste. It has been just a wonder for me to see him grow, one new layer upon new layer of profound musical thinking. . . .

"For *Hot House Flowers*, the music was written out, even though the solos were not, and it was easier for me to have something to latch onto. So that was closer to a classical session." Not everything Wynton would do would be written out as fully, as he went from one size group to another; Epstein had to work by instinct, usually guided by just chord progressions for the solos.

After *Hot House Flowers*, Steve Epstein worked on all of Wynton's albums, both jazz and classical. *Hot House Flowers* was an album of ballads on which Ron Carter played bass and for which Wynton received his second jazz Grammy. The honor notwithstanding, some reviewers thought the album was more stilted than his earlier ones. In the same year Wynton did a second classical album, *Baroque Music for Trumpet*, which also won a Grammy.

Wynton received more media attention than any other young jazz musician in the early 1980s. It was Wynton alone who had his chance at taking the historic blindfold test—a series that Leonard Feather had started for *Metronome*, and which *Down Beat* now owned the rights to continue. Feather had devised the test as a way of getting musicians to talk freely about the playing of others, without knowing in advance who was playing on any given track. It was also a chance to see if musicians could recognize each other's playing.

In Wynton's test, published in 1984, he missed recognizing several prominent musicians, including Idress Sulieman (who played with Thelonious Monk), Chet Baker, and, shockingly, Miles Davis.[7] His ears told him that trumpeter Sulieman, who had played with Monk in the 1940s, "really swung, soulful." Wynton was unimpressed with Baker, who was playing fluegelhorn on the selection made by Feather. Baker sounded, Wynton felt, "mellow and laid back, but the overall effect was like Muzak. Made me wish I was in a retirement home in Miami with a cigar in my mouth."[8] The biggest shock came when Wynton failed to recognize Miles Davis playing in a group co-led with saxophonist Jimmy Forrest in 1952. The track made Wynton think of Fats Navarro or a Davis imitator.

But Wynton did recognize Lester Bowie's performance of "Okra Influence" from an album called *The One and Only* on the ECM label. Wynton noted, "He gets certain timbres on trumpet that nobody has got since Miles. He's figured out something uniquely his, but even he says it's not jazz. On its own merits, it's good, but sounds somewhat European—German music of the '40s. . . ."[9]

Clifford Brown, leading on "Brown Skins II," and Duke Ellington on "Uppest and Outest" from the film score *Anatomy of a Murder*, with Ray Nance, Clark Terry, and Cat Anderson on trumpets, were easy for Wynton to identify. "Duke! The greatest of them all! . . . Miles Davis on that old '50s Blindfold Test was right—everybody should get down on their knees and thank Duke Ellington."[10] There was no mistaking Wynton's tastes and developing priorities from these pronouncements.

———————

In July 1984, Wynton had his first solo cover story in *Down Beat*.[11] Author Howard Mandel called him a "wunderkind" and captured the essence of the merry-go-round of Wynton's lifestyle. Within twenty-four hours, Wynton had traveled from New Orleans to New York to Philadelphia for a classical recital rehearsal. He had then visited the apartment he shared with Branford in Brooklyn, scheduled a concert with the Boston Pops, and rejected a summer tour of European jazz festivals so that he could travel through the United States and Japan with his quintet. Then he went to CBS headquarters, a black skyscraper at the corner of Sixth Avenue and 52nd Street, for his interview with Mandel. All it took for Wynton to muster up his energy was breakfast.

Then, "opinionated, goodhumored, and very personable," as Mandel characterized him, Wynton talked about the beauties of having known older musicians in New Orleans who loved music. Wynton made a point of describing each of the older musicians who had influenced him—not only his father, Ellis, but clarinetist Alvin Batiste and trumpeter John Longo, who had hardly ever gotten paid for the two- and three-hour lessons he had given Wynton. Wynton also singled out Clyde Kerr, Alvin Thomas, Kidd Jordan—"who put on a concert that brought together the World Saxophone Quartet," Wynton said—George Jansen, and Danny Barker.

Wynton wanted to make sure that his views on pop music at that time were truly understood. "I've never said popular music is not good. All I said was it's not jazz. That's just clarification for the purposes of education. . . . Man, I played in a funk band for four years; I know all those tunes from the '70s by Earth, Wind and Fire, Parliament/Funkadelic. . . . That's why I know it's not jazz. People think a simple statement like that is condescending to some other kind of music. But all music is better than no music."[12]

In response to a statement that he seemed to have a good idea of what he wanted to do with his life—play jazz—Wynton said he was just a humble student of music. "I'm embarrassed to admit it, but when I joined Art Blakey's band, I hadn't even listened to Art Blakey's records.

I was just playing scales on chords—I didn't know you were supposed to construct a solo."[13] Then, to explain what he was doing, he prefaced his remarks by saying he had to phrase them very delicately, since people were misconstruing him and missing "a great part of what my music is about.

"My music is a very intellectual thing—we all know this—art music, on the level we're attempting. Sonny Rollins, Miles, Clifford Brown, Charlie Parker—we don't have to name all the people, maybe just the main ones—Monk, Charlie Parker, Duke Ellington, Louis Armstrong. These were extremely, extremely intellectual men. Whoever doesn't realize that is obviously not a student of their music, because their intellect comes out in that music. It's obvious that the average person couldn't stand up and play like that."[14]

Wynton explained, as he would do many times in the future, how these great jazz musicians had both superior technique and the emotional resources to process what they observed and turn it into great art. In a very intellectualized, analytical way, he talked about how jazz musicians improved on pop music. He didn't reject the contributions of all pop musicians; he thought Marvin Gaye and Stevie Wonder were geniuses. But essentially he didn't think that music moved forward in the 1970s. "I think it went astray," he said. He decried the people who were trying to be pop stars at that time, and he didn't favor the music that sounded like European music of the 1930s. Don't get him wrong, he said in essence. He loved European music; he liked pop music. But neither was jazz.

However, in some of Wynton's comments, he seemed to be trashing pop music, despite many qualifications he offered: "To the young people who read this: we need young musicians trying to really learn to play the music and researching and learning how to play their instruments. Not all these little sort of pop-type cult figures talking-all-the-time heroes who have these spur-of-the-moment, out-of-their-mind, left-bank, off-the-wall theories about music which make no sense at all to anybody who knows anything about music. We shouldn't get rid of them—they're important, because we know through them what bullshit is. But musical terms are very precise; these terms have histories to them."[15]

Mandel asked Wynton if he was trying to express a particular idea when he composed; Wynton answered in a way that could guide people listening to all his music—or anyone's good music. He was trying to express "an overall feeling," he said. "It's difficult to translate music into language, because music is its own universe. You're just trying to write or play music. And there's so much going on, especially in jazz. Because jazz is the most precise art form in this century.

Mandel asked: "What does the precision attach itself to? Where can you hear it?"

Wynton answered, "The time."

And "What the jazz musician has done is such a phenomenal feat of intellectual accomplishment that most people don't believe it is what it is. What the musicians have figured out is how to conceive, construct, refine, and deliver ideas as they come up, and present them in a logical fashion. What you're doing is creating, editing, and all this as the music is going on. This is the first time this has ever happened in Western art. Painting is painted. Symphonies are written. Beethoven improvised, but by himself, over a score. When five men get together to make up something, it's a big difference."[16]

Mandel hypothesized that Wynton's band had a thoroughly understood idea of what was going to happen in a piece of music. But Wynton said: "No. There's a language of music present, but how that's going to be used . . . to achieve whatever effect you're after, we don't know what that is. First thing is, we don't have set chords all the time. We don't play on modes, ever."[17] Nevertheless, even his first album was filled with repeated themes, music that either was modal or suggested modes.

Wynton continued, "Whatever chord Kenny [Kirkland] plays, that's what chord it is. If Jeff [Watts] plays a certain beat, the beat becomes in that time. The form has to stay the same, the structure must be kept, but our understandings are very loose. We understand the logic of our language."[18] Wynton was emphasizing, in essence the way most small jazz groups work together.

Wynton continued to praise his band members, answering critics who said either that they were too young or too derivative of other players: "I love my band. Kenny Kirkland and Jeff Watts are the greatest young musicians on the scene, and they get no credit. People say Kenny can't do this, and Jeff can't do this, but they don't hear what they *are* doing, because they're too busy hearing what they've already heard. Then they say it sounds derivative."[19] There were many critics, of course, who extolled the musicianship of Kenny and Tain. These young musicians were assuring listeners that the art of jazz was not going to die out, as many jazz lovers had feared.

Finally, Wynton gave his philosophy of how to listen to, enjoy, and analyze a jazz composition: "What you have to do is not look at part of something and make that into the whole. When you hear my records, I want you to listen to the sound of each piece, the flow of it, just like you would with any music. I listen to the sound of music, then to textural changes. Then I think, what are they trying to say in this? And I figure out what's going on, not theoretically, but musically.

"When I study, I listen to certain things, specifically, for a reason. What's on this record? What chord is this? How does he get to this chord? What's the development section to this? What's the drummer doing here? What chord does this affect? How do these two people hear this? How can you achieve this effect?"[20]

Wynton believed that the theories of composition offered by modern classical composers couldn't help him understand jazz: "I can listen to [Arnold] Schoenberg and analyze those pieces. I've read *Structural Functions of Harmony*, and I know what's in that book—I'm not guessing; I know what he's saying. I sat down for hours until I knew what was being said.

"But the theories now hurt me more than anything, because these people are not sincere, and they don't want to pay the dues that it takes to learn how to play this music. They don't swing at different tempos. What you must learn to play our music is not being learned—and cats are getting over.

"The most important thing in jazz is swing. Rhythm. If it don't swing, I don't want to hear it; it's not important to hear whatever it is if it's not swinging, if it's jazz. There are different feelings of swing, but if it's swinging, you know it. And if you ain't swinging, you ain't doing nothing. The whole band must swing. You can't have weak links. Every musician in your band has to be as good as the others—has to hear just as well, understand the concept as well, think on his feet just as well. See, our music is really for the moment—that's what makes it so exciting. That's why it can either be sad or great.

"We're just trying to come up with an improvisation on the spot. Bam! D over E flat. What is that? You know immediately what the chord is. You're going to five, you know what the rhythm is, you just have to respond. But it has to be correct; it's not just playing any kind of thing. You don't just hit a chord 'cause you feel like hitting it—you got to understand the logic of the progressions of harmonies—the logic of sound, the logic of drums, the logic of how bass parts should go. Contrary motion.

That's what my brother and Kenny Kirkland understand real well. On those records I didn't write out any music for *Bell Ringer* and those long tunes. I just said, 'Branford, play contrary motion there.' 'Kenny, what do you hear on top of that, man?' 'Jeff, what rhythm do you think would fit there?' Good ears, man. Musicians."[21]

Wynton said he thought it might take many years for the music to get as good as he wanted it to be. He wanted young musicians—"cats like Charnett Moffett," only sixteen years old when he was visiting Wynton's house every day to learn about harmony on his bass—to learn about music. Asked by Mandel if Wynton felt pressure "as a guy who looks good, plays sharp, and studies," to represent the young generation of musicians, he said no, he didn't feel any pressure. Essentially, he remained himself.

"When I was going to high school, I never owned one suit," Wynton recalled. "I didn't know what it was to spend money. I went to school with the same pair of jeans on every day, a T-shirt and shirt from Sears on top of that. Alright? Now, when I come on, I do what I want to. I like to be clean, because I used to look at album covers of cats with suits on, and I'd say, 'Damn, look at that suit. Boy, let me get one. I wish I had a suit. . . .' I like suits. I like to be clean when I go to work, playing music that I think is important in front of people."[22]

In the end, the underlying thing for him was loving the music, he said. He didn't court publicity. He hadn't courted CBS and asked for a record contract. "Just for some reason, I started playing with Art Blakey, and then the next thing I know I got a record contract. Everybody's writing reviews of my stuff. I'm playing with Herbie Hancock and Ron Carter and Tony Williams. It happened just like that. I was still trying to learn how to play the music."[23]

There were, of course, those who criticized his notoriety for exactly that reason: that he was young and still learning about jazz, although he could obviously play the trumpet remarkably well. And Wynton downplayed his own drive: He could easily have stayed in New Orleans and never have become well known if he hadn't made the effort.

The biggest honor he had received by then, Wynton said, was to play with such musicians as "Ron and Herbie and Tony, Sonny Rollins, Dizzy Gillespie, to have the opportunity to talk with them and have them teach me stuff. I'm playing jazz because I want to play the music. I love this music, man. I stay up all night playing music.

"Now, you can say what you want to say; I've got such strong opinions because I love the music. . . . I know I'm not Louis Armstrong. I'm not fooling myself. When I hear jazz, great jazz, there's no other feeling like that for me. None. Beyond all the other stuff, the publicity and the hype will be gone eventually, but the music will still be there, and I'm going to still be playing it if I'm still alive—or trying to learn how to play it, because I realize how great the music is, and that's what's most important."[24]

Wynton's ideas would change as he continued to grow and learn. "We don't play on modes ever"—that idea would go out, and the style of music he played in *Black Codes from the Underground* and *J Mood* would come in, for a while. But essentially Wynton's character was set. Throughout his career he would hold dear many of the same principles he had set out with, as if they were guideposts.

One hilarious reaction to the Mandel article was published in the October 1984 issue of *Down Beat*, in the Letters to the Editor column, under the headline "Mother Knows Best."[25] The letter read, "After reading the interview with Wynton Marsalis, I must say that I felt very proud of this gifted, intelligent, and witty young man. The cover photo did melt my heart. However, I was disappointed that my son's memory has failed him so early in life.

"His reference to not having a suit and only one pair of jeans while in high school is ludicrous. For someone who started performing at the age of six, and continued until he left home, how he managed without a suit is confusing.

"Just for the record, the only ones who couldn't afford suits in those days were his parents. Dolores Marsalis, New Orleans."

This letter stood as an example of clever parenting. While correcting her son soundly, Dolores Marsalis praised him. No better technique exists for nurturing and imparting standards to a child. Of course, Wynton's friend Tony Dillon did recall that Wynton had few clothes because he spent all his money on music as a teenager.

Other letters in that column under the heading "Moreover Marsalis" took Wynton on from angles that were becoming more familiar. One said: "It was very tolerant of Wynton Marsalis to deign not to 'get rid of' the 'talking-all-the-time heroes' who've destroyed the jazz tradition. However, the only person in jazz who seems to be talking all the time lately is Marsalis himself. Being an ardent fan of his, I have read every interview with him I could find. All I ever learn from them, however, is that everyone from Louis Armstrong to Lester Bowie has done the music some grave disservice.

"It's obvious to me that Marsalis's love for jazz prompts these statements. It should be obvious to him that to say that nothing happened in jazz during the '70s is to spit in the face of every jazz musician who then practiced the art form without commercial concessions."[26]

By this time, too, there had already been occasional rumblings from critics that Wynton's playing was too cool or controlled or technically perfect, that he couldn't play the blues with authentic feeling, or even that he had a dead or flat tone at times—a tone that he did sometimes have and occasionally used to his advantage, because he could play with any type of tone that he wanted. Wynton's talents and versatility as a player could be used against him. There were some jazz critics who felt that to be truly soulful a player should not be "perfect."

The classical music reviewers seemed to have no reservations about Marsalis at all. One critic, Will Crutchfield, wrote in the *New York Times*: "The sensational young trumpeter Wynton Marsalis, who has appeared most often hereabouts as a jazz player, walked away with the show at the Mostly Mozart Festival's final program."[27] Yet Wynton was essentially still struggling to get his footing in jazz, to establish his own characteristic style.

Miles Davis, perhaps smarting from some of the darts Wynton had thrown at the electric, pop music Miles was then playing, did nothing to ease Wynton's way. In an interview in *Down Beat* magazine in December 1984, Miles commented, apropos Wynton's attitude toward chords, which Miles had left behind years earlier, claiming that jazz had become too thick with chords: "Like, where's Wynton Marsalis? Wynton's a brilliant musician, but that whole school—they don't know anything about *theory*, because if they did, they wouldn't be sayin' what they say, and doin' what they do . . . the only thing that makes Art Blakey's band sound good is Art. . . ."[28] Miles didn't have to single out Wynton Marsalis to make his point.

The influential *Village Voice* jazz critic Gary Giddins was also critical of the fast ascent of Marsalis. He had mixed feelings about the young trumpeter; he didn't feel that all the criticisms hurled at Marsalis were justified, and believed that, after all, he was still a young player who was developing his style and should be given some latitude. Giddins wrote: "Marsalis's cachet as a media star has produced a backlash. . . . Some of the carping is of the sort that greets anyone who makes it very young and doesn't have the decency to pretend it was all the Lord's doing. . . . Wynton gets it all on his own terms, and then has the temerity to savage the avant-garde as well as the whores—(seekers of commercial success). He's practically looking for a fall."[29]

Giddins didn't think that Wynton had "attained his enviable and well-deserved plateau just because he plays good trumpet." Wynton appealed to the media because of his image. "The media found its lead in his jazz/classical virtuosity, but it pursued the story because he looks, dresses, talks, and handles himself the way he does. As a personality, he's something new in jazz. Inevitably that part of the media entranced chiefly by the cut of his suit will shape his image to its own needs. *Esquire* chose him as its jazz representative for an upcoming issue devoted to movers and shakers under 40. . . . Marsalis provides just the role model *Esquire* requires—a black yuppie."

Nonetheless, Giddins was quick to point out that it was silly to criticize Marsalis just because he enjoyed a good relationship with the press: "Punishing an artist for his press . . . is also indefensible."

Finally, Giddins had mixed feelings about Wynton's then most recent album, *Hot House Flowers*: "I feel defensive about criticizing Marsalis, not wanting to fuel a backlash that is already branding him a cool academician (almost 23 and still not an innovator!), but *Hot House Flowers* is troublesome." Giddins found golden threads among what he considered to be many dull moments on this album. Wynton had decided to include strings in the accompaniment, and Giddins disliked them. It was not the first time that a jazz artist had been criticized for using that instrumentation. Billie Holiday and Charlie Parker had to defend their albums with strings, which they loved. Nonetheless, Giddins found the new album mannered at times instead of romantic as it was intended to be. And he was not alone.

Of more importance, Giddins thought it unnecessary to say that Wynton obviously owed a lot to Miles Davis. Giddins did say that Miles wasn't half the trumpet player at age nineteen that Marsalis was, but Davis's genius was to search for his own voice and concept, whereas Marsalis was a virtuoso whose "contribution is of another kind—consolidation, interpretation, popularization."

Giddins's review was a brilliant analysis of Wynton's situation, important commentary with artistic and moral perspective, and it would
become more fascinating and even poignant in the long run.

The majority of reviews at the time extolled Wynton's gifts and technique. The harsh criticisms of Marsalis that would come in later years,
when his life became filled with enviable and ideal opportunities, had
not yet emerged. Even trumpeter Lester Bowie mentioned Wynton
pleasantly in passing, and without any of the ire or pique that Bowie, a
famed experimentalist known especially for his work with the Art
Ensemble of Chicago, would later direct against Wynton. (Wynton
would criticize Bowie roundly, too.) In his early years in New York,
Wynton had played in one of Bowie's groups occasionally. As a sidelight
to discussing the equipment he used, Bowie said he played only trumpet.
He had had a fluegelhorn and a piccolo trumpet, but he had stopped
playing them. He might get back to the fluegelhorn one day, he theorized,
but probably not to the piccolo. He commented, "One time Wynton
came over here [to Bowie's Brooklyn apartment] for a rehearsal, picked
it up, and started playing his stuff. . . . I never could play it well. I couldn't
really see what was happening on this mother. But Wynton played so
much on this piccolo I started to give it to him. He played it seriously. I've
decided I'm too old for that."[30]

The next year, bassist Charnett Moffett played for the first time on
a recording led by Wynton, *Black Codes from the Underground*. Also on the
album were bassist Ron Carter, Branford, Kenny Kirkland, and Tain.
Though not spontaneous improvisation, the intense album—from the
first cut, the title tune—showed the influence of Wynton's listening to
modernists and experimentalists and presented an open style of music.
Many of the songs were based on modes rather than standard chord progressions. However, not everyone, possibly not even Wynton, would agree
with the idea that he was under the spell of the avant-garde or mod-
ernism. Instead, he described the album as preoccupied with form, with
Wynton still under the influence of Miles Davis in particular.

"I was using New Orleans music in *Black Codes*," Wynton explained,
citing as examples the funk tune "Hey Pocky-way," and the song "The
Magnolia Triangle" by the New Orleans drummer James Black. In any
case, recorded in January 1985, the fiery album became the favorite of
Wynton's projects among some experimentalists and modernists; they
were delighted when it won a Grammy. In turn, Wynton thought the

inspiration he had gotten from New Orleans music incorporated in the album underscored his philosophy that "all jazz is modern."

———<span>》●<</span>———

In later years, Charles Fambrough offered a critique of Wynton's bands, taking a somewhat darkened view of Wynton: "[The first band] didn't have the freedom that Art Blakey's band did. It was all about what Wynton thought the music should sound like. He didn't give any real consideration to the individual musicians. The band I was in was actually lucky. You can hear the cats playing the way they wanted to. But he was standing behind, saying: 'Don't do this, don't do that. . . .' That was the beginning of a problem Wynton was going to have in the future."

It's a moot point whether there actually was a problem. Wynton's detractors have said that it was not a good idea for him to start hiring young musicians whom he could totally mold, direct, and nurture, as he would soon do. Instead, he should have hired seasoned musicians with mature, creative, and set ideas of their own. On the other hand, Wynton's champions thought he had done exactly the right thing for his music. And not all his sidemen were pliable young things. Many were seasoned musicians who were happy with Wynton's directions and never thought them excessive.

Fambrough did think that the musicians in Wynton's bands, from Kenny Kirkland to trombonist Wycliffe Gordon, who was yet to come, were fantastic—"killer musicians." But Fambrough thought the individual voices were never strong enough in Wynton's band, even though Wynton continued to develop and become a more skilled musician and a better trumpet player. Certainly, Wynton was not the only leader to exert so much control over his groups; other very popular musicians had done the same thing. Fambrough's opinion joined the pantheon of pronouncements pro and con about every aspect of Wynton's musical development as a trumpeter, composer, leader, standard-bearer, and showman.

Wynton's next album, *J Mood*, continued to reflect his modernist bent, including "Insane Asylum" by the pianist and composer Donald Brown. Like *Black Codes from the Underground*, the music showed off Wynton as a brilliant trumpeter and exploratory mainstream player. But *J Mood*, recorded in December 1985, constituted a major departure from Wynton's earlier albums, because neither Branford nor Kenny Kirkland played on it.

Branford and Kenny had begun playing with the British pop singer and bassist Sting and wanted to tour with both Sting and Wynton. According to Kenny and Branford, Wynton foresaw that problems with scheduling would arise; he wanted his own group to be the priority, without conflict or tension, for his sidemen. Wynton recalled that he wanted to keep Branford and Kenny in his quintet so much that he told his manager, Ed Arrendell, to work around them and "do whatever they want." But there was no way to work around them. Sting's group worked all the time, not just a few months of the year. The scheduling problems would have been insurmountable. Kenny and Branford couldn't possibly work with both groups, and they chose to go with Sting.

"They didn't want to work with me," Wynton recalled. He was terribly hurt. "They even told Leonard Feather [then the jazz critic for the *Los Angeles Times*] that I fired them. How am I going to fire someone who has another job?" Nevertheless, Wynton instructed Ed Arrendell, "Take care of my brother." Arrendell worked out lucrative contracts for Branford and Kenny with Sting.

But Arrendell always was mindful, he said, that he "could have negotiated a deal, which would have allowed [Kenny and Branford] to finish the dates already scheduled with Wynton, as well as play with Sting, but Sting would have initially had to schedule fewer dates. . . . But Kenny and Branford said: 'Give Sting whatever he wants' [and] left Wynton without a band."

Arrendell admired Wynton for still being concerned about his brother, despite what he viewed as Branford's abandonment of the group: "I saw something very special about Wynton's humanity. He knew I would take good care of Branford, because you can get hurt [in this business]. It would have been a lot easier on Wynton if they had functioned in both contexts. To me it's the kind of consideration you would give someone you have toured with for years."

Kenny Kirkland later reflected about his time with Wynton's group: "I have such respect for Wynton. He is probably the most serious musician I ever played with. I was very impressed with him and very proud to be part of his thing. He had a very strong vision. He is the way I would want to be, someone very correct and serious about the music." Of course, Kirkland was an exceptional pianist and composer in his own right, whose contributions to Wynton's albums were striking. "Wynton didn't want to have any distraction," Kirkland remembered. "He said, 'You guys are going with Sting. I have to keep my band going.'

"Sting came to some gigs," he recalled. "Wynton gave him the eye, the cold shoulder backstage. He knew it was in the cards. Branford was more open to different forms of music. Leaving Wynton was something he needed to do for his own individual voice. He's older, but Wynton was always determining what Branford should be playing. I don't think it was a conscious thing so much. Branford was more interested in rock. It turned out to be his stepping-stone to being his own man. It just came on that way. Branford doesn't sit down and worry about anything. He saw something good in that opportunity."

Branford and Kenny Kirkland went with Sting. Nonetheless, Kirkland would say later, "In my heart I always felt Wynton was right. And for a long time I kind of felt guilty. But I did it anyway. We had the talent to play that music. So we did it. Wynton kind of understood that with me. With Branford, it hurt him a little more."

Branford recalled the incident: "He felt betrayed, which he shouldn't have felt." However, Branford could understand Wynton's insistence on Branford's and Kirkland's leaving well in advance of the Sting tour, Branford said. It "made a lot of sense. 'I might just as well get on with my thing now,' Wynton thought. What's the difference between January or June? If he has to get his thing together, he might just as well pull the trigger now."

Wynton was just as clear in his memory that it was completely Branford's decision to leave. Branford couldn't be in two places at once, and he chose to go with Sting. Any claim to the contrary, Wynton said, "is disingenuous type of shit." And "the hurt I feel is personal, like when your best friend sleeps with your old lady."

"There was no rift from my end," Branford said, "but you know, I wasn't disapproving of things he had to do. It was very funny, amusing, seeing other people's take on it. Everybody, even though there's empirical evidence to the contrary, the most basic being Cain and Abel—people, even relatives and complete strangers, seemed to think we should put on the illusion of cooperation because we happen to share the same last name. People were more interested in the outward facade than in finding a real relationship there. That was something that I never forgot. That it was more important to people that we put on the illusion of togetherness rather than actually go through any sort of emotional difficulty.

"You know, it's a lot like a marriage, being someone's brother. And then add the fame factor in it. It's tough. It's ridiculous. That's why there are so many families messed up now."

Branford mentioned the family of Ozzie and Harriet Nelson; Ozzie insisted that his sons appear on the family's TV show, even though the boys wanted to do other things, "because Ozzie needed them to continue that illusory picture" for the American public. "That's what I'm talking about," Branford said. "I had all sorts of stuff going down in my life, and that was a whole lot more important to me than whether or not Wynton approved of my playing pop music. [His approval] was important, you know, because we grew up around each other, and you know, you want the approval of your family, and your brother, but there comes a point at which I had to let that go. I truly believed in what I was doing, as I do now. And I figured there would be a time when Wynton would come around. We would just be brothers. This other bullshit doesn't matter, because it's truly bullshit."

In any case, if some people would think, a dozen years later, that a rift still existed between the brothers—who actually worked together a lot behind the scenes, and occasionally onstage, too—Branford said, "Who cares? People really have no interest in my relationship with my brother. . . . If people would only spend a third of the energy on their own personal lives and with the people that they supposedly love, that they spend talking about other people's lives. . . ."

Tain would say years later,"Wynton was heartbroken, I would say. And in a way he may not have ever wholly recovered to this day." Tain knew that Wynton had to miss playing with Branford. "They had a way of playing with and off each other," Tain recalled about the brothers. "That's [why I say that] the group was more than the sum of its parts, like Miles and Wayne Shorter, and Bird and Dizzy; they found their own way of phrasing." By the time he made this assessment, Tain and Wynton were no longer close. But at the time the quintet broke up, from Tain's vantage point as the band's continuing drummer, Tain was aware that Wynton was on a "mission," and he had to regroup.

Tain commented, "Wynton spent a certain amount of time by himself and more time with music and tried to find other musicians. Even with people not related to you, [the group] turns out to be a family thing. So you look for people you can just trust yourself to share music with."[31]

Trumpeter Justin Cohen, Wynton's old friend from Tanglewood, thought it must have been hard for Wynton to part from his brother. Cohen also knew that "Wynton could separate his feelings about music from everything else. For Wynton it was cut and dried. But his family had character."

A number of people were aware of tensions between Wynton and Branford at the time the band broke up. Wynton had sometimes been very critical of Branford for not being more serious. But as time passed, Wynton realized he had been wrong; he should not have told Branford what to do, Wynton said. Branford was right about doing exactly what he wanted to do—and not just because Branford should do what he pleased, but because he knew what was best for him. That didn't mean at all that Wynton felt Branford always made the best choices.

Wynton eventually reflected upon their complex, even tumultuous relationship: "They said he had more talent than I. There were certain things he could learn quicker than I could, but the overall understanding of a thing, I always had. We had different skills. So technical things he could understand much easier than I could, but other things I could understand easier than he did. But there was no comparison. It wasn't so much a comparison. I was always very serious. He did what he did. But I never compared myself to him one way or the other.

"When we first came to New York, people said he could play better than me. It was just interesting to hear that. People who were writing said that." Some, of course, said the opposite. Some musicians, too, occasionally said that they preferred the way Branford played jazz, and others said that Wynton was better. But Wynton claims this never created jealousy between them.

In his overall assessment, Wynton recalled his earlier belief that Branford should have been a more serious musician: "He didn't like to practice or work on stuff. That's not what he wanted to do. When I was younger, I used to think that's what he ought to do. But now that I'm older—I know you have to do what you want to do. That's a lesson I had to learn.

"And then everybody makes it seem like he should have been practicing. But he should have done what he wanted to do, not that he's obligated to practice. Why should he be obligated to do that? . . . He's himself. He should do what he does. But I didn't understand that at that time. . . . I was the cause of some friction between [us], that I thought he should have been practicing, or doing this, or doing that. It wasn't my place to believe.

"He shouldn't have been doing nothing. I should have been grateful that he was there to do whatever he did."

The breakup turned out to be a learning experience for both brothers and would pave the way for better personal and professional dealings between them behind the scenes in the future.

Billy Pierce later speculated: "They were brothers and very close. Through the years maybe a little of their personalities rubbed off on each other, because obviously Branford came to be a lot more disciplined and organized than when he was real young. I guess Wynton may have come not to take everything as seriously as he did when I first met him. Both did so well in the business and in music, and so the things that people need—a certain amount of flexibility and a certain amount of substance—both seem to have developed that."

Both certainly survived the separation and developed more as individuals and musicians. On his own, Wynton sought and found ways to thrive, becoming a connoisseur and a man of the world, developing a greater sense of independence and security in his tastes and projects.

Even the sadness of his brother's parting gave him new insights into dealing with the changes that inevitably occur in life: "Someone calls me and says he or she is depressed. I say: 'Enjoy it. Don't let me ruin it.' Sometimes you can't even get to that kind of feeling. You want to be depressed and can't be. All you end up doing is pitying yourself.

"A real, true depression is something. You've got to enjoy that. I'm not talking about something serious, chronic depression, a medical condition; I'm not poking fun at that. But I'm talking about the common things that happen, the normal things, when you go up and down. That's a part of life. That's the beauty of it really. Enjoy that kind of thing. Some people want to be the same all the time, without change. That's interesting, if you're into that. But I like the extremes of everything."

CHAPTER NOTES

1. Robert Palmer, "Concert: Sonny Rollins Meets Wynton Marsalis." *New York Times*, June 5, 1983.
2. Eric Copage, "For Kool Trumpet Star, Jazz Is Next to Classical." *Daily News*, June 30, 1983.

3. Article about Wynton Marsalis, by Whitney Balliett, *The New Yorker*, June 20, 1983, quoted in *Current Biography Yearbook*, 1984.

4. Unsigned piece, "Wynton Marsalis: Is He the One?" *Daily News*, August 26, 1983.

5. John Szwed, "Wynton Marsalis's Burden." *Village Voice*, September 6, 1983.

6. Rushworh M. Kidder, "His Jazz Trumpet Does Everything But Talk." *Christian Science Monitor*, December 20, 1983.

7. Leonard Feather, "Wynton Marsalis: Blindfold Test." *Down Beat*, December, 1984.

8. Ibid.

9. Ibid.

10. Ibid.

11. Howard Mandel, "Wynton Marsalis." *Down Beat*, July 1984.

12. Ibid.

13. Ibid.

14. Ibid.

15. Ibid.

16. Ibid.

17. Ibid.

18. Ibid.

19. Ibid.

20. Ibid.

21. Ibid.

22. Ibid.

23. Ibid.

24. Ibid.

25. Letters to the Editor, *Down Beat*, October 1984.

26. Ibid.

27. Will Crutchfield, "Trumpet: Wynton Marsalis." *New York Times*, August 26, 1984.

28. Howard Mandel, "Miles Davis," *Down Beat*, December 1984.

29. Gary Giddins, "Young Jazzman of Our Dreams." *Village Voice*, August 16, 1984.

30. Interview with Lester Bowie, *Down Beat*. It was a piccolo trumpet that Wynton used for the "Brandenburg" Concerto, which took him to Tanglewood; it was one of many trumpets he had bought with his earnings in New Orleans since his teen years.

31. In classes in New Orleans, Ellis had taught multireeds player Victor Goines, who would join Wynton's group in 1993: "You should never get on the bandstand with someone you're not willing to get into a foxhole with." Goines interpreted that to mean a musician is vulnerable and wants to be on the bandstand with supportive people.

TEN

THE SEPTET

A t the Joyce Theater in December 1985, Wynton led his new quartet—Marcus Roberts on piano, Robert Hurst on bass, and Jeff "Tain" Watts on drums—through a concert of beautiful music, with his impeccable tone, technique, and swing. The music, however, didn't quite burn with the fire that some seasoned jazz fans and critics in the audience were looking for. Miles Davis's influence was still palpable in Wynton's sound and approach. Wynton himself said the group was working on its vocabulary.

For the new group, Wynton chose Marcus Roberts very carefully. They had met at a National Association of Jazz Educators Convention in Chicago in 1982. Marcus had taken part in a young artists event there. He was a student of classical piano performance at Florida State University and had been selected to represent the school at this meeting. After Wynton heard him play, they stayed in touch by telephone. Marcus called to ask questions; Wynton sent him records by Thelonious Monk and others. Monk's music would become very influential for Marcus's work in Wynton's group.

"During one conversation that we had," Marcus recalled, "I was complaining that it was very difficult to get gigs, and it was hard to learn to play if you can't get gigs.

"Wynton said, 'I have a great pianist already, Kenny Kirkland, but if Kenny can't do some gigs, I'll call you.'"

When Kenny left in 1985, Wynton called Marcus.

"I knew I loved jazz and would always play it," Marcus said. "But I didn't have any real expectations that I could actually survive and take care of myself doing it."

He played his first gig with Wynton in Salt Lake City, Utah. At that time, the group was a quintet with Kent Jordan, a flutist, in the band, along with bass player Charnett Moffett, Tain, and Wynton. Kent left right after that when the group was supposed to play at Carnegie Hall.

The group played music from "Black Codes from the Underground" and from "Think of One." Marcus knew the music. "The only difficulty was having enough time to absorb the concept. But playing with Wynton was really like an agenda. I knew he had been sent here to lead the entire movement of jazz music. I was clear on that. So for me, learning his music was not a big deal, because he was who I was interested in playing with. It was just an objective, artistic decision. We became friends later. But the core of it was the music. I just made sure I knew it. It is very detail-oriented music and an intricate philosophy of playing. But it isn't insurmountable."

Marcus had played in several churches as a child, one of them Baptist, and his educational background was in classical training for basic, fundamental piano playing. "Jazz was certainly clearly what I was interested in playing," Marcus said, "and Wynton was very instrumental in exposing me to a lot of the fundamental concepts of playing jazz. Like the first time that I really became familiar with [John] Coltrane's music was in Wynton's group. We played a lot of Monk's music. We basically explored the history of jazz music in that vein. The first time I played solo piano was with Wynton.

"I think the important thing to know about Wynton as a bandleader is he always knew how to work with what was there. He knew how to organize it and get the most out of it without being antagonistic or hostile. I think that's a very, very important quality to have as a leader. The second important thing to understand is that he always made sure the musicians were taken care of and there was no question that he found what the musicians were doing had real value. I think that has made a big difference in his having the top position in the music. He treated people in a very good way. And it was simply a glorious period of time. I enjoyed it."

Marcus's mother had lost her eyesight from glaucoma when she was sixteen years old. Her eldest son had normal vision, but the next child, Marcus, went blind as a result of cataracts when he was very young. Inspired by his mother's positive attitude, he said, he never had any self-pity: "The point is for you to do what is within your capacity to solve a problem and then make peace with the outcome, because otherwise you'll never be satisfied. You'll be a martyr, or whatever, and there's no point in that." Marcus appreciated that Wynton "was not a whiner and a complainer," either. Marcus knew that when Wynton did complain, it was "like a front, and meanwhile he's getting a lot of stuff done. Generally, the whiners and complainers get nothing done," Marcus said.

Marcus found his way around the world by learning the layout of his environment. When he didn't know it, he needed a guide. On the road with Wynton, someone went to Marcus's room, took his arm, and "we would just go," Marcus said. In other situations, when there had been no one to help him, he simply started out on his own and hoped somebody along the way would help. That was how he had functioned in school when his usual route to a class was barricaded for repairs.

"A lot of it is just fundamental physical survival. It's a choice. You just sit there or do what you can. It's not that big of a deal. It's just a matter of negotiating an interface that will get you from one place to the next. It sounds a lot more mysterious than it is," he said. Commended for his calm outlook, he said, "Unfortunately you don't have much of a choice. You can do further destruction, or you can uplift yourself. With adversity, choices are very simple, stark and real."

The first record Marcus made with Wynton was 1985's *J Mood*. "That was really where we started exploring and learning how to play the blues, and that was what that record was all about," Marcus said, "trying to get more of a real sound of romance, purity, and beauty in the music." With *J Mood*, Wynton was slowing down, leaving behind his modal mood. As Skip Morris, his friend from Detroit said, Wynton now turned his attention to dealing with the "rudiments" of what he believed "jazz" to be, "with the blues and swing." *Standard Time, Volume One*, was recorded in 1986. "That was designed for us to work on playing standards," said Marcus Roberts. "We did some very hip arrangements, for example 'April in Paris,' 'A Foggy Day,' and we'd always play these things on gigs.

"Then we did *Live at Blues Alley*, which was a compilation, a consolidation of all his work until then. Here we just dealt with the original music.

Out of all his records, people seem to talk about that. They don't talk about his other albums. Musicians talk about it. It seems to be the period they can relate to, because we're playing long solos and a lot of rhythms, and a lot of things are going on. It was kind of like a modern expansion of the bebop conception. We played the melody, everybody soloed, and we could play our rhythmic and harmonic conception over the form. I think musicians related to that, because a lot of them went through that, playing long solos. After that record, it just moved very quickly."

⸺∍●⋲⸺

Live at Blues Alley had a very Monkish sound in its harmonies, particularly apparent in such songs as "Juan," a blues that sounded as if it had been written by Monk, and Wynton's own "Skain's Domain." By now Wynton had clearly moved away from the overwhelming influence of Miles and digested the lessons of the revolutionary bebop players.

But Wynton was still sufficiently associated with Miles's influence that a confrontation between the two trumpeters on a bandstand constituted a publicized mini-scandal at this time. Jeff "Tain" Watts recalled how Wynton's band arrived in Vancouver, Canada, a day early to play at Expo '86. Miles was playing on the day Wynton arrived. Wynton's band—Tain, Hurst, and Marcus—got into a limousine at the airport and headed toward the hotel. The driver may have been the one to show the band a local newspaper's interview with Davis.

"Miles had said something like: 'I can play one note and just cancel him out.' Wynton saw this and was kind of upset," recalled Tain. "The guys in the band juiced him up," as Tain recalled the moment, "to challenge Miles. Wynton said he didn't want to disrespect him. 'I don't feel comfortable with that,' he said."

It may have been Tain, or it may have been the collective group, that convinced him, saying in essence: Hey, man, you can sit in on him. Anyone can sit in on anyone. "And so finally he got his nerve up," Tain recalled. "And what Wynton did—he asked Miles if he could play. Miles said, 'No.' Wynton went up to play anyway. Miles cut the band off. Wynton said nothing specific one way or the other when he came off stage. He may have regretted it. I am sure he got a little charge out of being that audacious. Maybe he felt embarrassed, too."

Both Wynton and Miles would present their versions of the story. Miles told his side in his autobiography, saying that, at least at first, he had heard good things about Wynton: "Even though the jazz scene seemed to be stagnant, there were some good young musicians coming up, like Lester Bowie, and the Marsalis brothers. . . . Wynton played trumpet and everybody was saying that he was one of the best trumpet players to come along in a long time. . . . I think it was around 1981 that I first started hearing about them. . . . Some of the new developments in music were kind of interesting, but I found the most interesting stuff happening in white rock music. . . ."[1]

By 1985, feeling slighted by George Butler and Columbia Records, Miles wrote, "I really liked Wynton when I first met him. He's still a nice young man, only confused. I knew he could play the hell out of classical music and had great technical skills on the trumpet, technique and all of that. But you need more than that to play great jazz music, you need feelings and an understanding of life that you can only get from living, from experience. I always thought he needed that. . . .

"But the more famous he became, the more he started saying things—nasty, disrespectful things—about me. . . ."[2] Miles said he was particularly annoyed because he knew how much he had influenced Wynton's playing. "When he started hitting on me in the press, at first it surprised me and then it made me mad.

"George Butler was the producer for both of us, and I felt that he was more concerned about Wynton's music than he was about mine. George likes that classical shit, and he was pushing Wynton to record more of that. Wynton was getting a lot of play because he was playing classical music and by this time he was winning all the awards, both in classical and in jazz music. A lot of people thought I was getting jealous of Wynton because of this. I wasn't jealous; I just didn't think he was playing as good as people said he was playing."[3]

Miles criticized Wynton for playing classical music. "Dead shit," Miles called it, "the kind of stuff that anybody can do. All you've got to do is practice, practice, practice. I told him I wouldn't bow down to play that music, that they should be glad someone as talented as he is *is* playing that tired ass shit." Miles also thought Wynton should watch out for people who were just waiting for him "to miss one motherfucking note."[4]

As for the "incident," as Miles called it, in Vancouver, "At this outdoor amphitheater that was jam-packed . . . I was playing and getting off on what I was doing. All of a sudden I feel this presence coming up on me, this body movement, and I see that the crowd is kind of wanting to cheer or gasp or something. Then Wynton whispers in my ear—and I'm still trying to play—'They told me to come up here.'

"I was so mad at him for doing that shit like that, I just said, 'Man, get the fuck off the stage.' He looked a little shocked when I said it to him like that. After I said that, I said, 'Man, what the fuck are you doing up here on stage? Get the fuck off the stage!' And then I stopped the band. Because we were playing some set pieces and when he came up like that, I was trying to give the band some cues. He wouldn't have fit in. Wynton can't play the kind of shit we were playing. He's not into that kind of style and so we would have had to make adjustments to the way he was going to be playing."[5]

Miles complained that Wynton had no respect for his elders. (Miles, of course, didn't mention the hatchet jobs he had done in his autobiography on his elder, Charlie Parker, and a few others.) Furthermore, Miles said that he—and musicians in his own age bracket—would have asked each other beforehand if they could play. (That was the accepted way it was done.) To Miles, it looked as if Wynton was competing with him. Miles hadn't seen any respect from Wynton or "hardly any of the other younger musicians today. They all want to be stars right away. They all want to have what they call their own styles. But all these young guys are doing is playing somebody else's shit, copying all the runs and licks that other guys already laid down. There are a few younger guys out there who are developing their own style. My alto player, Kenny Garrett, is one of them."[6]

It must be said that nobody could usurp Miles Davis's place in the pantheon of jazz stars. But the more things change, the more they stay the same. Dizzy Gillespie, for one, used to organize raids with other young beboppers on 52nd Street in the 1940s. They'd charge onto bandstands in clubs where swing era musicians were playing and "challenge" them by playing bebop. They even had a name for this mischief: "ambushes." The audiences loved it, and the art of the ambush makes a good story to this day. So does Wynton's lone, aborted ambush of Miles. To carry it out successfully, Wynton probably should have taken his whole group, especially because his sidemen had convinced him to go on the bandstand.

Wynton's side of the Vancouver incident differed considerably from Miles's. First of all, the men in Wynton's band bet him $100 each that he wouldn't go up on stage to sit in with Miles. "Man, you're scared of Miles," Wynton recalled them saying. But really, the band was just "sitting around, joking, bullshitting," he said. "It wasn't serious, when they suggested: 'You're scared of Davis.'" Wynton didn't have to get his nerve up at all.

When he went on stage, according to Wynton, he didn't whisper in Miles's ear. First of all, the music was too loud for anyone to whisper anything and be heard. Wynton wouldn't have tried that, and he certainly wouldn't have said that anyone had told him to go on stage. No one controlled him. That was Miles's idea. But Wynton had it in mind to play on the bandstand with Miles "to address the dumb shit" Miles had said about him, Wynton said. Miles was playing the organ on a blues, "C C Rider," when Wynton started to play. Miles told Wynton, "Come back tomorrow." That was when Wynton was supposed to play with his group. Wynton was already playing when Miles stopped his band. "I definitely did not feel embarrassed," Wynton recalled.

Wynton didn't even like going to sit in with Miles's band, but he disrespected the music that Miles was playing, believed Miles didn't respect it either, and refused to sit back and let Miles insult him. "And the guys in my band did not pay me my money, either," Wynton added, putting a comical twist on the story.

Through the years, Wynton would have "very interesting, private conversations" with Miles about their differences about music. "He said he was bullshitting," Wynton said. "He knew. . . . How could you play all that music and not know?" Wynton had listened to Miles "constantly demean his earlier music, saying it wasn't shit, and jazz wasn't shit." Then, not long before he died, Miles played a jazz concert in Montreux, Switzerland. "That was a very complex decision he made," Wynton said about that last concert. "He didn't want to go out without at least trying to do it."

Wynton never altered his opposition to Miles's playing electronic music. "He sold his power to become popular," Wynton said. Wynton would always be vociferously and adamantly proud of his decision to play the music he played.

A confrontation between Miles and Wynton was bound to get a lot of media attention, and it did. Controversy sells papers—and brings the writer extra attention. Furthermore, Wynton noticed that he might say many things in interviews on many different subjects; some of his comments were inflammatory, and some were not. Writers would use only the inflammatory parts of his statements and little or even none of the mitigating, or even humorous, portions, he said. "Sometimes they sabotaged me outright, and sometimes they just misquoted me," he said.

When he had something strong to say, he passionately believed he should say it. Other people spoke their minds. He had a right to his opinions, too: "Why should I shut up? That's like not voting." Sometimes writers used already published material to get their controversies going and judged Wynton secondhand, he noticed. "They would write all this crazy shit . . . to make me seem like some kind of weird extremist running around, telling people how to play. Most of the time, when I was around musicians, we didn't even talk about how to play. We were into clowning, and talking about whatever musicians talk about, a little light conversations, mostly about women."

Wynton was not just developing a sometimes confrontational relationship with writers, he was providing them with a field day. But it was a mutually beneficial relationship in some ways; everyone was getting attention. When he ruffled the feelings of other musicians—those whose music he didn't like or respect, even if he thought it was interesting or amusing at times—he didn't see why he should mince words. "And I never tried to keep people from hiring them," he added. He was glad they were working wherever they found audiences. About one musician in particular, he said, "There's nothing wrong with being a con artist and working. It doesn't benefit me if he's not working."

<hr />

Just as passionately, Wynton lavished love and attention on his own music and his new group, struggling to develop. Marcus Roberts recalled of this period: "We did a record with Joe Henderson," said Marcus, "that later became part of a three-CD set, *Soul Gestures in Southern Blue*. The first part was called *Thick in the South*, done in 1987, the year Wynton filled Branford's seat with Todd Williams, a fine tenor saxophonist and a quiet, deeply religious man. Then the two most important records that that band did were *The Majesty of the Blues* and *Levee Low Moan*," said Marcus. The group played the title song from *The Majesty of the Blues* everywhere, Wynton recalled. That was a very important, definitive song. Marcus continued: "Those records, I think, defined and consolidated everything that had happened up to that point and laid the groundwork for what eventually became *Blood on the Fields* [Wynton's Pulitzer Prize–winning oratorio]. "Those are the two very important anchor recordings."

It's true that Wynton's playing evolved even more at this time. Critics tended to view his recordings in this period as a transitional stage for Wynton, until they would pronounce him a mature artist by 1989. For the CD *The Majesty of the Blues*, Wynton used the Second Line tradition of New Orleans—the funeral tradition—as a parable for the death and resurrection, as it were, of the blues as an eternally enduring art form.

By then, Wynton was turning more obviously in the direction of earlier jazz styles—not simply further away than ever from experimental music, but back to the swing era's standard tunes and riches. He was drawing on the lessons he learned from the compositions of Duke Ellington and to the New Orleans heritage that he had disdained as "museum piece music" in the early 1980s. Listening to earlier music was inspiring and instructing him about the right direction for him to take.

At the same time he was trying to incorporate the older music into his own modern conception, to extend his lessons in fresh ways. He believed that the title track of *The Majesty of the Blues* began to show how old and new can come together. It wasn't pure New Orleans music, he said; "[it] began in 6/4 time and modulated into different time signatures, went into different keys, had an open-ended vamp, with the drums playing a riff, and the bass and piano flowing around that in an improvised fashion. Even though it was still the blues, it didn't sound like anything that had ever been done." That was his new conception of experimental music.

Wynton changed his bassist and drummer by the time the band recorded *The Majesty of the Blues*. The powerful, modern drummer Jeff "Tain" Watts left, probably released by Wynton; Tain would go on to play with guitarist George Benson, then pianist McCoy Tyner, and soon with Branford in a group including Kenny Kirkland. New Orleans–born Herlin Riley, a drummer, and bassist Reginald Veal joined Wynton's group. *The Majesty of the Blues* was not their first recording with Wynton, but on that album, the sound of the new rhythm section became fully mature to fit Wynton's conception, in Marcus Roberts's opinion. "Also, there was the arrival of Wessell Anderson [the alto saxophonist] for that recording and also on *Levee Low Moan*, and his presence in the horn section, along with tenor saxophonist Todd Williams, who was already there, gave Wynton the foundation as a composer that he needed," Marcus said. There were traces of Coltrane in Williams's playing. "[Wynton] was very comfortable writing for that particular sound. And whenever the thing jells that way for a composer and bandleader, he can get a whole lot done."

Todd Williams, Marcus said, "was always very serious and dedicated, and he pretty much could play anything that Wynton wrote for the tenor saxophone and clarinet. He and Wynton could play and think exactly alike and phrase exactly together—and incredibly well. When Todd joined, it went from Wynton and me playing to me accompanying Todd and Wynton, since Todd could essentially play counterpoint with him on another wind instrument. That was a big thing."

Marcus couldn't separate the music from his personal relationship with Wynton. "The biggest thing is that he saw I had the desire to play, and he was willing to act on very little information as far as allowing me to play at first. It's not like I went there and set the world on fire. I had a lot to learn about the piano and a whole bunch of other stuff. But for whatever reason, we just had a certain connection. If he said something, I had an innate understanding of what he was trying to do, and vice versa. Some people just like to be around each other. And if there were things that needed to be dealt with as far as the band went, I could deal with it.

"As an example, if there was a new direction he was interested in going into musically, a lot of times these things have to be discussed. Though you can make a person play a part musically, whether he really believes in it is another thing. My role was a lot of times to facilitate, to explain what was going to be done. I'm not saying in any way that there was any confusion about who the real bandleader was. But I provided that extra 10 percent he needed sometimes. I think I provided it. If any extra explanation was needed other than what he had clearly articulated, I would try to articulate what I thought he was saying. But it was real unspoken and nothing official about it. He probably would be more qualified to say whether it helped or didn't. My sense of it was that as musicians came in, it helped."

Wynton commented succinctly some years later: "Marcus Roberts really knows my music."

To Marcus, Wynton's music was a very intricate and subjective topic, "and overall, in the scheme of the late twentieth century, very important, based on the fundamentals established by all the masters of jazz music.

We spend our lives trying to expand it." He saw Wynton's music as a philosophy. "I think *The Majesty of the Blues* was a very important piece in the development of that group's philosophy. I think it was a piece that really unlocked the group's interaction, the one piece where it seemed like we could play essentially whatever we wanted to without getting in each other's way, and everyone's strength could be developed. There were things that Wynton could play, and I could hear exactly what he wanted. And Reginald Veal could play New Orleans stuff that he had figured out on the bass. There was this modern framework that Wynton had figured out. We could hear just who we were inside of this very modern sound. Every night that piece of music was just totally different. I would say that was my favorite piece. That and 'Down Home with Homey,' a blues which he wrote for Herlin Riley on *Uptown Ruler*."

Wynton would often reflect that he was always trying to make the music more interesting and was most interested in working with forms. "Forms. So it's not just a tune, and a head. I use all the forms of jazz. 'Blue Interlude' [which he recorded in 1992] was my first attempt to deal with the extended form. But even before that I was writing all the different blues. I would try to put different forms on it, different bar phrases, signify the harmonies, the interludes in the song. Then I would try to change the mood more and keep the same thematic material, and then each of the pieces after that was just an attempt to make the music more interesting, with two or three people soloing at one time, with interesting modulations.

"I would write the harmony a certain way, work with different types of harmonic structures, integrate the groove, like the rhythmic groove with the melody and harmony and the form, and do a lot of different things with form and harmony, and with rhythm. Something like 'In This House, On This Morning' [also recorded in 1992]. And come up with really good, integrated thematic material."

———

By late 1986, Wynton had won praise for his new group's performance in a trendy Manhattan jazz club, Whippoorwill. Chip Deffaa, reviewing this performance, called Wynton the "definitive younger jazzman of the 1980s."[7] In trying to explain Wynton's success, Deffaa stated that the music was easy to understand and devoid of embellishments, and Wynton played directly to the audience.

The quartet's recording of *J Mood* in December 1985 had begun this period. During his annual gig at Blues Alley in Washington, D.C., that year, Wynton recorded the double-album set *Live at Blues Alley*. Critic Scott Yanow particularly liked it, giving it a five-star review. He called Wynton a "great" trumpeter and also praised Marcus Roberts. He cited a variety of songs—the standards "Just Friends," "Do You Know What It Means to Miss New Orleans?," and the little blues that Bird used to play, "Au Privave"—as among the better performances, along with Kenny Kirkland's composition "Chambers of Tain."

Still, despite Wynton's obvious progress as a musician, many critics continued to focus on his controversial positions as jazz spokesperson. Howard Mandel, who had written a sympathetic cover story about Wynton for *Down Beat* in 1984, two years later expressed his concerns in an article for the *Village Voice*. As he recalled in a conversation about that article, Mandel felt that Wynton was drawing the line on who was a jazz musician and who wasn't, excluding "the gut bucket crowd, David Murray, Muhal Richard Abrams [whom Wynton would soon hire to play in the new jazz program at Lincoln Center], Lester Bowie, Joseph Jarman, Roscoe Mitchell, the Art Ensemble of Chicago, and all the Chicago musicians, and probably Cecil Taylor and Ornette [Coleman]. . . ." Mandel thought that Wynton might have liked Ornette's music between the years 1959 and 1964, but not after that. "I don't think Wynton believes there's much validity to Ornette's harmolodic principles [Coleman's theory of music that is very difficult for most readers of his ideas to comprehend], or his electric band, or his orchestral pieces. . . ."

Mandel was also concerned that all of Wynton's sidemen in his small groups had been African American. For his little groups, Wynton didn't hire a white sideman, bassist Ben Wolfe, until 1993, six years after Mandel's article came out. Yet even before Mandel's article appeared, Wynton began to hire many white musicians and other professionals for other projects besides his quintet.

Some years later, Mandel moderated his views somewhat of Wynton. He would reflect that Wynton had undergone "quite a bit of development in his thinking. I'd like to hope so. And I think at that time he was feeling the full oats of his youth, and he was quite dismissive." At the time of Mandel's article, Wynton took umbrage at it, Mandel recalled.

Mandel knew that Wynton tried to analyze his work and jazz in general "to apply certain standards. To me, his standards are blanket condemnations. He doesn't like electronics in music, and I believe that he doesn't like modal music. . . ." His work bore no resemblance to the avant-garde and didn't show its influence at all, Mandel thought. Wynton's music was "highly structured, compositional, founded in composition and not in free group interplay, not in spontaneity. They may be playing, inter-acting within some outlines, but I have always thought [Wynton's groups'] improvisations are highly constrained, and their structures are not loose. If you look at the interaction between his drummers and him, not even as powerful a drummer as Tain has ever made Wynton cut loose.

"I never felt that Wynton ever cuts free and just plays. He is not like [trumpeters] Don Cherry or Lester Bowie or Miles. And true to his classical training, I believe, he pays close attention to composition. That's not necessarily a bad thing." Nevertheless, Mandel thought that Wynton was shackling the music. Mandel liked *Think of One*, Wynton's second album, but not the third, *Hot House Flowers*, which he thought was "con-trived"—"a pretty album" but "self conscious." As just one example of a critic who disagreed with Mandel's opinion, Scott Yanow praised Wynton's playing as melodic and subtly creative, with a consistently beautiful tone.

Eventually, after Wynton had become the artistic director of Jazz at Lincoln Center, Mandel would say that, though he was never a huge Wynton supporter, Wynton was "a superb technician. I have heard him play several different styles of jazz superbly in a week. He can go from playing Louis Armstrong and King Oliver duets to Rex Stewart parts in Ellington's band in the 1930s, to Coltrane, to like-Miles, hard bop, and post bop, in a few days. I've heard him play dynamite solos. But I don't feel and I have never felt that he sustains a program of originality, and I do not find myself returning to his music to listen to it for pleasure. . . .

"I find him an intriguing personality. . . . He works very hard, he's a very responsible young man, and I think he is in a position where he is carrying a load of responsibilities, and it's stressful. . . ."

These views of Wynton, who had even once confided how tired and exhausted he was to Mandel, accumulated over a period of years. They were mild, compared to some of the more audacious attacks by other crit-ics, who seemed motivated primarily by jealousy and self-defensiveness, without Mandel's heartfelt efforts to be honest and clear, particularly as Wynton's fame and influence grew.

Stanley Crouch predictably always took the opposite position. To Crouch, Wynton was the epitome of the gut-bucket musician, a person playing authentic jazz with deep feeling. Crouch forsook his former admiration and attachment to avant-garde musicians such as the energetic, elemental saxophonist David Murray, with whom Crouch had previously performed as a drummer. Crouch's switch of allegiance naturally earned him Murray's ire.

Another writer, Tom Piazza, who wasn't particularly mesmerized by Wynton's early albums, became attracted to Wynton's work at about this time. Piazza had originally been a jazz critic who turned to writing fiction. A lover of New Orleans music, he moved to that city and returned to writing about jazz. Soon he became one of Wynton's most valuable and reasonable supporters, attempting to analyze the competition that arose between Wynton and his most negative critics. Piazza never joined the extremist factions of writers and musicians who ran the gamut from claiming that Wynton couldn't play at all to insisting he was a god who walked the earth.

Unintimidated, Wynton kept making his views known. And it was true that nobody could really tell him much about music. To writer Leslie Rubinstein, Wynton commented, "Sometimes a jazz critic will say such-and-such sounds like Debussy. Debussy wouldn't know swing if it came up and hit him. . . . When people say, 'Classical music is more technical, more intellectual,' or 'Jazz is more emotional,' I refer these guys to Bartok's Music for Strings, Percussion and Celeste, to the majesty of soprano Kathleen Battle, to [Gustave] Mahler and Hummel and [Krzysztof] Penderecki; the answers are right there.

"I try to help them hear the sophistication in jazz; the techniques of sax players Charlie 'Bird' Parker and John Coltrane, drummer Art Blakey, pianists Art Tatum and Thelonious Monk, for instance, require more understanding of composition than Bach or Bartók. It is harder to play good jazz well than classical. Jazz is the classical music of our century."[8]

Wynton said misconceptions were spawned by elitist classical musicians who put down jazz without listening to it, and jazz musicians who bragged that they didn't know anything about the classics.

"There's no giant chasm between classical and jazz, just two different ways of thinking, like checkers and chess. Classical is obviously interpreting someone else's music, learning everything you can about and being faithful to your instrument. Jazz, on the other hand, requires, at its best, more intense listening. It is in constant motion. It's the first Western music in which the audience, as well, participates in the creative process.

"What the two styles do share, however, is a spirituality, and the ability to elevate the audience. That's what music is, elevation and improvement. Just as Beethoven improved folk melodies, Charlie Parker improved 'I'll Remember April.'"[9]

In 1988 Wynton also wrote an article entitled "What Jazz Is and Isn't," published in the *New York Times*.[10] It would show up again in a curtailed version in *Grammy* magazine in January 1990, and, in paraphrased versions, the ideas put forth would appear as part of Wynton's crusade throughout his career. Essentially, he said that jazz had been encumbered with the racist idea that the founders of the art hadn't known what they were doing. Early writers about jazz were to blame: "Because of these writers' lack of understanding of the mechanics of music, they thought there weren't any mechanics. It was the 'They can all sing, they all have rhythm' syndrome. If that was the case, why was there only one Louis Armstrong?"[11]

Wynton went on to reiterate his opinion that "rock isn't jazz and new age isn't jazz, and neither are pop or third stream. There may be much that is good in all of them, but they aren't jazz." He stressed the musical erudition of Armstrong and Ellington and made it clear it was long past high time they got their due.

The 1988 article in the *Times* was one of the few instances of a prominent African-American jazz musician stepping into the role of critic. Wynton's ability to wear two hats would act as a kind of clarion call. Critics would have to make room for an authority hailing from bandstands and concert stages. Critics who disagreed with his views would often clamor to state their own, and there was much of interest, intelligence, and experience to support their ideas about what was jazz and what wasn't. There were also critics who simply resented Wynton's newfound authority.

Wynton was, essentially, not saying anything wrong or even new. Close observers of the jazz scene had always known the truth about the hard work and artistry of jazz musicians. But what they had often said behind the scenes among themselves had now become headline stories. That was why Wynton gladly dug in his heels and never retreated. A month after Wynton's story appeared, *New York Times* critic Peter

Watrous referred to him in an article as a "trumpeter and critic." Naturally, that didn't end the controversies.

———————

By 1988, with the addition of alto saxophonist Wessell Anderson, Wynton's group became a sextet. All of its key players had connections in various ways to Ellis, Wynton, or their associates. The new drummer, Herlin Riley, had been playing with Wynton's father for years. Reginald Veal, like Herlin, came from New Orleans. Brooklyn-born Wessell Anderson went to college in Baton Rouge, ostensibly to major in accounting to please his father, but really to study with Alvin Batiste.

First, Wynton invited bassist Reginald Veal, born in New Orleans in 1963, into the group. Veal had begun studying seriously with Ellis Marsalis at NOCCA in the days when Ellis used to go to schools and recruit students for his program. Reginald was fascinated by Ellis's explanation of what NOCCA did and bucked the disapproval of his regular school's teachers, who said he would be hurt academically if he spent half his day at NOCCA. (Drummer Herlin Riley had had the same experience.)

Veal, who was playing electric bass and didn't begin playing acoustic bass until he was twenty, chose as his favorite bassists Charles Mingus, Jimmy Garrison (who played with John Coltrane), Paul Chambers (who played with Miles), Ray Brown, and Ron Carter. Eventually, Veal studied the work of Jimmy Blanton, regarded as the first modern bassist, whose solos provided a taste of honey for everyone else to learn from.

Ellis hired Veal in his formative years for gigs. "I can't think of any other way to learn to play besides being on the bandstand with him," Veal said. "Aside from all the things that he taught me [about music and] life, Ellis sets a great example: very spiritual, honest, intelligent, and smart. Almost any situation that you're in, he either has experience or has read about it. And it seems as if you could talk to him about anything, any problem in the world of any kind. He gives you an intelligent answer."

Veal met all the Marsalises by the early 1980s and became especially friendly with Ellis III, who was quieter and less flamboyant than his brothers and perhaps a little shy. "He could be by himself; the others love people and want people around them," Veal noticed. Veal played on his teacher Ellis's albums with Terence Blanchard and Donald Harrison. When that band wasn't working, Veal did other gigs. One of them was a concert at the Joyce Theater in New York with Wynton. After a few more jobs, Wynton said to him, "I'd love for you to be in the band." So Veal joined it in December 1987.

Veal thought that Wynton was a lot like Ellis. Wynton often said the same thing about himself, especially when asked about his love of teaching. "My daddy is a teacher," Wynton explained. Furthermore, he had grown up in a city where all the older musicians were eager to teach youngsters. Wynton also had mannerisms that reminded Veal of Ellis: "certain things he does with his mouth, his expressions, his eye movements signifying seriousness sometimes or just relaxation. And they have it in common that they're serious about the music.

"I think you cannot grow up in that family and be a dummy. I think Wynton has a lot of knowledge. He has studied a lot. He and Ellis were from different generations, and different opportunities were available for Wynton that hadn't been available for his father. Racial discrimination is one of the major differences between the generations. And so Wynton was very fortunate that he could do many, many things."

Before Veal married in 1991 and set up home base in Atlanta, the group was his family: Todd Williams, Marcus Roberts, then pianist Eric Reed, Herlin Riley, Wessell Anderson, and eventually Wycliffe Gordon, the trombonist. Wycliffe's entrance in 1989 made the group a septet. Marcus Roberts left in 1991, and Wynton was very sad. Then "there was a lot of crying going on when I left the band," Veal recalled. "I didn't cry in front of anyone. I never really cry. It was a hard decision. I expected to take a year off and go back. But it didn't work out that way. . . .

"At times it was hard [in Wynton's group]. Ten months on the road is not all glamour and glitz. It was very difficult. [But] it was such a good situation, almost perfect, and [we were] being paid." After leaving Wynton's group, Veal didn't work for about a year. He wrote music, went fishing, and visited family members around the country. That was how much he needed a vacation.

Veal was on most of Wynton's recordings beginning with *The Majesty of the Blues*, and even appeared on *Midnight Blues—Standard Time Vol. 5*, done with strings and released in 1998. He was also on some material recorded at the Village Vanguard and never released, which Veal thought was a great example of what the band was playing in those days. After leaving the group, Veal, who kept in touch with Wynton, would work with him in the future for individual jobs. Notably, this included the November–December 1997 "Love Supreme" tour of Japan, in honor of

John Coltrane, featuring only Coltrane's compositions. The other side-men included Elvin Jones and McCoy Tyner.

Herlin Riley, born in 1957, came from a musical New Orleans fam-ily. He was surrounded by music and played several instruments, study-ing trumpet at various schools. But he always returned to the drums, which he found he could just naturally play. While at Southern University, he got a gig on Bourbon Street, where he played drums in a burlesque club, behind strippers, comedians, and novelty acts. Actually, he subbed for the drummer one night, the trumpeter the next. That opened the door for him to work with various bands in town, including Al Hirt's. In the early 1980s, he was called to play for the show *One Mo' Time* in New Orleans, then went with it to London.

There, in 1981, at saxophonist Ronnie Scott's renowned jazz club in the Soho section of town, Herlin heard Branford and Wynton play with Art Blakey's group. Branford, ever the tireless socializer and circulator checking out the musicians on the jazz scene, heard Herlin play in London. Returning to New Orleans, Herlin got a call to play in 1982 with the illustrious pianist Ahmad Jamal's group. Then Wynton heard Herlin play at Fat Tuesday's in New York. "He complimented me," Herlin recalled.

A few years later, Herlin was playing with Ellis in a trio for the New Orleans Jazz and Heritage Festival. Wynton, who was working there, too, went to sit in with his father. All the while, Wynton was keeping Herlin in mind, and on February 16, 1988, a day after Herlin's birthday, he called the drummer to join the group. It was a quintet at that time, with Veal, Roberts, Wynton, Todd Williams, and now Herlin. Following Tain Watts into the group was no small job, Herlin recalled. "Wynton had to sit back and hear the difference [between Tain and me]. He was very patient and intelligent about it. I tried to play in Tain's style. It took a while before I could find my own niche inside Wynton's music.

"At that time, he was playing standards, 'Black Codes from the Underground,' 'Delfeayo's Dilemma,' 'Knozz-Moe-King,' those pieces, very interactive music, with the drums and trumpeter very interactive, and all the musicians, too, interactive. It takes a special consciousness to be able to interact intelligently. You can always just play stuff, repeat what someone else plays. But it takes something else, instead of doing that, to respond to what someone else plays, to answer it and complement it, and so you have call and response.

"The music goes by very, very fast. A lot of things are very subtle. It took me some getting used to. I did it to some extent with [Ahmad] Jamal's trio, with the piano as the nucleus, and Jamal would always just give the signal, a hand signal, and so forth, when he wanted a change in the music. Wynton was different. When he wanted a change, there were musical cues that came up. Subtle ones. While playing you had to listen for the cues. I wasn't used to them."

Herlin observed the close relationship between Marcus Roberts and Wynton. "It was incredible to watch Marcus playing in the band, because a lot of the music Wynton wrote was very, very difficult, especially the long-form stuff he did. We had our own problems playing it. Marcus memorized everybody's part. The rest of us had to read music, but Marcus managed to retain it. I was always amazed and flabbergasted at how he did that.

"We had pieces that would last thirty minutes. I think 'Blue Interlude' was the first long-form piece we did. Marcus learned that music from start to finish flawlessly. We were all still struggling with our parts. Wynton would play the music for him in sections, and he would explain chords to him. 'First of all, we're going to have two measures of D minor, a measure of G, a measure of A flat, two of B flat, D minor for one, A flat minor for two beats.' That's not exactly what it was. That's just an example of how he would break the music down and explain it to Marcus, and Marcus would just retain it.

"That was amazing to me. I guess it was a matter of learning each section. Often times the sections were related, but so different I had to read it. Even now, to be exact, I have to go back and read it, after playing it for five years," he said in 1998.

Wynton had a way of becoming very close with the members of the septet, Herlin noticed, and managed to adjust to many changes in personnel that naturally occurred over the years. For example, Wynton adjusted to the changes brought with bassist Ben Wolfe, who replaced Reginald Veal, and reed player Victor Goines, who came into the band after Todd Williams left. Although Marcus had already left the group before Williams, Marcus thought Williams's departure left a void. Then Victor Goines stepped in and established himself as a particularly soulful and exciting reeds player, whose work on clarinet Wynton loved.

Herlin thought that Wynton was blessed with tremendous intelligence. "It allowed him to become a great trumpet player and bandleader and to accomplish everything he accomplished over the years. Although the trumpet was the vehicle for his success, first and foremost was his intelligence." Herlin didn't always agree with all of Wynton's philosophies, but he felt that Wynton meant so much to music and musicians, to Herlin personally, "and to our culture in America, because he gave jazz another shot.

"I don't know if there would have been so many musicians out here today," Herlin said in 1998, "who actually could have arrived at their level of achievement if it hadn't been for Wynton. When he came along, music was headed strictly toward a backbeat, in rock and fusion. A backbeat. Uh gat. Not the tain tain tu tain tain, tu tain thing—that was diminishing. But today you have trumpeters Nicholas Payton and Roy Hargrove, saxophonist Joshua Redman, bassist Christian McBride, fine musicans, just to name a few, and many other people Wynton met when they were still in high schools and in transitional stages in their lives. As the result of his coming along, they were inspired.

"All of this I have come to realize was a conscious effort on his part. He was quoted in his high school year book as saying he wanted to make a difference in the world. Something to that effect. He was very systematic and organized, a person with a plan. And not only with a plan but with the diligence and drive to stick with his plan. He doesn't give up. That is inspiring to me.

"I sit back and watch him," Herlin commented. "I've been on the road and seen him, when we were doing one-nighters, every day in another city, with another hotel, and a plane or a bus. And he would get to a city in the morning at 10:00 A.M. and conduct a noon to 1:30 P.M. master class, make a three o'clock sound check, and after that do a lecture before the gig. And after the gig, he would sometimes stay backstage and give a guy a lesson on the trumpet for thirty minutes or sign autographs. And when it's quiet, and he's finished with the public, he'll go back to the hotel room, get to the piano, and write until two or three in the morning."

"Until he gets tired," said someone listening to Herlin describe his boss's lifestyle.

"I can remember," Herlin continued, "when he was writing 'Blue Interlude.' We were on a tour, a grinding kind of tour. Every night he would just write and complete different parts, drum parts, bass parts. We had four horns at that time. They didn't just play head solos and out.

There were intricate parts like fugues with parts interwoven. Then he would get up the next morning and do it all over again. He went at this kind of pace for a month. I was just flabbergasted at the amount of energy and intestinal fortitude he has, the drive, and always with intensity. It kind of put me on a vibe that I should aspire to be more like that.

"Maybe his intelligence and drive were nurtured by his early family life," Herlin mused. "Wynton saw his father work and try to support a family of six kids and a wife as a musician with jazz gigs, which weren't very lucrative in those days. The father remained true to the instrument and to the music. Some of that commitment may have rubbed off on Wynton. When Wynton decided he wanted to play, he could come out and earn a living at doing it.

"But he never took it for granted, because he had seen his father and others in New Orleans struggling to make ends meet. And Wynton is very thankful for the opportunity. I think he realizes that when one is given a lot, when you have a gift, you have a moral obligation to pursue it.

"There has been a rippling effect from Wynton's efforts," Herlin said. He, for one, had been invited to visit Copenhagen to coach and teach. "Before I joined Wynton, these people didn't know me from Adam's house cat. So now I'm exposed to a lot of musicians around the world, and they have been exposed to me, and we respect each other. It's strictly because of my association with Wynton. And that's just one small part of it."

Others in Wynton's groups would have the same experience. Most of them would not have an easy time establishing successful groups on their own, however. Wynton would dub the problem "the curse of Skain." Nevertheless, "the bottle has gotten to Japan from New York harbor," Herlin said.

A year before Herlin joined the group, Wynton became involved with a week of performances at Lincoln Center for the Performing Arts, Inc., in its program called Classical Jazz. Wynton had dreams of building it up. "When I first joined the band, he was talking about his five-year plan, his ten-year plan. And sure enough," Herlin reflected in 1998, "I am here to witness this. He would say: 'Just you watch.' He's such a visionary."

Wynton brought the same vision to training his band members, Herlin recalled. "When Wycliffe Gordon [the trombonist] first joined the band [in 1989], he would miss notes, and his solos didn't sound as good as they should have. I asked Wynton, 'Why did you hire this cat?' Wynton said, 'You just watch and wait and see how he sounds in a year or two.' He could hear something. He knew Wycliffe had a lot of personality, and it was just of matter of [his] playing with musicians who could bring that out of him. Sure enough, a year or so later, Wycliffe was playing with so much conviction, personality, and humor. Wynton is one of those people who can shake away all the frills and fluff and get right to the core of what's going on. He can get to the core of your personality."

Many times, Wynton said to Herlin, "Man, you just need to. . . ." If Herlin was playing New Orleans music, using a lot of bass drum, Wynton would tell him to stick to that technique and develop it. "I would incorporate the bass drum into the playing and the swing. In New Orleans, the drumming comes from the bottom up. The drumset is played from the bottom up, with a lot of bass and snare drum. Bebop is played from the top down, with cymbals." Time is kept on the cymbals, and the bass drum is used for accents. "So that's the basis of the styles," Herlin noted. In New Orleans music, there's the feeling of playing in two, or 2/4 time, though it's actually 4/4 time, the same as in swing era drumming. But in the swing era, in bands such as Count Basie's and Duke Ellington's, the feeling became more fluid.

"That's just one little thing," Herlin said. "He would say things like that to people on every instrument. He can identify the personality and the characterstics of every individual: 'Those are the things you should do. That's your direction.' He can tell you things that identify you as an individual player: 'Try to exploit those things.'"

Wynton would eventually advise Victor Goines about the brilliance of his clarinet playing and tell him that was his primary instrument. Not all musicians would like Wynton's tendency to tell them what to play and how to play. However, his methods were working brilliantly for him, for his music and groups, and for many, if not all, the critics.[12]

Wynton's brother Branford was clearly coming into his own by this time. He and Wynton made occasional guest appearances in each other's groups. "We're still brothers," Branford told writer Cathleen McGuigan.[13] But Branford's decision to wend his own way, relying on his own musical talent and social adroitness, was paying off. Wynton's contract at Columbia had paved the way for Branford's.

By 1989, Branford put out his third album, *Renaissance*, which went close to the top of the jazz charts. He found himself performing pop music with Sting for huge audiences one night, then leading his own group in small, packed jazz clubs the next. He had already played on two Sting albums, appeared in a documentary with Sting, and had his first movie role in the popular comedy *Throw Momma from the Train*. In February 1989 he was seen in Spike Lee's *School Daze*. McGuigan called him "the class cutup who surprises everyone by becoming valedictorian."[14]

In December 1989 Branford led his own group for the first time in a weeklong club engagement at the Village Vanguard, with pianist Kenny Kirkland, drummer Jeff Watts, and bassist Bob Hurst—essentially his brother's former rhythm section.

Reviewing for the *New York Post* on December 15, 1989, Lee Jeske wrote about a set that lasted eighty minutes, half an hour longer than the usual set in a jazz club: "The Branford Marsalis Quartet dug in and burned. . . . Coltrane's still the jumping off point, but this time they've also harnessed some of the Coltrane band's heart. The Vanguard's bandstand was alive with energy. Watts has developed into a titanic drummer—his polyrhythms enveloped the band, squeezing extraneous notes from everybody's solos. Marsalis, switching from tenor to soprano, and Kirkland never sounded leaner; their round robin solos during the first three songs, presented as a 45-minute medley, were hard bop at its hardest, unsentimental and vibrant. . . ." Branford included the early jazz classic "Royal Garden Blues" in the set—a nod to Wynton's historical bent, perhaps. "[He] is still developing his own recognizable tenor style, but he finally seems comfortable as a leader," wrote Jeske.[15]

Actually, Branford had already made it clear a little earlier in the decade that he had arrived, playing with power and intensity in a group headed by pianist Ronnie Mathews in the trendy jazz club Whippoorwill. *New York Times* critic Robert Palmer wrote in 1986 about Branford's playing in that group: "The classic tunes and straight-ahead swing showed off his warm sound and mercurial phrasing to perfection. On record, playing tunes by his brother Wynton Marsalis and by other young writers heavily influenced by John Coltrane and Wayne Shorter, he has sounded like something of a Coltrane and Shorter copycat. At Whippoorwill, he sounded like himself."[16]

Although he always considered himself a jazz musician and composed jazz, Branford would soon lead *The Tonight Show*'s jazz-rock band when Jay Leno took over from Johnny Carson. That job would give Branford a very high profile with an audience that liked neither jazz nor even rock but watched television. Some people started to confuse Branford with Wynton, calling both of the brothers "Winston." And Wynton had people tell him that they knew him very well from *The Tonight Show.*

⸻⸻

Wynton was happy with his horn section for his septet, including Wessell Anderson and Wycliffe Gordon.

Wessell Anderson's father had played drums and listened to bebop records. Wessell would always recall the blue-and-white label of Blue Note's records spinning on the turntable. And when his father put on one of Bird's recordings of "Embraceable You" on another label, Wessell said he wanted to play "that instrument." He didn't even know what it was. Taking lessons and trying to play like Bird, while hanging out with other budding musicians in Brooklyn and New York, he met the ubiquitous Branford Marsalis. Branford told him to go to Southern University and study with Alvin Batiste.

Off Wessell went to Baton Rouge, Louisiana, where he fell in love with the area's manners and courtesy, its culture and ambience. Batiste helped Wessell convince his father to let him switch his major from accounting to music. When Wynton went there to teach a clinic in 1985, he heard Wessell and said, "I like the way you sound. I want you to do a gig with me in Cleveland."

Wessell said, "Okay." Vernon Hammond, in partnership with Ed Arrendell in Wynton's management company, called the next day to give Wessell specific instructions for travel. Wessell expected that he would be going on the road with Wynton's group forever. His friends threw a party for him at school. The gig lasted a week at a club, where Wessell earned $500. Even though Wynton sent him back to school to study more, Wessell was riding high on the thrill of what he had done. He was tipping people ten and twenty dollars. "I was Mr. Moneybags. That was a shock to me to get $500, just to see what type of wages a professional musician was making."

After school, Wessell went to New York, where the usual sideman wages were $50 and $75 a night at that time. Then he began working for Betty Carter, the singer, who often took young musicians into her groups and under her wing. Wessell thought of her as a second university. He called Wynton to ask for referrals to jobs. This time Wynton said, "Come to work."

Wessell said, "This time you can't get rid of me."

Wynton said, "No, I've been listening to you; I've been following you."

Wessell joined the group in 1988, when it included Wynton, Todd Williams, and the rhythm section of Marcus, Veal, and Riley. Wynton used a number of tenor players that year: Charlie Rouse, Don Braden, James Carter, and Walter Blanding. (Blanding, along with Victor Goines, would go to work for Wynton regularly later.) Wessell noticed right away that Wynton wanted a certain feeling. He wanted excellence in music, but he wanted a band that would stay together for a long time, not just a collection of great musicians.

Wessell was so excited to be playing in the group that he didn't realize the extent of Wynton's goal—to build an ensemble of young musicians at Lincoln Center. Wynton set the musicians to learning about jazz history. "None of us had really understood how great Louis Armstrong was," Wessell recalled. "He was just a figure we had heard of, an icon, like Duke Ellington, and so far away [in time] we had no relationship to him. We had a good relationship with Miles Davis. He was much closer to us.

"When we had gotten into jazz, we got into it for the hang of it, the social atmosphere of the clubs," Wessell noted. "When we go to clubs at first, we are going to be with other people who like the music. And then we realize we all play, and this is the kind of music they're playing, and we imitate. Then we are involved with the music. Then we realize we have to learn the ins and outs, the history, and how certain devices work, and what's going on on the bandstand, and what to do—the whole thing. So after a while it's part of your life, for the only way you can learn is to do it 24–7 [twenty-four hours a day, seven days a week].

"You learn about the personalities in music. I didn't realize that Duke stayed on the road fifty years. People were with him for thirty years. They didn't speak to each other. But when they were on the bandstand, you found out what made that band so great. Duke was a genius. He had the vision. He had to get specific people.

"He got Johnny Hodges; that was the sound Duke wanted. Others had to fit around Hodges. For Harry Carney, Duke wrote music. For Clark Terry and others. They weren't just the best, but their personalities brought their parts alive."

For his band, Wynton wanted people like Duke's men. "You know, there are other excellent sight readers and improvisationalists in New York City. You can get them, but you have to have someone in the band with the same vision you have and the same voice. And that's the individuality that jazz music has. Each person brings his personality to the music. And it's as if he's talking to you, showing his true personality," said Wessell.

"The band was so close, like a family. We did everything together. We had a bus, and we had to be in close quarters all the time. We did a lot of one-nighters. In a typical day we would leave after the first performance, say, in New York City, and if we were at Lincoln Center, go to the Green Room reception and meet with people. At midnight, we went back to the hotel, dried out our tuxedos—they would be soaking wet with perspiration. The next performance was, say, in Charlotte, North Carolina, for which the bus would leave at 2:00 A.M. So we packed our clothes and readied ourselves for the eight-hour drive. We might have a coffee, take a nap," Wessell recounted.

"The bus would be cold in February. A tour bus has bunks. It's very comfortable, but still you're in a moving vehicle for eight hours. You have to get along with people. You watch movies, listen to tapes. By the time we get to the hotel, it's noon, and the reserved rooms aren't ready. So the guys get together in a restaurant and wait. We have to do a sound check. We get to the room at 1:00 P.M., and by the time the luggage arrives, it's 2:00 P.M. We unpack, rest, shower, and go to the sound check half an hour away. Most of the day is spent with other things than music, until the 8:00 P.M. performance. All the time we're together, talking. And on the bandstand, we transfer our emotions about each other to the music."

"A lot of us came from backgrounds of listening to pop music on the radio," Wessell said. "We had to learn how to approach jazz. Older musicians understood the blues, but we didn't. Maybe we knew James Brown, but Lester Young came up in Kansas City, where they were playing the blues. So we're the third or fourth generation of blues players, and we have to digest the information to play the blues. That's why we have to go back and listen with a close ear and say, 'This is why jazz went this way and that way.'

"After King Oliver, you get Armstrong, and after that you get Harry 'Sweets' Edison, then Dizzy, and then Miles. We always discussed that as a band. Some people go to work from nine to five and say, 'See you later.'

But we're together all the time. If someone is pissed off about something that happened on the bandstand, we discuss it. If someone is not playing to the best of his ability, we discuss it. That makes the band develop quickly. We depend on each other, people playing together with the same concept. It's not just Wynton. The people are coming to see us, though it's Wynton Marsalis and his band. We realize he's a person who passionately wants to swing and play jazz music, not just to look good or get attention or publicity."

On the road, Wessell, gifted with such a warm tone that he was nicknamed "Warmdaddy," often hung out with Wynton after the gigs and went to jam sessions. "We realized we had the same passion about music," Wessell said. "The day didn't stop. If there wasn't a jam session, we would go to his room and listen to tapes and records or we would talk. Others would come and talk about the gig or what we would do the next night. We got close. It was a competition, too. I wanted to see what made him tick. And he wanted to see the same thing about me."

If the band wasn't working and had time off, Wessell and Wynton called each other long distance and started playing the blues. "Whoever won, that person would laugh and hang up. We got very tight. We were on the road three weeks every month, twelve months straight. That went on for six or seven years.

"Wynton likes basketball. He would sometimes take time off to play," Wessell noted. "He is a musician trapped in a sportsman's body. If he didn't play music, he'd be an athlete." In Brooklyn, Wessell's parents had never wanted him to play sports in the street; there were too many cars there. "So my escape was into music. In my spare time I listened to music and went to the movies. I still do. I used to go to movie theaters, but sometimes it's too noisy in the theaters, and I get a video in a rental store."

In March 1989 critics noted that Wynton was broadening his musical reach, incorporating with great artfulness the influences of his New Orleans roots with the mute work of the Ellington band, and with his own familiar, pure-toned, agile, melodic style. The entire sextet was swinging and polished, meeting the leader's exacting standards. Wynton's return engagement at the Joyce Theater that spring was a success.

When trombonist Wycliffe Gordon joined the group, making it a septet, he continued the trend for Wynton to take in youngsters and nurture and mold them into virtuosos on the job. To trumpeter Jon Faddis, Wynton confided that he did it because "I like their vibe, man." That is, he later explained, they were eager to play.

Wycliffe had lived until he was ten years old in Waynesboro, a town with dirt roads, about thirty miles from Augusta, Georgia. He was handy, having learned as a child to do everything for himself. Wynton would say the band members called him "Pinecone" because of his country background; he had the sterling quality of being able to fix things, for example a broken hinge, with the most rudimentary of tools such as chewing gum or gum wrappers. In the country, a person had to be self-reliant.

When Wycliffe was a child, he decided to play the trombone, because his elder brother came home with one from the school band one day. The family inherited jazz recordings from Wycliffe's great-aunt. Of all the songs, including slave chants, Dizzy Gillespie's big band playing "One Bass Hit," and Sonny Rollins playing "Sonnymoon for Two," Wycliffe loved Louis Armstrong's "Keyhole Blues" best. He played it over and over, learning all the parts as his initiation to jazz. He knew about the groups Earth, Wind and Fire, Rick James, and Kiss, but Armstrong's Hot Fives and Hot Seven bands had all the charisma, in Wycliffe's opinion. He decided to try to improvise, before he knew what the word meant.

In college, during his sophomore year at Florida A&M, Wycliffe played for Wynton in a clinic, and Wynton liked a riff that Wycliffe invented. Wynton took him to the hotel, where they talked about music.

Wynton knew another musician in Wycliffe's class and called him to say, "What's the trombone player's name?"

"Wycliffe," the other musician replied.

"What kind of a fucking name is Wycliffe?" Wynton wanted to know.

Wynton called Wycliffe and told him to get together with Marcus Roberts, who lived in Tallahassee, to practice. But Marcus spent most of his time on the road with Wynton. Wycliffe found few places to play jazz in Tallahassee and became discouraged.

Then one day, Marcus called to say that Wynton wanted Wycliffe to play a gig at the Caravan of Dreams in Fort Worth, Texas. Wycliffe did it, but he didn't feel that he had played very well. The experience awakened and frightened him. "I wanted to find the back door and walk back to Florida," he later reminisced. But Wynton and Marcus gave him a list—four sheets of paper covered on both sides—with the names of records to listen to.

"So there's someone out here still playing jazz and playing the hell out of it," Wycliffe told himself. He bought a cheap stereo and the recommended records and kept in touch with Wynton and Marcus. At the end of 1988, Marcus called to say that Wynton wanted Wycliffe to play with the band again, this time at Blues Alley in Washington, D.C. At least Wycliffe had been listening to the right records, even if he couldn't play that well yet, he thought.

Wynton, who was working on the album *Crescent City Christmas Card* at that time, asked Wycliffe to play for the recording in early 1989. Some other gigs followed, then Wycliffe went to Aruba with the band on June 9. Eric Reed was the pianist in the band then, filling in for Marcus. Soon, Wynton's invitations to Wycliffe to play for one engagement or another turned into a steady gig.

Wycliffe got annoyed, he said, when security guards saw him in airports with a horn and asked him who he played with. Then they said, "Oh, Wynton Marsalis; he's arrogant." "Everyone has a degree of arrogance," Wycliffe told them, "but, no, he's as nice as you ever want to meet."

Developing a friendship with Wynton, Wycliffe even tried to teach the trumpeter how to swim. Wynton never did learn. "He damn near drowned me in a pool in a hotel," Wycliffe said. Except for that novel experience, Wycliffe observed exactly the same things about Wynton that Wessell and everyone else in the band had seen. And Wycliffe began learning more about jazz history from the study sessions on the bus and in hotel rooms with videos and tapes of Armstrong, Coltrane, and other musicians whom Wynton loved.

Wynton nurtured Wycliffe until he was playing the way Wynton envisioned Wycliffe could play, with great technique, understanding, and excitement. "I don't know if he has a third eye," Wycliffe would eventually say. "He is a great visionary. He can see a stone that has to be [polished] and can be made into a jewel."

Marcus officially left the band in May 1990 but actually played with Marsalis on and off throughout 1991. "I didn't really leave," he said. "Various piano players came and went. I recorded *Citi Movement*, even though it was redone. I may be on one song. I would say as far as the discography goes, the [first] record I feel that I didn't contribute to the origination of, the development of, was *In This House, On This Morning*. That was [pianist] Eric Reed. . . . Up to that point [1992], I was pretty much in some way a part of [all the recordings]."

Despite the fact that Wynton was upset when Marcus decided to leave the band, Wycliffe noticed that Wynton told Marcus, "If you want to go on your own, I'll help you." Wynton bragged about Marcus all the time. Wycliffe thought that made Wynton special. Two years later when Reginald Veal left, Wycliffe cried. But Ben Wolfe arrived, at first to replace Veal when he was having dental work done, then to become a regular member of the band. The first white man to join one of Wynton's small groups on a regular basis, Ben became good friends with Wycliffe.

"I don't think a lot of things happened the way Wynton wanted them to happen," Wycliffe reflected. "Guys got married, and then there would be pressure on the homefront. The guys were willing to take a pay cut just so they could be home." Working, working, working—there was never a dull moment in Wynton Marsalis's band. After six weeks in Japan one year, Wycliffe himself was glad to get back to the United States. "The gigs were good, but I can't speak any Japanese," he explained.

Wycliffe never considered quitting to stay home. "Musicians in my generation want to be like him," Wycliffe said about the inspiration he drew from Wynton. "They want to be in his shoes. I've heard musicians, young and old, talk about him. I am one of those who wish to give him his flowers while he's living. Sometimes you run into animosity. It's hard to look at your peer and say, 'You're doing something great,'" Wycliffe said about the jealousy he perceived in criticisms Wynton sometimes faced over the years.

"We've been called Wyntonians," Wycliffe would say, once the Jazz at Lincoln Center programs began to emphasize Ellington's music. "As if we didn't have minds of our own. We may agree but we don't necessarily agree on everything. But all in all, I don't think I could have been in a better situation musically, because Wynton is always open musically and always helps the musicians. He loves music and musicians. I've yet to run into anyone as serious about music and what he does as Wynton is."

Wynton was not impervious to critical heat. Some of it he could dismiss easily, and he claimed that he did—though he was actually always sensitive to it. But sometimes his feelings were actually hurt, or he was puzzled by a writer's perception of him. Wycliffe noticed that Wynton became very upset one night in Los Angeles while reading an uncomplimentary article about him. It had some facts that "were screwed up and negative," Wycliffe recollected.

Wessell Anderson contended that Wynton didn't mind the negative remarks of some critics. "He loves it," Wessell said. "His thing is to get everything out in the open. People would think he's stressed out. He says he loves it. He has been in combat, or has had combatants [for years], and it just makes him stronger. I never saw him get nervous or angry. He prepares for them. He does research, or he just knows what he's talking about, or he gets all the articles and gets a red marker and makes sure he marks everything they said wrong, and he starts exactly with that. [He's] talking about something that [he] knows deep down and that he has to get out. He says he's just another cat slaying the dragon."

Wynton clarified his position: "I think the thing that bugs me the most is pettiness, the petty quality of bitchery, someone nitpicking. Most things make me happy. I have to complain to people so they won't know how happy I am. Ecstatic. I complain to keep them from subjecting me to bitchery. I say that it's rough and tough out there. A lot goes on that's against people coming together. People are trying to keep people down—poor people, black people, anybody who doesn't have something—people are always trying to keep people from getting more. That whole cycle is just fear, fear of people having something that you don't have, and keeping them down is not going to help you get it."

He didn't like people "fucking over teenagers." He found it "unbelievable" and "major rough" to see that happen. There were people who wanted to "make you accept less and be less than you actually are. That creates depression. Be nothing. Look where I'm from. Everyone is sensitive.

"But I ain't complaining about it," Wynton claimed. "It is what it was. It could be anything, not having money. It could be having money. There's always something. I'm happy just to be out here participating in life. Even the stuff that I don't like. I'm happy just to have a chance to participate and reflect some of the creativity that comes from God and to have the opportunity to work, to work with people and play music, to speak and be heard, to have some kind of influence on anything. My main thing is to help. I'm happy and grateful—not for what I do, not for living by some archaic moral code, but because I'm trying to create something to make people feel better. Just to be a part of something as great as jazz music. That's enough to make you ecstatic."

His views on the difficulties faced by teenagers, particularly black teenagers, didn't negate another opinion he delivered to writer James Brady, for a *Parade* magazine article. Wynton told Brady, "I've been hustled by the police. You grow up in this society as a black, you get that. But the greatest menace in the black community is not the police. It's all these young black men who beat up old ladies and kids. Whenever you elevate hoodlums to heroes, you've got trouble."[17] His comments came in the wake of the Los Angeles riots, when both black and white teenagers looted and set fire to ghetto neighborhoods.

As for the many writers who said that Wynton disliked electronic music, Wynton tried to correct the impression he had given: "Electronic music is okay. A lot of times, the things you grow up with, you like. I grew up with electronic music. My [point] is: I like some things I don't want my kids to like. I may like dope, but don't tell my kids it's good.

"It's crazy to go to the extreme of saying I would run out of the room [when electronic music is playing]. Who would I have known or dated that didn't like pop music? And the media tried to make me seem like I was crazy and frothing [at] the mouth. It's just untrue."

As for criticism leveled at him by other musicians whom he knew, Wynton simply said: "It's jealousy." He noticed similar feelings held by the fans of superstar basketball player Michael Jordan: "[They] don't want [Jordan] to win, just because he's better than other people. They curse when he does well. . . . And that happens more often than not. I say: 'What is that type of petty thing that creates that type of feeling? Men are so competitive. Where does that come from? Who is enjoying life?' That type of pettiness creates misunderstanding.

"I played in a pop band in high school. That's what we did. We played hundreds of gigs. Other [young musicians who criticize me] didn't do that. I don't like the direction that American pop music went in. But that won't change the direction, nor will it change the beauty of being in the world."

A lot of times, Wynton didn't know what was true himself. Sometimes he heard a tape of himself playing music, and he realized that he hadn't known he was that good or that bad. "Or there might be a tape of a conversation someone had," he said as an example of his point.

"A man might come home and cuss out his wife one day. And people might say that's how he was. But what about the other days? So a lot of times in your life, other people don't know what's going on. Who knows what's going on between a man and a woman when many times they don't know themselves? Life is so varied, so full of complexities. It's easy to get lost. I could honestly not know what I did. So how could someone else know?"

Sometimes the criticisms of other musicians seemed to Wynton to be "comedic—like someone throwing beer on a boxing ring, and it doesn't deserve to be commented on."

⟶⟶⋗●⋖⟵⟵

As Wynton's fortunes rose, so did Stanley Crouch's. Crouch was a volatile man. When he was working at the *Village Voice*, he got into a physical fight with another writer. After this incident, Stanley was fired. Yet, Crouch was also sensitive; in his *New Yorker* profile, the author noted, "For all his bravado, Crouch retreated to an editor's cubicle after being given notice, and wept. 'Now I've really done it,' he moaned."[18]

After leaving the newspaper, however, Crouch brightened up considerably. He seemed to have no financial worries, turning down the offer of a small gift of $100 from another writer. He would later comment in his *New Yorker* profile, "The two best things that have ever happened to me were being fired by the *Voice* and being hired by the *Voice*—in that order."[19]

Perhaps getting fired *was* the best thing that could have happened. Within two years, his essay collection, *Notes of a Hanging Judge*, was being praised by the kinds of people who never read the *Voice*. He received a Whiting fellowship and a MacArthur "genius" grant—the famous "no strings attached" grant that many artists coveted. And in 1987 Marsalis asked Stanley to help get the program called Classical Jazz on its feet at Lincoln Center. It would turn out to be the accomplishment that Crouch could point to with special pride.

By the time Herlin Riley joined Wynton's group, Wynton's friendship with Stanley Crouch had for a long time been cemented on an intellectual level. But they related to each other on a more basic level, Herlin noticed. They could talk to each other about any subject. Wynton could turn to Crouch for emotional support. Herlin agreed with people who thought that Stanley was quite feisty and said what was on his mind—whether others wanted to know or not. Herlin thought Crouch was also very strong in his convictions. "Wynton is the same way. I think Wynton was always that way, and Stanley may have fortified it."

━━━━━━◆◆◆━━━━━━

It is impossible to recount all of Wynton's activities by the late 1980s in chronological order—or at all. For one thing, many events took place simultaneously. He continued to lead his septet, record music, teach, lecture, win awards, and work with some classical musicians. He wrote the book *Sweet Swing Blues on the Road*, immortalizing his septet. He let Tom Piazza come along on a tour for an assignment for *Esquire* magazine, for which Piazza praised the septet as one of the "greatest jazz groups of all times." Wynton also acted as host for a highly praised video, *Trumpet Kings*, written, directed, and produced by Burrill Crohn. He also hosted the PBS special *Wynton Marsalis, Blues and Swing*, which eventually aired in February 1989. Wynton also performed with classical musicians such as the lyric coloratura soprano Kathleen Battle.

But one small project that began as a weeklong jazz festival at Lincoln Center in the summer of 1987 gained momentum. Eventually it would take priority in Wynton's life. After a gig at the Village Vanguard at the end of 1994, he disbanded his septet to turn his attention to this project full time. It was, of course, the new jazz program at Lincoln Center.

CHAPTER NOTES

1. Miles Davis with Quincy Troupe, *Miles: The Autobiography.* New York: Simon & Schuster, 1989.
2. Ibid.
3. Ibid.
4. Ibid.
5. Ibid.
6. Ibid.
7. Chip Deffaa, "Wynton Marsalis: The Simple, Clean Sound." *New York Post,* September 19, 1986.
8. Leslie Rubinstein, "Creative Spirit: Wynton Marsalis." *Stagebill,* March 1987.
9. Ibid.

10. Wynton Marsalis, "What Jazz Is and Isn't." *New York Times*, January 28, 1988.
11. Ibid.
12. Peter Watrous, the influential critic of the *New York Times*, wrote particularly flattering reviews of the Lincoln Center program that Wynton was helping to establish.
13. Cathleen McGuigan, "Branford's Two Worlds." *Newsweek*, January 4, 1988.
14. Ibid.
15. Lee Jeske, "Elder Marsalis Hot to Trot." *New York Post*, December 15, 1989.
16. Robert Palmer, "Jazz: Ron Matthews Quartet." *New York Times*, August 24, 1986. Mathews's last name was misspelled in the paper.
17. James Brady, "In Step with Wynton Marsalis." *Parade*, August 16, 1992.
18. Robert S. Boynton, "The Professor of Connection." *The New Yorker*, November 6, 1995.
19. Ibid.

JAZZ AT LINCOLN CENTER

From Classical Jazz to a Year-round Program

I n New York City in the 1980s, jazz pianist Barry Harris, known since his teens in Detroit as a great music teacher, was running a storefront jazz school, called the Jazz Cultural Theater, on Eighth Avenue in Manhattan. His school was funded, according to legend and lore, primarily by the Baroness Pannonica de Koenigswater, at whose house Barry lived, as well as by some fees from students. The baroness served as a patroness of many celebrated jazz musicians, including Thelonious Monk, Art Blakey, and Charlie Parker.

A young woman named Alina Bloomgarden began to attend Harris's school. Alina's boyfriend, a tenor saxophonist who studied with Harris, took her along.

"I would go and just hang out there," Alina recalled. "I found it so healing. I couldn't believe how it just transformed my state of mind. We celebrated birthdays at Barry Harris's Jazz Cultural Theater. Barry played. He also proselytized about jazz being the great American art form, and young people today weren't going to hear it, he said, and all these great older players were going to die off. It was a very endangered art. I was hearing this subliminally without feeling I would have any role to play at all.

"I was [working] at Lincoln Center, and I still am, as director of Visitors Services. I do all kinds of programs to break down barriers to the arts and make Lincoln Center more welcoming, to welcome new audiences to Lincoln Center. That's the way I've interpreted what I do," she said.

"I heard they were trying to think of uses for Alice Tully Hall for the summer. I proposed to Nat Leventhal, the president of Lincoln Center, that we start a jazz program." Alina told him, "Jazz is a great American art form. We could have a role to play in how it's received and respected in its own country, the way it's respected in Europe and all over the world. We could present jazz in the way we present classical music, with informative program notes, thematic programs, repertorial programming."

He said, "Write me a proposal."

"I wrote it, and it was presented, I think," Alina said, "to the management committee. Months went by. I went to see what happened. Nat said, 'Well, I liked it, but management thought the jazz audience would be wild.' I said, 'Come on, that's not what the jazz audience is like.' He said, 'Okay, write me another proposal.'"

So she wrote another one and emphasized that a jazz program could pay tribute to great jazz composers and bring together musicians who played with them or were greatly influenced by them. "This proposal died, too," Alina reflected. "I had started making proposals in 1983. By 1987, we had a new chairman of the board at Lincoln Center, George Weisman. And Weisman said, 'You've been thinking of doing a summer program at Alice Tully Hall, so what are you doing?'"

It had suddenly become imperative to Weisman to bring jazz to Lincoln Center. Retired in 1984 as chairman of the board of Philip Morris Companies, Inc., he had become chairman of the board of Lincoln Center in 1986. Connected to the arts center since its planning in 1958, he had been part of the film society, then had gone on the parent board of Lincoln Center in 1970. He loved opera, the ballet, and the symphony in particular. He even had some peripheral interest in jazz; that is, he had taken pleasure in hearing it, beginning in the 1930s.

Weisman had gone to the Village Vanguard and to Eddie Condon's jazz club originally in Greenwich Village; at Condon's, for the price of a glass of beer, he had stood at the bar and listened all night. He had heard Benny Goodman at the old Pennsylvania Hotel, and Tommy Dorsey and Glenn Miller, too. After World War II, he sometimes still frequented jazz clubs. He heard Marian McPartland at the Hickory House in midtown Manhattan, soul singer Nina Simone in Los Angeles, and saxophonist John Coltrane in Greenwich Village. Weisman was a casual jazz fan, who went to hear jazz if he happened to be in the neighborhood of a club. Ordinarily, he traveled in circles filled with the sort of people who went to European classical music events at Lincoln Center.

One night in 1987, he and his wife, who live in Rye, New York, attended a jazz concert by Marian McPartland and two other pianists at the State University of New York at Purchase. Weisman thought it was a "marvelous" concert. He noticed that the audience, which was "balding, graying, and WASPy," he said, reacted enthusiastically. "They tore the place apart." Weisman had never seen people in those social circles react that way before. He told Nat Leventhal about it and added, "Bring in jazz." The center wanted to use the name Classical Jazz, Weisman recalled, to "get it by the other constituents," who were eager "to keep up the image of Lincoln Center as a place where classics were presented," with a nice orderly group of people performing and attending.

"So Nat convened a meeting of all the usual suspects," Alina said, "the people who typically would produce at Lincoln Center, along with me. Everyone looked at me and asked: 'What is she doing at this meeting?' Nat went around the room and asked: 'What is your idea?' and 'What is your idea?' Then he looked at me and said, 'Okay, Alina, this is your chance.' So I restated my idea. He looked at me and said, 'If you're going to present jazz, what will you present?' Now, I had never thought I would be the one producing jazz concerts at Lincoln Center. But he threw the ball back at me. I said, 'Okay, I'll come back to you with ideas.'

"I did a couple of things right away, one of which was to call WBGO [the public radio station in Newark, New Jersey, that specialized in jazz]. I knew people there would have the phone numbers of people who could help me. I didn't know anything or anyone. I talked with Dorthaan Kirk [the widow of the highly regarded multi-instrumentalist Rahsaan Roland Kirk]. She didn't want to give me the time of day at first, but then we talked. We were conspirators for the first year, beginning in February 1987. We agreed we would do it, and by August 3, we produced the first concert.

"I wanted to put on three concerts, Ladies First, then a tribute to Bird, and a tribute to Monk. I had these ideas. Carmen McRae had put together a Monk album. She was supposed to be a very unapproachable

artist (for people whom she didn't know.) So Dorthaan helped me. When
I said, 'How do I get to Carmen McRae?' Dorthaan gave me Carmen's
phone number. I called and said, 'Hello, Carmen, this is Alina
Bloomgarden.' Dorthaan always teased me after that, imitating me saying that. And that's how I got Carmen McRae to do it. She said yes. It
seemed very easy.

"It was a good idea. We put together wonderful people. We had the
group Sphere [with pianist Kenny Barron, bassist Buster Williams,
drummer Ben Riley, and tenor saxophonist Charlie Rouse] that first year.
And pianist Marcus Roberts, and Carmen McRae. Just for the Monk
night. For the Charlie Parker night, we had Red Rodney, the trumpeter,
and others. Then we had Ladies First as the first concert, with singers
Carrie Smith and Betty Carter. Betty had her own struggling jazz label,
Bet Car, at that time. Then I started learning more, going out, meeting
people, hearing them.

"Someone said: 'Call Wynton Marsalis.' So I contacted Wynton's
manager, Ed Arrendell, and his partner Vernon Hammond. And I said
to Ed, 'We can really put jazz in Lincoln Center and put ourselves in the
service of Wynton's vision.'" Somehow, Alina knew, or was told, that
Arrendell, Wynton, or both could be a little tough. But Arrendell set up
the meeting. "I didn't know Wynton had a vision [for Lincoln Center].
I knew he had a vision for the classicism of jazz, for wearing suits and
jackets and dignifying performances. Ed set it up. Wynton came to me
in my office.

"I told him, 'I want to present jazz in a dignified manner and really
do repertorial programming, great composers, and musicians who never
get a chance to play with each other."

Wynton said that he loved the idea, and anything he could do to
help, he would.

I said, "Okay, I'll tell you how you can help. Will you act as artistic
advisor?"

He said, as Alina recalled, "You don't want me; nobody likes me."
Wynton recalled saying something different, advising her not to tell people he was the artistic advisor, because not everybody would want to work
for him. Some people had their reservations, he believed. Alina said,
"Don't worry about it. I want you." She told him that they had a very
small budget, "maybe $100,000, certainly not much more. [It was
$146,300 the first year.] He said he would perform for free for me, and

Simeon, Wynton, Sr., and Wynton, Jr. on September 6, 1997.

Wynton Jr. at the piano
and Simeon on clarinet,
1997.
Photo by Pavin Carter

Jasper Armstrong Marsalis, Wynton's youngest child.

Jazz at Lincoln
Center banner show-
ing Wynton Marsalis.
Photo by Leslie Gourse

Conducting the orchestra, 1994.
Photo by Jack Vartoogian

A 1993 performance.
Photo by Jack Vartoogian

Marsalis Family concert, 1990. Jason, Reginald Veal, Ellis,
Wynton, and Branford.
Photo by Jack Vartoogian

Ellis and Wynton at the Blue Note, June 1990.
Photo by Jack Vartoogian

Delfeayo Marsalis, undated photograph.
Photo by David Gahr

Jason Marsalis, undated photograph.
Photo by David Gahr

Wynton reading to children.
Photo by David Gahr

Wynton at the Village Vanguard, 1993.
Photo by Jack Vartoogian

he performed for free for two years. We wrote a contract letter together right then, at the end of the meeting."

Wynton signed it with his eccentric handwriting, in which his signature looks like an Arabic word. At the time, Wynton really had no idea how important Lincoln Center would become for him, and he had no special plans or dreams for the program, although other people would later ascribe them to him.

Alina told Nat Leventhal that she was going to get Wynton Marsalis as artistic director. People at Lincoln Center said disbelievingly, "Sure, she's going to get Wynton Marsalis." So she sent Wynton's letter around to everyone. Alina recalled, "Everyone started talking to me differently. 'Okay, I guess she can do that,' they said. And that's when I was suddenly producing. I did everything and depended a lot on WBGO for publicity, and commissioned original artwork for the brochures.

"The first year Wynton was too busy to perform. He was on the road. But we certainly conversed, and he gave me some suggestions. He gave me Stanley Crouch. Wynton said, 'Get Stanley to write the program notes.' And Stanley helped, also. We became like a triumvirate after that.

"The next year, in 1988, Wynton performed at a couple of concerts. First we talked about taking some Ellington records and having them transcribed. They had never been performed since they had been recorded. Stanley came up with David Berger, a noted Ellington scholar, copyist, and transcriber. And we thought of the orchestra we would get to perform. They suggested the American Jazz Orchestra, which had been performing at Cooper Union in the 1980s, an orchestra founded by pianist John Lewis and *Village Voice* jazz critic Gary Giddins, with Roberta Swan of Cooper Union. I said, 'Wait a minute, guys. This is Lincoln Center. Let's put together our own orchestra.'"

In the same period that Lincoln Center founded its own jazz orchestra, the American Jazz Orchestra, whose debut performance had been an exciting event in jazz circles in 1986, struggled for a firm foothold. It would cease operations in 1992, essentially for lack of funding, as Lincoln Center's program continually gained momentum.

"We brought in people who had originally played with Ellington," Alina remembered. She wasn't very clear about which year which musicians played during the first two years. But: "We brought in Britt Woodman, the trombonist, and someone from Sweden, and bassist Jimmy Woode, and baritone saxophonist Joe Temperley—Ellington alumni and others, a great orchestra. Wynton wanted to make sure that young people got a chance to play Ellington's music. And in a way that idea goes back to the original hope of Barry Harris. And it happened, the thing we set out to do. That music is not going to die now," Alina said with hindsight in 1998. "It really won't. Now it's in the center. Now there are younger people who know that music and see it as hip."

The first year of the Classical Jazz Festival was 1987, and the first year of the orchestra was 1988. From then on the festival was held every year. It was called Classical Jazz until the end of 1991. Reviews of the program had been very good. Alina noted, "Then they started Jazz at Lincoln Center as a separate department. The last year I produced was in 1990."

To do the programming every year during her tenure, Alina went to Wynton's house on 18th Street, where he was living with Candace Stanley, near Beth Israel hospital. "He was already prosperous and living in a very nice townhouse," Alina recalled of the house he owned. "Candace was really his girlfriend in those days. I told him how good the food was when I ate in his house. He said, 'Yeah, my girlfriend made it.'

"The thing that always impressed me: The phone would ring, and it would be a kid from Florida, or someplace. Wynton would take the phone and say, 'What? Let me hear that again.' Wynton would take his horn out and say, 'Listen.' And he would go—dodoo da da da. He would give a lesson. Wherever he went all over the world, he gave the kids his phone number at home, saying, 'Call me, let me know how you're doing.'

"He personally made such an impact just by making himself available. People can just call him, and he'll stop everything. For the music, he'll stop everything for some kid in Texas. Roy Hargrove, for example. I was always so impressed with that. And kids would bring their horns backstage. He would stop everything. 'Let me hear,' he would say. He would be teaching right then. He's so generous that way, so committed."

In Dallas, Texas, young trumpet player Roy Hargrove fell in love with Wynton's playing when he saw him in a spot on the evening news. "He talked about jazz and played a little bit," Hargrove recalled. He also saw Wynton perform the Haydn concerto for trumpet. "Wow, he's doing what I want to be doing, yeah, yeah," Hargrove told himself.

When Hargrove was nine years old in elementary school, he had heard the school's band play in an assembly. He loved hearing the band improvise; the band teacher had taught the students how to do it.

Hargrove knew he wanted to join immediately, and soon he was playing cornet in the band. "All I did was practice. Sometimes my mother would say: 'Go outside and play football.' But my father said, 'Let him practice.'"

Wynton was playing at the Texas jazz club Caravan of Dreams, when he decided one day to go to the Dallas high school where Hargrove was a student. Hargrove felt in awe of his presence. "Wow, this is the cat I was seeing on television. And he's right here, and it wasn't like we had to go and find him. He called the school. He said, 'Hey, I'm coming down there.' And there was no hoopla. They're not paying him. I was very glad to know there was someone on the planet like him. He was into making sure that the young cats knew about the music." Hargrove followed Wynton around, asking him for exercises to warm up with, Hargrove remembered years later. After hearing him play, Wynton invited Hargrove to go to the Caravan of Dreams and sit in with the septet. But Hargrove didn't go right away.

Nevertheless, Wynton told singer Carmen McRae's former manager, Larry Clothier, to go to hear Hargrove play. Clothier was then booking the acts at Caravan of Dreams. On the last night of Wynton's gig, Hargrove finally did appear with a few friends. Clothier thought at first that Hargrove looked like an unprepossessing kid. But when he got up on stage to play a little with Wynton on the tune, "Softly, As in a Morning Sunrise," Clothier perceived him instantly as a mature artist. Clothier asked Hargrove to accompany him to Europe to the summertime jazz festivals.

Hargrove told Clothier: "You have to ask my folks."

They said yes. So Hargrove went as a special guest to Europe to play with pianist Ronnie Mathews's trio with Benny Bailey and Frank Morgan on the front line. The head of the North Sea Jazz Festival, a friend of Clothier's, was particularly instrumental in giving Hargrove the chance to perform.

Back in Dallas, Clothier kept inviting Hargrove to go to the Caravan of Dreams and play with the groups passing through town; they were led by Dizzy Gillespie, Freddie Hubbard, Herbie Hancock, Bobby Hutcherson, with their rhythm sections featuring such people as pianist Larry Willis, bassist Walter Booker, and drummers Idris Muhammed and Jimmy Cobb. "These were all my teachers," Hargrove would reminisce. He followed them around, he said proudly, "even when I went to

Boston," where he studied at the Berklee School of Music for a year and a half, and later, too, when he went to the New School in New York City in 1990. By then Hargrove was working so much late at night and out of town that it was impossible for him to continue at school.

In New York, Hargrove went to Wynton's house to play and talk about music. While learning from Wynton, Hargrove was establishing himself as one of the brightest trumpet players alive. Wynton had paved the way for him. "I still use the exercises he taught me to warm up on," Hargrove recalled. "He also showed me a piece of music. It was all six-teenth notes and a couple of minutes long at least. And you had to play the whole thing in one breath. I was like, 'Wow.' He said, 'Yeah, play this in one breath.' I said no. He did it on the spot. This cat's amazing. I didn't take the music with me to try to play it. I was too afraid to even try. Now I could practice it, a classical piece, really challenging. You have to circu-lar breathe. That's another thing . . . Wynton's the cat."

"I don't get to talk to him that much," Hargrove said in 1998, by which time he himself had risen to become not only one of the best and brightest trumpeters in the jazz world but leader of one of the most praised big bands. "I always give him my regards and try to pick his brain when I see him. Really, just the best way to learn is to listen to him, to certain things he does when he's warming up. Trumpet players, they don't want to give up the information, but he's cool."

Hargrove would always recall how nervous he was when he first played with Wynton at Caravan of Dreams. "Because he is like the great-est trumpet player ever. He can do anything on the trumpet. People [are] criticizing him all the time, but I say anyone who can do what he does on that instrument, hats off. It takes a lot of practice to do that. You have to spend hours and hours to get to that level. I have to give him his props. If anyone mentions his name to me, I'm like, Wynton, shit, you know, he sits on that throne."

David Berger, who had first met Wynton when David called for a substitute in the trumpet section at the Alvin Ailey Dance Company about ten years earlier, met Wynton again when Alina Bloomgarden was producing Classical Jazz at Lincoln Center. Alina called Berger and said, "Stanley Crouch recommended you. Would you be interested in con-ducting a concert of Ellington's music as part of our summer series, Classical Jazz?"

"Sure," Berger said.

He and Crouch had become acquainted at a Duke Ellington Society meeting. Both of them showed up one night because James Lincoln Collier arrived there to talk about his biography of Duke Ellington. Some musicians were very angry at Collier for what he had written. "Scandalous," Berger called it. "A lot of musicians showed up to vent their anger at him."

Collier had written that Ellington was not really a composer, in essence; he was an arranger and a dilettante who had become famous through his personal charm and ability to use his musical and professional opportunities. Collier downplayed Ellington's abilities for playing the piano and reading or writing music. Berger recalled that Collier spoke, then people in the audience got up and said what they thought. Berger asked how Collier could write what he had written. "I just asked that question," Berger recalled.

"Then Crouch really lit into him. But Collier sort of deserved it," Berger said. Crouch and Collier would be at swords' points from then on. "So Crouch and I went out for drinks afterward," Berger recalled.

"That started quite a number of evenings when we went out and talked." Berger always liked Crouch. "He was a guest in my house many times. He's really intelligent, insightful, and he doesn't hold back. He says what he thinks. I don't always agree with it." Berger thought that Stanley didn't feel he had anything to lose by being outspoken, even contentious and abrasive at times.

When Alina Bloomgarden called Berger to conduct the jazz orchestra at Lincoln Center, she told him that Wynton Marsalis was in charge but would be playing in the band. Berger would have to meet Wynton. "Okay?"

"Sure, okay," he said.

So Berger met with Alina, Wynton, and Stanley Crouch.

Wynton said, "What would you do for the Duke Ellington concert?"

Berger said, "I would provide music for it, transcribe off the records, and conduct it." The music wasn't available. It may have been locked away in a vault by Duke's son, Mercer, Berger said, in the Chase Manhattan bank. Some music may have been lost. In any case, Berger and Lincoln Center had no access to it.

Alina said, "We have to put an orchestra together."

Wynton said, "What's your concept of how you want to perform this music?"

Berger said, "I don't want to perform it the way it is on the records. I want to perform the pieces. But I want the personality of the players that we pick. I want them to play their music. I don't want anyone to imitate."

Wynton said, "Great. That's exactly how I feel. I like this guy." Then he left to keep a pressing commitment.

———————⟫◆⟪———————

One of his obligations at this time was an album to be titled *The Majesty of the Blues,* which he recorded with Dr. Michael White, a clarinetist devoted to New Orleans music. Along with White, the recording group included trumpeter Teddy Riley, trombonist Freddie Lonzo, and Danny Barker on banjo in 1988—all veteran and highly regarded New Orleans musicians—and musicians from Wynton's group: Wessell, Marcus, Veal, and Herlin (no relation to Teddy Riley). Stanley Crouch wrote the sermon, and the Rev. Jeremiah Wright was the narrator. It was not only a remarkable album for the reverence and attention it gave to New Orleans music, it was an interesting, even pivotal album in Wynton's career, because of the way it combined Wynton's New Orleans orientation with his modernistic leanings, and a dream come true for Michael White. His path had crossed Wynton's several times in airports, as they had been traveling to their different gigs.

One night, in 1987, White dreamed that he saw Wynton playing traditional New Orleans music, and White had something to do with the performance. When he woke up, he thought his dream was ridiculous. Nevertheless, he started to send Wynton tapes of New Orleans music and talked to him about the music of Jelly Roll Morton and King Oliver. White told Wynton that even Duke Ellington had thought that Jelly Roll Morton's music had been important. He told Wynton that New Orleans music was a part of him whether he knew it or not, and there was no way he could move away from it. The spirit of all jazz was in New Orleans, White preached. It started there. "The most socially involving form of jazz is New Orleans jazz," White said. "It's a very spiritual thing. And the spirits are very much around us."

Wynton would later say that he had always been aware of the power of that music, and he had already been involved with it to a degree. He was influenced by White to the extent that he was influenced "by all musicians I'm around," Wynton said. "Certainly I respect him and what he's doing. But once Herlin Riley and Reginald Veal came into the band, two musicians from New Orleans in the rhythm section, naturally we're going to play New Orleans music."

Wynton asked White for some brass band tapes; White sent tapes that emphasized the oldest brass bands, he said. Wynton eventually called White and said he had an idea for a recording, for which he wanted some New Orleans musicians. Wynton played his ideas on the piano next to the telephone. White said, "I guess so." But he really couldn't tell how the different parts were going to work out.

Nevertheless, he and the other New Orleans musicians joined Wynton in a New York studio in 1988. "The whole concept sort of developed right there," White reflected. "He had an idea. He pointed us in a direction and let it happen. There were two New Orleans–type songs and a sermon in the background. There were a lot of things happening, instruments playing, responses to the sermon. And I realized my dream had come true.

"Just before the album came out, Wynton was set up to perform in the New Orleans Jazz and Heritage Festival. Miles Davis was supposed to follow Wynton, in the river tent packed with people. Near the end of the concert, without anybody knowing what Wynton was going to do, Wynton brought out the musicians who played for the recording. And there was pandemonium in the house. By the time we got to the slow part, 'The Death of Jazz,'" White recalled, "it blew everybody away. By the time we got to the 'Happy Feet Blues,' like a Second Line song [at the end of the entire piece], people were dancing. Nobody expected that. That created such a sensation. Then Miles came on. Wynton was a tough act to follow, especially in New Orleans. People were so charged up. They started to leave, while Miles played a few numbers. . . .

"I've done a lot of touring with Wynton or Lincoln Center musicians," White said—he toured with a Morton, Monk, and Marsalis project a few years later—"and I've seen it happen many times on concerts where he has done modern music and then New Orleans music; that seems to capture people in a way that other music doesn't."

For one thing, it's rarely played anymore outside of New Orleans, and people have little opportunity to hear it done so well; the novelty of the experience provided by fine musicians is extremely satisfying, even exalting. *The Majesty of the Blues* itself was a bright and interesting effort and a milestone in Wynton's development as a composer.

⟶➤●◄⟵

At the next meeting, with Stanley Crouch and Alina Bloomgarden, Wynton asked David Berger, "Who do you want to play in this band? If you could have anybody in the whole world, anybody, your wildest dreams, who would be the best guy to play a particular chair?"

Berger named "outrageous" people, he said.

Although Wynton didn't even know most of them, he said he would get them all for Berger.

"And you know what? He did," Berger recalled. "We had a ball. I'll never forget the first rehearsal. For one week, in August 1988, before the concerts, all these Duke Ellington guys showed up, my heroes from my childhood. It was a dream come true. It was just amazing. It was not only Ellingtonians but other great musicians, [saxophonist] Joe Henderson, [drummer] Kenny Washington, [bassist] Milt Hinton, [pianist] Sir Roland Hanna, Jimmy Hamilton on clarinet. What a thrill. Wynton played fourth trumpet. He was very unassuming, just trying to play his part, trying to learn from everyone else. He was very generous. He did a great job. 'This is it,' I thought. 'How could music get better than this?' My favorite music with the greatest players.

"All of them got the music ahead of time and rehearsed it. Everyone was excited. There was a real family kind of feeling. Alina ran it like a mom-and-pop store, the beginning of something great, the beginning of something successful.

"The next summer we did two concerts. Many of the same people played the next year. Norris Turney, Art Barron, and Britt Woodman were not available the first year, but they played the second year, and Buster Cooper who had played with Duke in the 1960s, a trombonist, and Willie Cook came all the way from Sweden, and Jimmy Woode came from Switzerland in the second and third years, and Jimmy Hamilton came from the Virgin Islands, and Chuck Connors on trombone, and Clark Terry played one time and did TV shows. It was fabulous. That's basically how the Classical Jazz Orchestra got started." Berger did the arrangements and conducted.

Early in this period, George Weisman was tremendously impressed the first time he met Wynton in the executive offices of Lincoln Center on the tenth floor of the Rose building on 65th Street. Weisman met with Wynton and Nat Leventhal. "I was impressed with his conception of jazz as a cultural phenomenon," Weisman said, "as the only real American form of contribution to music throughout the world. We're still living with the heritage of European western opera and symphonic composers, but jazz was really the first American expression that was authentically part of the cultural scene."

"I realized the importance of jazz when Wynton came on board and expounded his theories. I was impressed with his intelligence, and his well-spoken elucidation of what jazz was, and its place in America and world cultural life." From time to time, Weisman saw Wynton at committee meetings of Lincoln Center. "He would talk about his plans, his tours, his performances," Weisman recalled. "I also saw him at the galas."

Weisman remembered Stanley Crouch and Albert Murray at the jazz society meetings, too. "They were the philosophers and historians who sort of gave the institutional history to jazz and also to its place in society. They repeated or reinforced what Wynton said, basically. And it was sort of an interesting byplay. Sometimes they would talk, and Wynton would say, 'Yeah, man,' and 'Right on,' and agree with them. Stanley liked to talk. He was a big bear of a man, very articulate, bright, and he made very acute observations of people and things. Al Murray was a good guy, a friendly man, with a great deal of wisdom and knowledge, the kind of guy who wouldn't let the board do something stupid."

Weisman was behind Classical Jazz from 1988 to 1994, through its life as the Classical Jazz Festival produced by Lincoln Center and then during its existence as a separate department at Lincoln Center. In 1991 Alina Bloomgarden ended her involvement with Jazz at Lincoln Center and Rob Gibson—who had met Wynton while working as the producer of the Atlanta Jazz Festival—became the executive producer and director of the Jazz at Lincoln Center year-round program.

Alina had been very disappointed not to continue with the jazz program after the 1990 season. But during her few years of working with Wynton and Stanley, she had grown very fond of them. She observed that Wynton was a positive, driven man about his work, always doing something. Although his pronouncements and teachings made him seem extremely optimistic to many people, she didn't think he was. To her, he sometimes seemed to have the weight of the world on his shoulders.

"If you really know him personally," she said, "you know he's not always positive because he has an amazing amount of responsibility that he manages. In all the years I've known him, he was always managing a band. You have to be a psychologist par excellence to do that. And he's always dealing with trying to create, and he always is creating. He's also dealing with all the corporate situations that he's in. Then he's dealing with the public. He complained a lot . . . about all the things he had to coordinate, that kind of thing. . . .

"He and Stanley give each other an earful. . . . So whatever life [Wynton] tries to eke out for himself, his personal life is always on the back burner." His personal life wasn't given any priority. "He knows that about himself. He doesn't make any claim to anyone that he could make it a priority."

Alina also felt that some of Wynton's problems forming relationships with women were molded by his relationship with his mother. She was under the impression that Wynton's mother might have criticized him. Wynton thought that his mother simply didn't really understand what his life was like. She knew that, too. He therefore couldn't take any criticisms— if that's what they ever were—to heart, he suggested. As for Candace Stanley, Alina said, "I think they loved each other, but what she needed and wanted, he just couldn't give her in terms of that stable, normal life. But did he love her? Yes, I do think so. And did she love him? Yes, I think so. But she couldn't get over wanting what she needed, and which she had a right to have: a husband who is going to be there. And he can't be that."

Alina believed that Wynton had never taken a vacation—not a long one certainly, as far as she or anyone else knew. When Alina learned from a writer that Wynton had once confided, when he was in his early twenties, that he wanted to pack it all in and go fishing and live in a tent with a girl for a week or two, Alina said, "He hasn't done that yet as far as we know." He had, however, stolen a few days here and there to spend time with girlfriends.

Although Alina was disappointed that she wasn't included on the staff at all for the year-round jazz program beginning in 1991, she managed to make peace with herself about it to a degree. But she grieved for a while. "I had to understand, the most important thing was the music. That's where Wynton's commitment really was. He had to make this thing work. Somehow I understood that. Wynton is someone with vision and knows how to get things done."

Alina continued as director of Visitors Services. "I never could be angry at Wynton for some reason," she reflected. "I can say in restropect I contributed to something wonderful and very true to the original vision that I had. People who weren't playing and listening to jazz are now playing and listening to it. That part I can always feel good about. Wynton has a brilliant quality, a great way of working with people. That's why, despite my disappointment, I can never be angry with him. It's not about one person getting hurt. And Wynton talks straight from the heart, with no affectation. He could be president [of Lincoln Center]."

——————

On October 22, 1990, *Time* magazine featured Wynton on the cover with the headline "The New Jazz Age," calling him the inspiration for a youthful renaissance in jazz. Wynton had just turned twenty-nine years old. He was one of the few jazz musicians ever to appear on the cover of *Time*. The magazine named other budding stars, trumpeters Terence Blanchard, Roy Hargrove, Philip Harper, Marlon Jordan, pianists Marcus Roberts, Geoff Keezer, and Benny Green, saxophonists Branford Marsalis, Christopher Hollyday, and Vincent Herring, guitarists Mark Whitfield and Howard Alden, drummer Winard Harper, organist Joey De Francesco, and singer and pianist Harry Connick, Jr., who had just crossed over from his Monk-influenced, Ellis Marsalis–tutored piano style to become a crooner and bandleader. All these musicians owed their opportunities to Wynton's success, according to *Time*.

Time's writer questioned Wynton about his earlier criticisms of Miles Davis for playing fusion. Wynton excused himself on the grounds of his youth. "I was like 19 or something, man—you know, wild. I didn't care."[1] Pianist Billy Taylor defended Wynton as the most important young spokesman for jazz then: "His opinions are well-founded. Some people earlier took umbrage at what he said, but the important thing is that he could back it up with his horn."[2]

After 1991, the development and evolution of the jazz program at Lincoln Center was driven by Wynton, Stanley Crouch, Albert Murray, and Rob Gibson—"the core philosophers," as George Weisman called them. "I think a lot of the programming gets agreed on by them." (Gibson would say that he and Wynton did the majority of the programming.) When Weisman retired in 1994, the jazz program hadn't yet become a constituent on an equal footing with the other arts at Lincoln Center.

"But it was on its way," Weisman said. "We had prepared the board for it when I left."

By 1995, Weisman recalled, "it was felt that Jazz at Lincoln Center raised enough money to sustain itself, and it had a good organization in place, and it was well established in cultural circles as the outstanding jazz movement in America. It was known as the leader of all the jazz institutions, and it was copied.

"All of a sudden, Carnegie Hall formed its jazz orchestra." The Carnegie Hall Jazz Band, with several concerts a year produced by George Wein, founder of the Newport Jazz Festival, had Jon Faddis as musical director and band leader. Founded in December 1991, it made its debut on October 22, 1992, and sometimes competed with the Lincoln Center Jazz Orchestra. In George Weisman's opinion, "Jazz took on a whole new dimension in American cultural life, and Wynton was the pied piper." Jazz, within the parameters established by Wynton and his coterie, was attracting audiences.

David Berger's position with Jazz at Lincoln Center ended in the winter of 1994. "We were on a tour," he recalled. "Wynton was not with the band. He was with a small group [the septet] on tour. Marcus Roberts was basically the leader of the Lincoln Center Jazz Orchestra, and I was still conducting. Rob Gibson said, 'We're going to make a change.' I said, 'That makes sense.' There was no reason for me to be there. Marcus couldn't conduct. He was blind. But he was leading, making all the decisions."

Berger thought that he might have continued with the orchestra if Wynton had been in town. But actually Wynton and Gibson conferred all the time about any plan that Gibson put into action. Wynton's attention, of course, was diverted at times from Lincoln Center by his passion for his septet. Some issues he backed away from and let Gibson deal with.

Rob Gibson had been hired by a general consensus of several people, including Nat Leventhal, to serve as executive producer and director of Jazz at Lincoln Center. Gibson's responsibilities were pretty much the same as they had been at the Atlanta Jazz Festival, he said, but on an expanded basis, with concerts, lectures, films, children's programs, a radio series, and world tours.

When Jazz at Lincoln Center was accused of anti-white racism, Gibson vociferously defended himself and his decisions. He had the courage to describe himself as "completely white, as white as I can get. I burn and peel at the beach annually. I'm a white Anglo Saxon Protestant in the WASPy sense of the term. I have no embarrassment about that. I was born like that. I'm going to continue to be like that." Gibson adored Wynton as a great composer, player, bandleader, and friend. And there was no doubt that Gibson had a strong presence in his job. People around him were aware of his authority.

Wynton was delighted about the choice of Gibson. "When he came to Jazz at Lincoln Center, I knew we could have a world-class program," Wynton said. "It was another one of those providential meetings like the one I had experienced with Ed Arrendell—a meeting that had a spiritual connotation to it. When I met Ed, I knew I would be with him for the rest of my life. I could just tell that. And with Gibson, it was the same kind of thing, because he and I were interested in doing the same thing.

"We had already been doing it independent of each other. I hadn't really known him in Atlanta. But I knew whoever was in Atlanta had a comprehensive conception of what jazz was, because whenever you went there, you were doing radio shows; you played outside in the park for 40,000 people; and there were forums where people got together and discussed the music. He was doing all kinds of stuff, like the retrospective for Ed Blackwell. Gibson had so many skills. He ran a radio station. He's a presenter—he knows how to present concerts. He has been a salesman. He has myriad skills. And he is great at his job; not just good, he's great at it. And he has an unbelievable work ethic. So when he came into Jazz at Lincoln Center, it was a major step forward for us. We had someone with tremendous energy." Wynton admired the growth and the intelligence of the expansion of Jazz at Lincoln Center as time went on and felt a lot of the progress was "due specifically and solely" to Gibson.

Gibson brought in Robert Sadin to conduct the orchestra for a while. "It was easier for him to take directions from Marcus, I guess," David Berger reminisced. There had been no friction between Wynton and Berger personally. "Marcus and Rob Gibson had their agenda," he said. And "Wynton was going to take over eventually. I knew it was a matter of time until he wanted to conduct. He was always artistic director."

Berger had loved working with Wynton. They had hung out quite a bit, on planes, in airports, and bus trips. Wynton would always go over scores with him. They discussed personal issues, too—"our aspirations and how to go about achieving greatness. I learned a lot from him," said Berger, who at forty-eight in 1998, an attractive man, with gray hair and glasses, was about a dozen years older than Wynton.

Berger knew absolutely that Wynton wanted to become a serious composer. When he was starting out, Stanley Crouch and Albert Murray impressed upon him the importance of Duke Ellington's music. "It was the best music we could play. People loved hearing it." Berger felt the same way about it. "And it certainly was a side effect that Wynton could learn this music from the inside out and become a better composer. Wynton wanted me to show him certain things, and we frequently went over the scores."

Wynton's success stemmed from more than just his background, more than from his father and mother's nurturing. It came from something else than being touched by genius, Berger thought. "He just has so much energy. He truly has charisma. There's no question about it. It's just excess, positive energy, and he gives it off. It makes people feel good being around him. His attitude is that he'll dream of something and make it happen. And he does that. And he makes you feel: 'I could do that, too.'"

Berger continued doing a little work connected with Jazz at Lincoln Center, and eventually he would do much more: as an assistant to Wynton for *Blood on the Fields* and then as a copyist for Ellington's music. Although he wasn't Wynton's closest friend, in some ways Berger had a special sensitivity to Wynton.

There was always something a little mysterious about the trumpeter. He never told any one person everything. One friend knew that he wrote poetry; other friends had no idea. Even Branford didn't know that Wynton wrote poetry. (Ellis III more readily volunteered that he did.) But Branford knew that Wynton didn't make everything about himself general knowledge.

Stanley Crouch was once asked by David Berger, "Have you ever heard of a trumpet player named E. Dankworth?"

Crouch said, "No."

Berger said, "That's Wynton's pseudonym on labels he's not supposed to be on." Crouch pretended not to know—perhaps because Wynton wasn't just bending a note, he was bending a law, because he was under contract to one recording company and working for another. Berger thought it was especially funny that Crouch seemed not to know, because

Crouch had written liner notes for an album, *Deep in the Shed*, led by pianist Marcus Roberts on the Novus label. Wynton had played for Marcus's album under the Dankworth pseudonym. In his liner notes, Crouch praised the "great trumpet player" on the record.

Jazz players had been using pseudonymns for a long time to get around the limitations of their recording contracts. Wynton had done it more than once, Berger knew, although he wasn't sure how many times. Actually, Wynton and Crouch had discussed the pseudonym. Wynton had chosen Dankworth because he liked the sound of it and its Englishness; of course, he knew the saxophonist John Dankworth was English. "It's just some more stupidity that we do," Wynton reflected on the name choice. "I answer the phone a lot of times and say, 'E. Skain Dankworth.'"

CHAPTER NOTES

1. "The New Jazz Age." *Time*, October 22, 1990.
2. Ibid.

RADIO SERIES, TV SHOWS— AND PEABODYS ON THE SIDE

I t would have been impossible for anyone except Ed Arrendell to approximate a listing of all the events and side ventures in Wynton's professional life; probably not even Arrendell could come up with a complete list, because Wynton was in the habit of saying yes to most people who asked him to become involved in a project. And he liked the feeling of choosing his own destiny. Wynton was so busy that it was no surprise when people laughed at Alina Bloomgarden in 1987 for saying she could get Wynton to participate in Classical Jazz at Lincoln Center. Another major project that got under way at around the same time was a series for National Public Radio.

Murray Horwitz, originally from Dayton, Ohio, had lived in New York for about fifteen years, where he worked in musical theater, cowriting *Ain't Misbehavin'*, a musical revue based on the songs of Fats Waller. In 1987 he moved to Washington D.C. to work with the National Endowment for the Arts. A year or two later, he got a call from John Schreiber, who at that time was working in George Wein's Festival Productions office. Wynton Marsalis had agreed to do a young people's concert featuring the popular *Peanuts'* cartoon character Snoopy as part of the JVC Festival—also produced by Wein—at Town Hall. King

Features needed someone to write and host it. Because Murray Horwitz had begun his career as a clown in Ringling Brothers Barnum & Bailey Circus and had worked with children, Schreiber thought of him and asked him to write the show.

"I'd be delighted," Horwitz said.

The tough thing to do was to get in touch with Wynton, Horwitz recalled. During the summer that Horwitz needed to speak to him, Wynton was going to play Charles Mingus's *Epitaph* in a big band at Wolf Trap, the performing arts center in Vienna, Virginia. An assistant to Wynton told Horwitz that he could talk to Wynton at the sound check for the Mingus performance.

Horwitz said, "That's not enough time. We have a whole concert to write, and it won't work out that way." He thought for a minute. "When is this sound check?"

The assistant told him.

Horwitz said, "For the day before, I have tickets for the Berlin Opera's *Die Walküre*. Would Wynton like to go with me?"

Ten minutes later, the assistant called back and said, "He'd love it."

Horwitz met Wynton at his hotel to go to the opera. "It was a great experience. We hit it off right away," Murray recalled. At the opera, Murray talked about light cues, and Wynton said, "What a bad way to get to a 3/4." They liked listening to each other's insights. After dinner, they talked for a long time about the budget and other matters.

Despite his many other commitments—including recording his album *Crescent City Christmas Card* with such diverse musicians as clarinetist Alvin Batiste, saxophonist Joe Temperley, and opera star Kathleen Battle—Wynton managed to find time to work with Murray Horwitz to do the young people's concert. It was a success for the JVC. "In fact, the guy who runs the Berlin Jazz Festival liked it so much," Horwitz recalled, "that he had us over to do it at the Philharmonie—the big, modern concert hall in Berlin—in November 1989, a week before the wall came down."

In July 1989, when Murray was director of jazz, classical music, and entertainment at National Public Radio, he was told, "We have a special coming up, and we need a host." It was to be a re-creation of James Reese Europe's Clef Club orchestra concert, to be done at Carnegie Hall. "We'd like someone with one foot in classical and the other in jazz," Horwitz was told. He said, "What about Wynton?"

The NPR executives said, "Great, if you can get him."

Horwitz called Wynton, who said, "Sure."

Late that summer, on a rainy day, Horwitz and Wynton met at Carnegie Hall to discuss the project. Afterward, they walked together to Wynton's town house on 18th Street, where Wynton was still living with Candace. By the time they reached the house, they were soaking wet; yet they had come up with an idea for a radio series about jazz. Wynton kept saying over and over, "What makes the music what it is?" Their idea was to strip away a lot of baggage with which explanations of jazz had been freighted over the years and pare it down to its essentials, including what musicians thought about the music. Horwitz somehow retained the impression that he and Wynton had even come up with the series title that night: "Making the Music."

They intended to do a thirteen-part series, but in Washington, the NPR director of marketing told Horwitz it was much easier to sell the series if it had twenty-six parts. Horwitz talked to Wynton, who agreed. There was a long developmental process. They looked for approaches and for writers. In October, the radio producers at NPR told Horwitz to give them information that would allow them to figure out how much it would cost to make the series. The budget turned out to be about a million dollars, a lot of money for public radio, with most of it provided by the Lila Wallace Reader's Digest Fund and National Public Radio.

In the fall of 1991, Horwitz took three weeks off from his job and went home to write the series. He had talked to Wynton enough to know basically what Wynton wanted to say. Not only did Horwitz sketch out the series, he also came up with suggestions for existing recordings, new tapings, demonstrations, and musicians to interview. His sketch became an interim step. "The series turned out to be nothing like what I wrote. It helped for budgeting and for our thinking to get it together," Horwitz recalled.

"Wynton composed, and we recorded the theme song, a train theme, in Princeton, New Jersey, at the McCarter Theater. We put together a pilot show to get some funding. We did a recording at the Village Vanguard and did some musical demonstrations there about what makes a great solo; we talked to [saxophonist] Charles McPherson, Marcus Roberts, vibist Milt Jackson, bassist Bob Cranshaw, and tenor saxophonist Jimmy Heath." The pilot was produced by Steve Rathe, who was producing radio shows called "Jazz from Lincoln Center" by then, a series that featured Wynton about half the time.

Whatever Horwitz had written for the series, Wynton revised and reshaped. "Wynton was great at pushing everybody to think and work hard and find ways to do something in a fresh way. I am now and was then a middle-aged man. And as a playwright and lyricist, I try not to think conventionally. But at a certain age, you think in certain grooves. My first answer was conventional. Wynton would say, 'Why not try this?' And he was right. It wasn't always something that cost more money. It was just about thinking a little differently. You won't hear anything bad about him from me. It became real clear early on that he was one of the smartest people I ever worked with in my life. I told people: 'This guy is the real thing. He's going to leave all of us in the dust.'"

While the series was in production, Horwitz, at a lunch with the eminent critic and jazz scholar Martin Williams, raved about Wynton. Williams "listened patiently," Murray recalled, and said, "You get along so well with him, because that young man has grown up ten years in the last two. I don't know if it has to do with his having children, or what, but he has matured."

Wynton would later be surprised to hear that he had undergone such a metamorphosis in Williams's opinion, because Wynton had not met Williams at this time, and they would never have more than a passing conversation. Wynton had always been polite to Williams, once they actually met. Comments like these made him wonder how people could judge him and yet never have sat down with him.

Horwitz hired Margaret Howze, who produced the series; she had been an assistant producer at National Public Radio for several years by that time. "She had a very capacious musical mind and a very good radio head, and she was a very hard worker," he said. "We also hired Bettina Owens, who was our administrative coordinator; she handled the tens of thousands of details. The editor of the series was Dottie Green.

"Margaret and I and sometimes Dottie would occasionally catch up with Wynton on the road, or else in his apartment." By that time, he had moved and lived alone in his condominium on West 66th Street in a building adjoining Lincoln Center. "We asked ourselves: What do we want to achieve with this show on fusion, or bebop, and what do we want to say about Ellington? If we had three or four things to say about

Thelonious Monk, what would we say about him? And then we fleshed those answers out with Wynton.

"He was incredibly hard working at this. I say 'incredibly' because he was doing so much else at the same time. So all kinds of late-night telephone conversations took place. We held the phone up to the speakers to play music for him. In April or May of 1994, we went into production for the start of the shows for 1995. We taped Wynton at certain locations. At the time we didn't have great studios at National Public Radio. NPR was moving to better studios in new quarters. So we were taping the shows in New York at the old RCA studios on West 44th Street, and on the road, too," Horwitz recalled.

"Margaret went down to tape him in Birmingham, Alabama and elsewhere. We were faxing scripts back and forth. Once Margaret and I went to Chico, California, after flying to Sacramento, and recorded him in the NPR member station there in Chico, KCHO, with student engineers. Then we drove back, trying to beat the sun, so that I could make it for the Kol Nidre service that night in a temple in Sacramento. I dropped Margaret at the airport and got to the synagogue on time. Many road stories happened. We tracked several shows in Atlanta at the Peach State Public Radio station. But most of the work was done in Washington."

"Wynton loved being at NPR offices in Washington," Horwitz said. "He walked the halls and looked in people's offices. He even said, 'I've never really had an experience like this since elementary school, with hallways and rooms. I know most people live their lives this way, but I live my life in hotel rooms and buses.' At NPR he went to work in an office every day. People loved him. The classical people got the benefit, too. He talked to the NPR board one day. He was really part of the family. I'd like to think it energized him, too.

"The office I have now," Horwitz said in 1998, "is an expanded version of the office Margaret Howze had then. I'm pacing the floor now. I remember Wynton noodling on his trumpet, I writing at the computer, and Margaret at the machine, making a cut with a razor blade, for him to have in the studio. History will judge the series. To my ear, it's the only full-scale exposition of jazz music ever made to the American public. If you listen to all twenty-six parts, you'll know a lot about jazz.

"Wynton was really the heartbeat of the whole thing. It was Wynton who constantly said, 'It's not good enough,' when we would have settled for just okay. And we're NPR. We go for the A. But Wynton said it was a failure if it wasn't an A plus. We were looking for the exact Cannonball Adderley cut to play in an episode, and I said: 'How about this? This does it.' Or Margaret would stay up all night, listening to music and choosing a piece. He would say, 'No, the rhythm section is fucked up.' I said, 'It's okay.' And he said, 'Just listen to it.' And 'Shit, he's right,' I'd realize. He said, 'So keep looking.' He was never intransigent or unreasonable, but he was always demanding, exacting. Margaret spent some nights in the office. I spent three or four nights there. He may have spent nights here, or on the phone.

"It wasn't like doing a show at Madison Square Garden, where instantly you know if you have a laugh. It's not like being in the theater, where people scream at a show. In radio, it's as if we were throwing a note in a bottle that goes out to sea and hoping something comes back. At WBEZ in Chicago, the only public radio station there, the program director, Torey Malatia, reported that listeners called to say the series had explained the music to them. That's when I knew we had done something worth doing."

In the spring of 1996, Horwitz learned that the series had won the highest award in broadcasting, a Peabody, for excellence. The series was technically a collaboration between Wynton and Horwitz, but others wrote segments—Margaret Howze wrote the Monk show; Sonja Williams produced an Ellington show. Only one ticket was provided by the Peabody committee for the awards ceremony. Horwitz made sure that everyone involved had a ticket at a cost of $150 each. At the ceremony, there was a cash bar. Seven people connected to the show went to New York and "crashed on Wynton's floor," Horwitz recalled. "Wynton made gumbo for us, and Wynton and I made the acceptance speech.

"What Wynton got paid was miniscule. People would call from his office at Lincoln Center and Ed Arrendell's office. 'What are you doing?' they asked. There was so much work and so little money. Maybe there was a $20,000 budget for Wynton. It really cost him money to do this series."

In addition to the radio series, there were regular broadcasts of Jazz from Lincoln Center beginning in September 1993, produced by Steve Rathe. That series, which was hosted by CBS correspondent Ed Bradley and which often featured Wynton, also would win a Peabody Award, for its fifth season, in 1997. Like so many other people who eventually became involved in facets of Wynton's career and Jazz at Lincoln Center, Steve Rathe had met Wynton many years earlier.

In the late 1970s, Rathe had worked as a stage manager at a jazz tent at the New Orleans Jazz and Heritage Festival. Both Wynton and Branford were presented there, when they were in high school. But the real star at that time was Ellis. Wynton was playing in the NOCCA ensemble. Then Rathe saw Wynton go off to Tanglewood, Juilliard, the Jazz Messengers, and return to New Orleans in the early 1980s, by which time he had attained a degree of celebrity. A coterie of people trailed him, Rathe recalled: "Someone from *Life* magazine, with Annie Lebowitz shooting the story, followed him around. He was a homegrown celebrity." He still had no idea how far Wynton would go. The next year Wynton won his first two Grammys.

Rathe, who was doing some road managing, next crossed paths with Wynton on the road in Europe. "Sometimes we traveled with groups to the same festivals at the same time. For a few days, I hung out with Wynton and Branford. It was always a pretty agreeable experience. And it was remarkable what happened to him." Rathe wondered about "what would have happened to most twenty-one-year-olds if they had suddenly become the object of worldwide adoration, and people told them every time they turned around that they were geniuses. . . . Wynton was a young man who received a lot of adoration and hadn't yet had a lot of experience in the world." Experience would, over the years, improve Wynton's handling of his celebrity, Rathe believed. Wynton progressed from "a gifted young person . . . who didn't really understand . . . how people needed to conduct themselves in the world . . . to a young man who was as gracious as anyone could ask for, and with an enormous fondness for children."

Rob Gibson, who had been a radio station manager in Atlanta, called Steve Rathe and asked him to produce the Jazz from Lincoln Center radio shows. As early as the 1970s, Rathe had produced a series called "Jazz Alive!" for National Public Radio. Stanley Crouch had acted as a host for the shows in that series. When Rathe had come to New York, Crouch was always hanging out with the avant-garde musicians. "I liked the fact that Stanley represented a downtown voice in jazz a long time ago," Rathe said. So Rathe was moving in familiar territory, among people he knew, when he took on the Lincoln Center radio shows.

On the tape submitted for consideration for the Peabody Award were excerpts from current performances of Jelly Roll Morton, Thelonious Monk, and Wynton Marsalis, along with Jackie McLean playing a selection of music. Hosts and writers for the shows included a wide array of well-known jazz writers, such as Peter Keepnews, Joe Hooper, Neil Tesser, Stanley Crouch, and Howard Mandel. Mandel, who wrote some shows for the Lincoln Center series and provided interviews for others, observed that it was nearly obligatory for him to include Wynton in every show. "The shows, always about jazz, often using concerts played by the Lincoln Center Jazz Orchestra, also presented solo piano concerts and guest artists. A big selling point of those shows is to have Wynton on the air. In some cases, when he was not performing, he was not on the air, but otherwise, yes. Jazz at Lincoln Center is all behind him, and to be fair, he fronts for them. It's a symbiotic relationship. They have made quite a lot of the institution. And having a charming, talented front man is absolutely essential to that kind of institution," said Mandel, who was never thoroughly enamored of Wynton's leadership at Lincoln Center.

One of Wynton's best-known exploits in broadcasting, because it was televised as a four-part PBS series, was *Marsalis on Music*. In July 1994, Wynton traveled with a crew of about twenty-five Sony video producers, directors, recording engineers, cameramen, and stagehands to Tanglewood in Lenox, Massachusetts, and set up shop in a red barn across the street from the main music festival grounds. One writer, who took a dim view of the unusual commotion at normally bucolic Tanglewood, reported that the tapings of the show, done over a period of two weeks, disrupted the summer music school and caused a great deal of dissension among people connected with it. Nevertheless, the shows, aired in 1995, captivated television audiences, with Wynton explaining aspects of jazz history and performance, playing with his own group, Seiji Ozawa and the Boston Symphony Orchestra, and cellist Yo-Yo Ma and his cello quartet.

One show, entitled "Sousa to Satchmo," taught how music evolved from classical styles to Sousa marches to Louis Armstrong. As just one element on this video, Wynton explained how syncopation meant placing accents on unexpected beats. For illustrations of ensemble playing, he used musicians from the Lincoln Center Jazz Orchestra and the Liberty Brass Band with clarinetist Dr. Michael White, and showed how various instruments played their own melody lines in their own spaces: clarinets on top, trumpets and saxophones in the middle, and trombones on a lower plane.

For another show, "Listening for Clues: Marsalis on Form," Wynton taught about the forms of music and showed how different types of music related to each other. He used the classical sonata form and contrasted it with the thirty-two-bar American standard song form. He had uncanny ways of making clear what he was trying to teach. For example, he reminded kids that their school days had a certain schedule with classes, and weekends began with cartoons on television. If they knew what usually happened on a weekend, they could identify the day. Thus "knowing the form [of a piece of music] means you know what is going to happen. You can recognize it," he said. And recognition enhanced the pleasure of listening to music.

To teach the sonata form, Wynton used a whimsical analogy: A child goes to a pet store to buy a puppy but can afford only a hamster. So he buys the hamster and puts it in a cage. That's the statement of the sonata's theme. Then the hamster gets loose from its cage and runs away. The child chases it all over the store until he finally catches up with it— represented by an alternate theme. That ends the second part of the sonata. Then the restatement of the theme begins and proceeds to the end of the sonata.

For the American song form, Wynton and his jazz orchestra played "I Got Rhythm" by George Gershwin, a thirty-two-bar tune with the form AABA, signifying that the song is divided into four sections, with eight bars for each section. The first eight bars are repeated in the second eight bars; the third eight bars, which make up the B section, constitute the bridge, which is followed by a repetition of the A section for the end of the song. Wynton also taught that a song is referred to as a chorus, and there's great variety in the ways that choruses are played; one chorus may be a saxophone solo, while another may be an ensemble chorus. A song can continue with chorus after chorus until the musicians are ready to finish.

For the show called "Why Toes Tap," Wynton taught that rhythm is the most basic element of music. Without rhythm, there's no music. You can't even get from one note to another, because the change from one note to another sets up a rhythm. "Music is organized sound in time," he said. He contrasted the rhythm created by a driver honking a horn in traffic to the sound of cacophony—disorganized sounds. From there he explained two of the many types of time signatures—3/4 time and 4/4 time—and used an example from Tchaikovsky's *Nutcracker* Suite for 3/4 time, then a Duke Ellington adaptation of it in 4/4 time.

The most universally applicable of all the shows was "Tackling the Monster," done with Yo-Yo Ma, the classical cellist, and with Wynton's band members, including the rhythm section pianist Eric Reed, bassist Ben Wolfe, and drummer Herlin Riley. In this show, Wynton and Yo-Yo Ma discussed the skill of practicing, and their twelve-point program could be applied to nearly any endeavor in life. Wynton warned students not to practice just to please their parents or fill in time when they had nothing else to do. Yo-Yo Ma admitted he hated the idea of having to practice. But once he started, he liked to do it, because he loved to learn new things and challenge himself.

The twelve-point program included such principles as: seek out a good teacher who knows what you're supposed to be doing; write out a schedule for your daily practice, so you know what you are planning to do that day; set long-term goals for yourself, so you know what you want to accomplish over a period of time; concentrate when you practice, and if you can't keep your mind on what you're doing, stop for a while and come back to it so that you can clear your head; focus on your task; and feel good about yourself.

Take your time; you may not be able to play a piece fast at first, so teach yourself to do it slowly. Practice everything as if you were singing; that is, express yourself as much as possible and try to be yourself. (Sight-singing is an important tool in teaching people to play instruments. Wynton's father used it, and Wynton may have first learned it from Ellis.) Then, don't be too hard on yourself; don't feel bad about making mistakes, because you learn from mistakes. (The only people who don't make mistakes are the ones who aren't doing anything.) On and on the lessons went.

On the educational videos, Wynton projected a warm, friendly personality and used clever, comprehensible metaphors and examples. He made it easy for children to learn about the elements of music and want to learn more. He also educated and enthralled adults. On May 6, 1996, at the Waldorf Astoria Hotel, Wynton won another Peabody for the entertaining and profoundly instructive series.

On the videos, Wynton played an unusual-looking, custom-made horn crafted for him by Dave Monette. Monette, who lives in Chicago, has designed special horns for Wynton; one is so elaborate that it looks like a great filigree case with a trumpet tucked inside. It's very heavy, terrifically expensive, and Wynton doesn't use it very much. Mostly, he uses another Monette horn that bears a slight resemblance in its sleekness and angles to a supersonic transport airplane. In his book, Wynton recalled a time when he dropped a trumpet and destroyed its sound. Monette flew from Chicago to Providence, Rhode Island, where Wynton was going to make a record, and fixed the horn free of charge.[1] Wynton calls his friend "Doctor Monette," and Monette calls Wynton "Professor."

These were just some of the projects that Wynton fit into his brimming schedule.

CHAPTER NOTES

1. Wynton Marsalis, *Sweet Swing Blues on the Road*. New York: W.W. Norton, 1994.

THE CONTROVERSIES BEGIN

Wynton continued to maintain a heavy schedule in the late 1980s and early 1990s, alternating his time between his own group and his commitments at Lincoln Center. In 1989, Wynton, having toured the summer music festivals in Europe, felt distressed to find that most groups in the festivals weren't playing jazz.[1] But the promotors persisted in calling them jazz festivals, not music festivals, so they would draw an audience. Wynton thought this was wrong.

Meanwhile, the summer festival at Lincoln Center had presented the music of Jelly Roll Morton. Wynton enlisted many New Orleans musicians for the concerts, persisting in his emphasis on older music. Not all critics liked the idea of Wynton's choosing Jelly Roll's music, when there was so much more current music to present. Some critics felt that Wynton's interpretations veered too far from Morton's original versions of his works. On the other hand, one critic thought that Jelly Roll's music had never sounded so good before. Throughout the 1990s, Wynton would keep playing Jelly Roll's music.

On December 20, 21, and 22, 1989, Wynton played in a three-concert series at Alice Tully Hall, called "Classical Jazz Christmas With

Wynton Marsalis," which was broadcast on the program *Live From Lincoln Center* on PBS. Wynton played his own arrangements of holiday songs and carols and a Duke Ellington big-band arrangement of Tchaikovsky's Nutcracker Suite.

In June 1990, Wynton led his septet, on the same bill with singer Pearl Bailey, in a concert at Avery Fisher Hall. They performed "Uptown Ruler" and Wynton's first extended piece, *Blue Interlude*, compositions and performances that critics praised. They kept up the level of appreciation for the release of his album, *Standard Time, Vol. 3*, subtitled *The Resolution of Romance*. Wynton, playing many duets on standards with his father, had clearly moved out from the shadow of Miles Davis and developed his own personality, molded in part by his study of Louis Armstrong's work. By the summer, the album went to the top of *Billboard*'s Top Jazz Albums chart and stayed there for a long time.

That August, the Jazz at Lincoln Center program was much more varied than the 1989 bill. Saxophonists Von Freeman from Chicago and the estimable Johnny Griffin and Jackie McLean, all great improvisers, led their groups in concerts. The venerable alto saxophonist, trumpeter, arranger, and composer Benny Carter arrived to conduct a newly commissioned work for vibraphonists Milt Jackson and Bobby Hutcherson, backed by a fine rhythm section of James Williams, Ron Carter, and drummer Billy Higgins.

Still, there was a great deal of emphasis on older music. An all–New Orleans program was again a prominent feature at the festival. The program's orchestra, then called the Classical Jazz Orchestra, ended the series with two nights of Duke Ellington's music. The orchestra's members included trombonists Art Baron, Britt Woodman, and Buster Cooper, saxophonists Norris Turney and Joe Temperley, and bassist Jimmy Woode, all former members of the Ellington orchestra. They played Ellington's "The Far East Suite," "Toot Suite," and train pieces beginning with the 1924 "Choo Choo," continuing to "Loco Madi" from the 1970s. The performances as usual were hailed by most critics; audiences flocked to the concerts.

Meanwhile, Wynton and his group continued to tour and perform. Peter Watrous, reviewing Wynton's group at the Village Vanguard, praised the septet's work as vital and accessible.[2] Watrous heard references, presented with originality, to John Coltrane's early 1960s music. He also thought that Wynton's focus on history, on the blues form and standards, was based on a strong desire to preserve these musical high-points of American culture.

In short, Wynton was constantly featured in the print and broadcast media, as he proselytized for the rich music of the old masters and decried loud music, fusion, European music with a bit of blues trappings, and most of the avant garde. Once in a while, a reviewer or fan mentioned that Wynton was overlooking and criticizing newer music. Some said it didn't matter; many other people were playing newer music anyway and finding opportunities to reach audiences because of the general revival of the public's interest in jazz. But the issue of Wynton's field of vision—though it was filled with a range of music that he considered to be "pure jazz"—didn't go away.

Wynton really didn't need to worry. For one thing, the music that found favor with him was the music that had made most people fall in love with jazz in the first place. Audiences that bought tickets for seats at Alice Tully Hall weren't about to quibble with him. He had all the right critical praises in all the right places. By December, his original film score for *Tune In Tomorrow*, with its patently clear influences of New Orleans music and Duke Ellington and Billy Strayhorn, was winning high praise from critics for his playing and his compositions. That album, too, had a commercial success on various jazz charts.

George Kanzler was one of the many jazz critics who voiced his appreciation of the film score, writing that Wynton displayed "a sensuous richness in his lyrical conception and a glowing tone."[3] In essence, Kanzler wrote that Wynton's adventures with New Orleans–based music were joyous romps invoking the spirit of the old music rather than just a dreary revival for the sake of nostalgia. Kanzler heard Ellington's influence most of all in Wynton's composing: "such Ellingtonian devices as shifting tempos and time signatures, elaborations of basic blues forms; interlocking, overlapping and call-response solos; themes voiced by and identified with individual instruments, and characteristically Ducal harmonies."[4] Kanzler loved the performance of Wynton's suite, *The Saga of Sugarcane and Sweetie Pie*, essentially a love story, a particularly good example of Wynton's use of Ellingtonian techniques.

Even more, Kanzler liked *The Majesty of the Blues*, "built on one of those . . . amorphous, exotic rhythms that Duke Ellington loved."[5] Kanzler thought the work lived up to its name "in a compelling series of solos supported by ensemble passages, each building inexorably to a dramatic climax through judicious use of dynamics and harmonic tension."[6] Kanzler praised the group's horn players, noting their mastery of the way Ellington's band members had used mutes. (Wynton had taken advantage of every possible opportunity to learn. Somewhere in the midwest, Joe Temperley had watched Wynton sit in with veteran trumpeter Joe Wilder for an hour and a half, while Wilder taught Wynton how to use the wawa hat.) Kanzler also praised pianist Eric Reed for providing great comping support.[7]

Another important 1991 work was Wynton's score for Garth Fagan's dance piece *Griot—New York*. Griots are West Africans who keep the culture and tradition of the people alive in music and dance. It was as if Fagan conceived of himself, Wynton, and a sculptor, Mark Puryear, whose works were utilized and integrated into the ballet, as contemporary griots along with the dancers.

Any attempt to analyze Wynton's score for the three sections of the modern, profoundly expressive ballet has to be left to musicologists. However, Wynton established themes, set up improvisations, and used forms as diverse as the waltz, the calypso, and the feeling of African music, which thoroughly supported every flutter, twitch, undulation, and eccentric twist and turn of the dancers' hands and bodies.

Fagan said he had wanted to show a new way of moving, and he seemed to accomplish that. When Wynton first saw the dancers going through their erotic, perfectly synchronized paces, he was intimidated and challenged by the sensual and mature depiction of relationships between men and women. His age group had trivialized the relationships, he said. But he could see the naturalness and purity in Fagan's creative vision.

The collaboration of the trumpeter and the choreographer turned out to be a mesmerizing experience for the audience. Not only did Wynton acquit himself as a brilliant composer and player, but his band rose to the occasion. Reeds player Victor Goines, who was usually praised for his clarinet artistry, outdid himself with his splendid tone on the tenor saxophone.

By August 1991, the Classical Jazz Festival began its fifth season at Lincoln Center. Gordon Davis was chairman of the board of directors for Jazz at Lincoln Center. It was now part of a year-round program, with a plan for over twenty concerts, lectures, and film programs during the season scheduled to last until April 1992. The season was launched with a beautifully designed brochure, put together by Rob Gibson, including a liberal sprinkling of photographs of the great musicians Wynton admired: Duke, Louis Armstrong, the Bennie Moten Orchestra in Kansas City, John Coltrane, Count Basie, Charlie Parker, Jackie McLean, Claude "Fiddler" Williams, James P. Johnson, who had been one of the foremost Harlem stride pianists, and old time New Orleans clarinetist Johnny Dodds. Not surprisingly, Albert Murray and Stanley Crouch were key contributors to the booklet. Crouch wrote about "Jazz Criticism and Its Effect on the Art Form," essentially praising African Americans for inventing jazz. He focused on his heroes, Ellington and Armstrong, as key figures in creating a music that had international and cross-ethnic appeal.

As a nod to contemporary jazz, photos of Freddie Hubbard, Branford Marsalis, drummer Roy Haynes, and the illustrious trombonist and arranger Melba Liston, who worked closely with pianist Randy Weston, showed up in the brochure, too, with announcements of concerts.

Whitney Balliett reviewed the proceedings for *The New Yorker*.[8] Wynton's band, comprised mostly of New Orleans musicians, played the music of Joe "King" Oliver in Chicago in the mid-1920s, when Armstrong was in the band, as well as Jelly Roll Morton's music and the repertoire of the Creole Jazz Band. Balliett pointed out that at the time these musicians and groups originally recorded their classic works, their music was already going out of date. Louis Armstrong, emerging from Oliver's band, and Sidney Bechet and Coleman Hawkins were about to convert jazz into a soloist's paradise in the 1930s. Nevertheless, Balliett praised the music played with faithfulness to the original repertoire.

Singers Shirley Horn and Abbey Lincoln (Aminata Moseka) reigned for the second night's concert. Horn was accompanied by Wynton, harmonica virtuoso Toots Thielemans, and saxophonist Buck Hill, while Lincoln used the great rhythm section of pianist Cedar Walton, bassist David Williams, and drummer Billy Higgins, joined by guest saxophonists Jackie McLean and Branford Marsalis.

The third night's program, an homage to Basie's band in Kansas City in the 1930s, fell short of re-creating the original band's sound, Balliett thought,[9] despite the presence of such legendary Kansas City musicians as pianist Jay McShann and violinist Claude "Fiddler" Willams, Ted Dunbar, the guitarist, and Aaron Bell on bass. Wynton, leading the Lincoln Center Jazz Orchestra with fifteen pieces that night, added momentum to the program, with Britt Woodman on trombone, Norris Turney, Joe Temperley, Charles McPherson, Frank Wess, and Todd Williams on saxophones and other reeds, Sir Roland Hanna on piano, and Kenny Washington on drums.

The next night, the program staged a fascinating tribute to John Coltrane—"A Coltrane Serenade"—with Wynton's young musicians playing for some of the program, joined by Coltrane's famed group pianist, McCoy Tyner. Wynton was ubiquitous throughout the concerts, impressive with his vaunted versatility. The next night offered "Portraits by Ellington," played by an eighteen-member Lincoln Center Jazz Orchestra, with music ranging from "Black Beauty" written in 1928 to the "New Orleans Suite" of 1970 celebrating Armstrong, Bechet, bassist Wellman Braud (who was Dolores Marsalis's relative, predating the first modern bassist, Jimmy Blanton, in Duke's band), and gospel diva Mahalia Jackson. Balliett commended David Berger for his transcriptions and conducting.[10]

Balliett observed that Wynton had become "a conservator" in his jazz festivals. Clarinetist Bob Wilber made the interesting remark to Balliett that the tables were being turned. Traditionally, white musicians and scholars were the moving forces behind researching and preserving the old music, while black musicians "have almost exclusively practiced the cult of the hip."[11] Now Wynton was bringing the music of King Oliver and Louis Armstrong to the attention of the general public, including young black musicians, who usually knew little about jazz history before John Coltrane and Miles Davis.

While Balliett praised Wynton for "attempting to teach a new generation of black musicians where they came from," he felt uneasy about the proceedings, because "[I]t appears that [Wynton] is reviving not only the older music but also the reverse racism popular among black musicians in the fifties and sixties. Just six of the fifty-four performers used this week at Lincoln Center were white. Blacks invented jazz, but nobody owns it," Balliett wrote.[12]

Thus Balliett sounded a new alarm. Not only was Wynton eschewing fusion, the avant-garde, and post-1965 modern jazz, but he was eschewing whites. Other writers soon joined the fray and accused Wynton— sometimes with a sense of steaming fury in their attacks—of racism. Wynton could point out that Jazz at Lincoln Center's executive producer and director Rob Gibson was white, and so was David Berger, and there were at least some white musicians in the Lincoln Center Jazz Orchestra.

Some historical perspective could have helped illuminate the situation. Jazz groups had usually always been either all white or all black, or a mixture of races but still with one or the other race predominating. Blacks and whites could not even play on the same stage together in the South. Norman Granz, the producer of the traveling concert series, "Jazz at the Philharmonic," in the late 1940s and early 1950s, had struggled mightily to make sure his integrated concert offerings were presented to integrated audiences. Duke Ellington had managed to hide his dark-haired, white drummer, Louie Bellson, in the back row of the orchestra.

The history of jazz was shot through with indignities based on racial separation. Some musicians had worked to counteract the problem. Rarely had the cause of segregation in jazz groups been racist feelings among musicians, though, of course, musicians were not exempt from prejudice. It was simply that, historically, music venues had been segregated, and, particularly in the South, it was not acceptable for blacks and whites to appear on stage together.

In 1997 jazz writer Thomas Sancton conducted an extensive interview with Wynton. He asked the trumpeter, "How do you answer critics who say, for example, that you don't use enough white musicians, that you run the Jazz at Lincoln Center program on the basis of cronyism, and so forth?"

"I feel that is just part of the history of our nation," Wynton said. "If you go back in the history of jazz, you'll see that kind of thing many times. It's a response to the perception of me using power the way that I want to use it as artistic director of Jazz at Lincoln Center, to present my vision of it, which is what I am hired to do. And that's something that makes a lot of critics uncomfortable—much more than they would be in another field. You can be sure that other artistic directors don't have to put up with that.

"But I thank the Lord for the opportunity to be attacked. . . . I thought the attack that my critics mounted was pitiful. It was poorly researched. It wasn't based on facts. It was really just emotion. Fear. Anger. Ignorance. It hasn't changed how I do my job. I am ready to confront them at any time. I was hired to do a job and I am going to do it. You know I'm from another era. A lot of the time, with jazz, they're used to dealing with a different kind of political era where black musicians had to bow down to them—not exactly bow down, but you know what I'm saying. So they're thinking I would do the same thing. But I won't. . . ."[13]

Wynton's groups had been made up of only young black musicians. And if they reflected the conditions under which he had grown up, that didn't necessarily mean he was a racist. He ordinarily played with people he knew best. He did say that African Americans had created jazz. But Wynton said that nobody owned jazz, and anyone who could play jazz could be a great jazz musician. It was not until 1987, however, when he connected with Lincoln Center, that he began hiring many white people for various jobs with the Classical Jazz programs. (His inclusion of whites had no effect on the classical world, where orchestras traditionally employed few or even no black musicians.)

Wynton had personally chosen Steve Epstein, a white man, in the early 1980s to work as producer on virtually all of his jazz recordings. And, at age twenty, Wayne Goodman, a white trombonist, was hired by Wynton as a copyist for the Classical Jazz Festival. Goodman had been a student of David Berger's, which led to his job at Lincoln Center.

Fascinated by Art Baron's masterful work with the plunger trombone style from Ellington's band, Goodman began studying Baron's technique. Developing a rapport with the older musician, Goodman was extremely excited to find himself invited to substitute for Baron at a rehearsal. To his great disappointment, the rehearsal was canceled. Later on, Berger invited Goodman to work in a band, with Wynton as guest soloist, for a concert of Ellington's sacred music given in December 1993. Wynton heard him play there and eventually invited him to join his band for the premiere of *Blood on the Fields*, an oratorio that would win Wynton a Pulitzer Prize.

Goodman was first asked to substitute for Jamal Haynes one day in a rehearsal for the oratorio. Then Goodman returned the next day. Wynton looked at him and said, "What are you doing here?" Goodman said he had been hired for two days. Wynton replied, "Why don't you just stay on the gig?" The music was hard. Wynton needed the men to attend rehearsals. Goodman was available. After that, he stayed with the band, where he learned that it was okay "if you fuck up a little," as long as you correct yourself. "There's no room for mediocrity," Goodman recalled. "[Wynton]'ll just keep working it until he gets it where he wants it to be. He has a definite idea of how [the] band should sound, and he tries to bring this out of [the] musicians."

Goodman was thrilled with the opportunity to play with the great players in the band, the young and the old, at Tanglewood and at Lincoln

Center. He never detected any feelings of racism or resentment against him from Wynton or anyone else in the band. He felt the charges of racism against Wynton were absurd.

Bassist Ben Wolfe, a white man, came to Wynton's attention when Wolfe played in Harry Connick, Jr.'s big band in 1989. It was impossible to miss how wonderful he sounded and what a strong player he was. Wolfe was already traveling in the right circles. He had met Branford and played with him first. Then Wynton asked Wolfe to substitute for Reginald Veal in the septet in the early 1990s, when Veal was having dental work done. Wolfe recalled the first piece he played with the band was "Citi Movement."[14] He remembered, "They were really impressed that I could learn it so fast. I was really excited to be playing for Wynton. I didn't want to show up and sound like a sub. So I rehearsed, and for a month I played in the septet, once with a quartet, and for little things here and there. And I was playing with Marcus Roberts. It was kind of like the Marsalis family opened up."

When Veal left the band permanently, Wynton tried out a few other bassists, but soon returned to Wolfe and hired him as the regular bassist for the septet for its last year of existence.

As Rob Gibson recalled, "In August 1992, Ben Wolfe played 'In This House, On This Morning,' and Ben came on the show and read his butt off, for this two-and-a-half-hour piece. We [at Lincoln Center] had commissioned that piece [by Wynton]. It was probably the first long piece commissioned by Jazz at Lincoln Center. And Ben went on the road with us for the summer, to France, and played with us a lot, actually. [Wynton's critics] never talked to him [about racism]. That's astonishing. And they never talked to me about the subject."

Wolfe himself, who is Jewish, said that he never so much as detected one iota of prejudice in Wynton or any other member of the septet. He had no idea that one of his best friends in the group was, if not prejudiced, at least aware of Wolfe's difference; Wolfe did not have the same church background as the rest of the fellows and didn't know the hymns that they sometimes sang together to pass the time when they traveled in the buses between performances, Wolfe's friend said. But to be aware of a difference is not to dislike it. And Wolfe could play the group's music; there was no question of it.

Wynton had the right to hire whomever he wanted, Rob Gibson said, adding, "I think when you're in a position of power in an institution like Lincoln Center, people are going to be jealous no matter what your skin color is."

Ben Wolfe recalled the ease with which he dealt with Wynton: "When I went to his condo at Lincoln Center [to which Wynton moved in the early 1990s], a lot of people were always going in and out. It's very nice there, beautiful. I get along with him great. I got along with everyone in the band. I really enjoyed it as one of the best experiences I had on the road. Wynton always treated the band very fairly. Aside from being a great musician, he's a great bandleader. Everything was very organized. You never had to worry about getting paid, nor about any issues, or anything. I never worried.

"I've been in bands where I've had arguments with the artist's manager or was robbed or treated unfairly. But never with Wynton. In fact, I would have played with Wynton for free. Not really. Symbolically. I learned so much. And he was very inspiring, very busy, nonstop. . . . It was interesting.

"I was probably the first white musician regularly in his band. He has been accused of racism. That's a little thing that comes up with him. But it's actually an issue that never came up with him. In the nucleus of the band it never came up. I never thought about it. Whenever the issue of racism came up in a magazine, no one ever called to ask me about it. It makes me think that people just like to have it in their magazines. Not one interviewer ever asked me about it. Wynton only hired black musicians, they said."

Joe Temperley, the white baritone and soprano saxophonist, a virtuoso on both instruments, was invited right away into the Classical Jazz Orchestra as soon as it started. He was a former Duke Ellington band player. He had the same experience that Ben Wolfe did, which is to say no experience of any racism. It seems reasonable to theorize that the start of Classical Jazz gave Wynton the opportunity to expand his horizons, or anyway his hiring practices. Of course, when the chance came for him to give young, African-American musicians a chance to play, he took it. He very much wanted to do that.

Gibson said: "We never judged anyone by skin color. I know, because I've selected a whole lot of [musicians] myself, and we always select people who we think are the best. We had Lew Soloff play lead trumpet in 1992, for the reason that he was the best guy we could get."

Some writers said there was a measure of truth in the charges of racism. As the years passed, although there were many compositions by white composers played under the aegis of Jazz at Lincoln Center, only one program was devoted to a white composer: Gerry Mulligan. Some writers suggested that Wynton should devote nights to composers or players who had much less influence on the development of jazz than the African-American composers whom Wynton did choose. Wynton replied, quite correctly, that he wanted to get the masters presented first.

Some writers mentioned that the omission of Benny Goodman and his great Carnegie Hall concert was a gross oversight. Rob Gibson, a jazz history teacher at Juilliard, who could be very outspoken, responded to this criticism in his own spirited, feisty way: "And I say, what did [Goodman] write? It wasn't that [Goodman] wasn't a great clarinetist or bandleader, because he was. But it's a matter of what did he write? Now we can go out and do Benny Goodman, and [we'd] be doing a lot of Jimmy Mundy, Horace Henderson, Fletcher Henderson [all African-American band leaders whose arrangements Goodman used], and people who wrote charts for [the Goodman] band. And we've done it in different ways. And that's the devising of a canon, a representative and definitive anthology of jazz creation. Then you get into opinions, and absolutely that's what being an artistic director is about.

"Nobody ever gave George Balanchine a hard time for not putting Martha Graham on at the New York City Ballet.[15] It was his prerogative, just as it's Wynton's prerogative to do what he wants to do. It's about the taste and the authority of the artistic director. But critics want to dismiss it sometimes. Well, it's America. They can write whatever they want to."

For a while, Wynton managed to stand at a distance from the controversies that swirled around him for his pronouncements about music, his inflammatory attempts to codify a jazz canon defining what was jazz and what wasn't, and the charges of racism that didn't go away. The list of complaints against Wynton and Jazz at Lincoln Center would grow to include the number of commissions for composing that Wynton received. Rob Gibson stated that he was responsible for Wynton receiving one commission a year; it was written into his contract. However, Jazz at Lincoln Center made about twenty commissions a year, Gibson said. Wynton wished that people would simply pay more attention to his music. It seemed to him that his music was getting lost in the shuffle at times, when writers concentrated on these other issues.

Those critics who stayed away from the controversies—the nattering back and forth about whether Wynton was a racist or an exemplary humanitarian—did manage to keep writing perceptive analyses of his development as a musician and composer. Meanwhile, audiences at Lincoln Center kept growing and enjoying the jazz program.

———>●<———

During the last week of May 1992, Wynton's septet premiered his original composition, an evening-long work that Jazz at Lincoln Center had commissioned, *In This House, On This Morning*. It was a complicated, very long piece that Wynton hoped would take people through all the passions of a day in church. Wynton may not have had enough time to work on the piece, and its sheer length didn't hold the attention of the whole audience throughout the night. Many people left after intermission.[16]

Gary Giddins, jazz critic for the *Village Voice*, in retrospect wrote about the piece, saying it was under-rehearsed and seemed unfinished.[17] On the other hand, Stanley Crouch predictably regarded the piece as a "masterwork." Other critics of the piece to a degree gave Marsalis the benefit of the doubt.

Wynton took the septet on a tour with *In This House, On This Morning*. At the request of his good friend Carol Clarke, he gave a memorable performance of the work at the Baptist Church in Alabama, where four little girls had been slain by a bomb during the height of the civil rights movement and its attendant violence in the 1960s. The performance raised funds for the church and programs to memorialize the civil rights era.

In the sixth season of Jazz at Lincoln Center, between July 31, 1992, and May 6, 1993, the Lincoln Center Jazz Orchestra set out on its first national tour to over twenty-five cities. People showed up in considerable numbers to hear the orchestra. Part of the reason was the prestige of Lincoln Center, which the tour represented. Furthermore, some of the concerts took place in already well-established programs, such as the Monterey Jazz Festival in California. There young people screamed in the middle of tunes. Clearly the band was being promoted intelligently.

The 1992–1993 season of Jazz at Lincoln Center, still featuring Ellington and other old masters in its official brochure, paid tribute to Thelonious Monk, including the Thelonious Monk International Jazz Competition. Jazz at Lincoln Center then launched a new, educational program for kids: Jazz for Young People. The first one made its debut during the Christmas season in 1992; the second concert was entitled "What Is American Music?" in January 1993; the third, "What Is a Big Band?" in March; and the fourth, "What Is New Orleans Jazz?" in May. Because of the success of these first programs, four Saturday mornings and afternoons every season would be turned over to the children's shows at Alice Tully Hall. Wynton led all of these concerts, illustrating his points with the band.

In these first programs, Wynton taught musical forms by using the songs "Happy Birthday," a blues, and finally "I Got Rhythm," which he demonstrated had provided the chord structure for Thelonious Monk's complex, classic bebop song "Rhythm-a-ning." When Wynton and pianist Eric Reed made a mistake while playing the blues, Wynton laughed it off and showed the kids an example of an incorrectly played blues. Not only did critics write about the series in glowing terms, but word of mouth spread the message. Within a short period of time, tickets for the Jazz for Young People concerts became scarce; as the years passed, sometimes children had to be turned away for lack of space.

—————

From the point of view of audiences, critics, and Lincoln Center's directors, Jazz at Lincoln Center enjoyed rousing successes. Each year the program expanded. In January 1993, Wynton supplied music for the New York City Ballet's production of *Jazz: Six Syncopated Movements*, choreographed by the ballet's director, Peter Martins. Intended as a very ambitious portrait of America, Wynton's score won critical praise, although the choreography was not as well received. The weeklong August festival of Classical Jazz in 1993 featured events on Thelonious Monk and Billie Holiday, and commissioned pieces by pianist Geri Allen playing with her septet—probably the first time a woman instrumentalist had been included in Jazz at Lincoln Center—and Marcus Roberts with his nonet. (Female singers were of course included.) The Lincoln Center Jazz Orchestra performed suites by Ellington. Pianist Renee Rosnes was invited to play for some Ellington concerts, too.

As the program continued in September, trumpeters Terence Blanchard and Roy Hargrove performed their commissioned pieces. Now the critics raised charges of cronyism about the awarding of commissions. Although many musicians would receive commissions—ranging from the elder statesman Benny Carter to saxophonist Wayne Shorter, both famed as composers and without connections to Wynton—many other well-known composers in the jazz world were overlooked, while younger musicians found favor. The avant-garde and fusion players and composers, who did not fit into the jazz canon of Lincoln Center, remained particularly aggrieved. A pithy recital of these criticisms appeared in an article by Richard Harrington in the *Washington Post*, showing how this internal jazz war was being covered as news in the mainstream press.[18]

Rob Gibson offered one seemingly reasonable answer: There was just so much music available that the young program was having a hard time fitting in even a small percentage of it. Gibson also pointed out that canons lay at the heart of the Metropolitan Opera, the New York Philharmonic, and the New York City Ballet.

But jazz differed from these arts. Jazz was still fairly young and growing. And other criticisms of Jazz at Lincoln Center militated against general acceptance of Gibson's answer about the traditions of canons.

Then the situation got even hotter.

CHAPTER NOTES

1. Wynton Marsalis, "What Jazz Is and Isn't." *New York Times*, January 28, 1988.
2. Peter Watrous, "Wynton Marsalis at the Village Vanguard." *New York Times*, November 10, 1990.
3. George Kanzler, "Marsalis Film Score Ranks Among the Best Ever." *Newark Star Ledger*, December 23, 1990.
4. Ibid.
5. Ibid.
6. Ibid.
7. Other critics wrote along the same lines as Kanzler in this period. Scott Yanow said that Wynton had finally found his own voice.
8. Whitney Balliett, "Jazz: Wynton Looks Back." *The New Yorker*, October 1991.
9. Ibid.
10. Ibid.
11. Ibid.
12. Ibid.
13. Thomas Sancton, "A Conversation With Wynton Marsalis." *Jazz Times*, March 1997.

14. Rob Gibson recalled instead that it was "In This House, On This Morning," an attempt by Wynton to take the audience back to church. Reginald Veal played for both recordings, but Ben Wolfe played for live performances of these pieces.
15. Actually, Balanchine and Graham collaborated on one work presented by the New York City Ballet in 1959.
16. "Blue Interlude," Wynton's first extended composition, which was released on a CD a few weeks before the premiere of *In This House, On This Morning*, was also performed that night.
17. Gary Giddins, "Shackling Surprise." *Village Voice*, October 12, 1993.
18. Richard Harrington, "The Canon Wars Come to Jazz." *Washington Post*, February 20, 1994.

THE SKIRMISHES OF '93 AND '94

R ob Gibson sent a letter dated May 31, 1992, to the older musicians in the Lincoln Center Jazz Orchestra, including trombonists Art Baron and Britt Woodman, alto saxophonists Norris Turney and Jerry Dodgion, multi-reeds player Bill Easley, and Joe Temperley, the soprano and baritone saxophonist. All of them had played in the bands of Duke Ellington, Benny Goodman, and Count Basie, the Thad Jones–Mel Lewis Orchestra, and other historic big bands. Gibson's letter told them they were being replaced, at least temporarily, by musicians under age thirty.

"It is with mixed emotions that I tell you about an experiment we're trying this summer with the Lincoln Center Jazz Orchestra," he wrote. "We're making across the board changes in the orchestra personnel by hiring an entire band of guys under the age of 30—I hope you'll understand that the decision to not utilize your great talents this summer has nothing to do with artistic ability or any personal issues—this is simply an attempt on our part to try and get some of the younger musicians to learn more about this music and begin to play it with some authority. Obviously, we had that authority with you, and that's why this has been a tough one. However, the artistic decision that was made in this instance is something we hope will have benefits for jazz music, its future, and for the young men who'll be learning to play it." The letter also stressed that dismissal of the elders didn't signal their "permanent disassociation."[1]

The letter announced a shockingly illegal move that nearly provoked a lawsuit against Lincoln Center by some of the older players who were in danger of losing their jobs. Wynton was traveling with his septet at the time. According to Rob Gibson, Wynton knew about the impending change in the orchestra, but he had no idea of the wording of the letter. On June 10, Gibson sent out a second letter retracting his first one.

It was a low point for the jazz program, which already had enough headaches. Gibson later explained that he alone had written the letter "that talked about some changes we were going to make in the orchestra and an experiment we were going to do to use some younger guys. The press got hold of it and made a big deal. And not everyone older in the orchestra got the letter. It was a dumb thing [for me] to do and a dumb way to phrase the letter."

Even five years later, Gibson was angered by the memory of the fiasco: "The press misreported it and quickly flip-flopped it into a race issue. They flip-flopped age to race pretty quick and blamed it all on Wynton, when in fact it was my fault and never Wynton's fault. He knew about it, but he didn't know I phrased one sentence very stupidly. He knew that after he read about it in the paper. This happened in 1993. I was thirty-four years old then. . . .

"Race has been central in the press's *angst* toward our program. The bulk of the press has been very positive toward our program, all over the world. But it's easier to remember the negative things than the positive. I can easily remember those negative things written about us, and I can easily tell you that there's a great amount of untruth."

Exactly how the issue of race intertwines with the fiasco of this letter fraught with ageism may not seem to be immediately clear. But in general all issues lead to each other when criticisms heat up about Lincoln Center.

Despite the problems this letter created, Wynton would continue to defend Gibson and his actions. "The point to make about the letter," Wynton said years after the incident, "was that it didn't reflect the view of Lincoln Center." The wording was radically wrong. "But the fact is that the tour [the Lincoln Center Jazz Orchestra was] going on would be featuring a different style of music. We were going to be playing Ornette Coleman's music." Jazz at Lincoln Center wanted younger people to play it; they were the ones who could play it best, Wynton had decided. The older musicians in the Lincoln Center Jazz Orchestra played Ellington, not Ornette Coleman, an avant-garde musician and composer, who represented essentially a different world. "But when we went back to Ellington, we would use the same older musicians. When this [letter] is used as a reflection of our hiring practices, it's not true." Exactly who the personnel would have been in the temporary orchestra was never stated, but Wynton always wanted to give young African-American musicians a chance to play jazz.

Wynton wished that people would pay attention to all the wonderful things that Gibson had done for Jazz at Lincoln Center. It dismayed Wynton to see people "try to attack Gibson's ego and make him seem like he was inconsequential," he said. There was some suggestion at the time of the letter incident that Gibson simply did Wynton's bidding. However, Wynton and Gibson were doing the job at Lincoln Center together, and it would be impossible for anyone to separate them, Wynton affirmed.

In New York, some critics fixed on this bizarre event, assuming, undoubtedly correctly, that the decision was made by Gibson, Marsalis, Stanley Crouch, and Albert Murray as a consulting entity. Actually it was taken by Gibson, he said, with Marsalis. A few critics tried to stage a little dinner party with Gibson as guest of honor, as it were, to find out exactly how the power was wielded for the program. At first, Gibson thought a dinner meeting would be "a great idea." But the corporate structure of the arts complex would be, at least by inference, involved, and Gibson may have decided he couldn't or didn't want to act unilaterally. Other people stepped in to join in his defense: Stanley Crouch and Marilyn Laverty of Shore Fire Media, Wynton's publicist. She had left Columbia in 1985 and opened her own firm, with Wynton as one of her most important clients. Jazz at Lincoln Center hired her with her firm in 1992 to do publicity. Half a dozen writers regularly on the jazz beat in New York City were invited to the event.

Gibson cooked rice and beans and chicken and served drinks in his own apartment on Manhattan's West Side. Marilyn Laverty baked a batch of brownies.[2] After the meal, Gibson and Crouch reportedly discussed the program and answered questions. No one criticized the speakers, according to an article by Richard B. Woodward published a year after the dinner. (Woodward hadn't been there, but he was assigned to write a story about the ongoing controversies surrounding the Lincoln Center program.)[3]

Some of the chitchat at the dinner party was supposedly off the record. However, Gene Santoro, who now works for the *New York Daily News*, wrote a story divulging embargoed information—information postponed for release for a later date. Stanley Crouch was incensed by what he considered to be a breach of professional conduct. He reportedly berated the errant writer the next time they met face to face. According to Santoro: "[Crouch] started to harangue me for about 15 minutes. It was a nonstop torrent. He started by telling me I was a nobody, that no one in the jazz community cared about anything that I wrote, that I had balls writing about music I knew nothing about. I let him talk. It was pretty clear it was not supposed to be a dialogue but a diatribe. . . ."[4]

After Crouch's lecture, the writer complained directly to Lincoln Center. Someone in a position of authority at Lincoln Center said he had asked for Crouch's side of the story and was satisfied that all had been smoothed over. Then Santoro met Crouch again and faced another tirade of sorts. Crouch kept calling him "a liar," Santoro said.[5]

Woodward attempted to interview Crouch for his article, but Crouch declined on the grounds that it would be a waste of his time. Woodward did report that Crouch threw in a remark reiterating "his low opinion of almost all jazz critics."[6] Another jazz writer, whom Crouch has never criticized much, noted that he has been heard to say that most jazz critics are "arrogant," and has developed a condescending, antagonistic relationship with writers from whose ranks he sprang.

This incident showed how easily the controversies swirling around Lincoln Center's jazz program could be stirred up into a conflagration. The ill will that had long been festering between the jazz critics and the managers of the program was increasingly coming out into the open.

One writer, Tom Piazza, who had not been present at the dinner, suggested in his book *Blues Up and Down: Jazz in Our Time* that critics were zeroing in on Lincoln Center because the critics were white, while three out of four of the main players at Lincoln Center's jazz program—Gibson, Wynton, Crouch, and Murray—were black. (Really, the main players were Gibson and Marsalis, Gibson corrected.) In any case, white critics weren't accustomed to having their positions of authority usurped by any African-American musicians—to wit, Wynton. That idea seemed to have something to recommend it, even though Gene Seymour, an African-American critic for *Newsday*, may have been the first writer to wonder why early jazz trumpeter Bix Beiderbecke, who was white, hadn't been paid tribute to at Lincoln Center.

Piazza also thought that the directors of the program may have made matters worse by their lack of tact and defensiveness with critics. He believed that some of these criticisms had been at times belabored, excessive, personal, and even occasionally vitriolic. Nevertheless, perhaps Jazz at Lincoln Center's administrators should have stood above the fray and turned the other cheek, as it were, so great had been audience acceptance. They had little to fear from a small group of disgruntled jazz writers.

Perhaps the tensions were aggravated between the center's program directors and the press because critic-writers of any race weren't about to suffer gladly while watching nonwriters earn so much authority. Furthermore, critics are born to criticize and speak up—or at least bound to do those things. There was so much activity at Jazz at Lincoln Center that it was a gold mine—and a natural focal point for all that was wrong with the jazz world. In short, there were no easy answers to questions that arose about the management of the program, perhaps because nobody really seemed to want solutions and everyone had his or her own personal ax to grind—or ideas to air.

The quarrels seemed to have crossed a line and metamorphosed from criticisms into a grisly sort of entertainment, melees with a carnival atmosphere, for those—primarily those at a distance—who could maintain a sense of humor about it, or a running gun battle for those caught up in the situation. Positions were hardening on both sides; Woodward quoted Wynton as saying "I will never bow to these men. That will never happen. . . ."[7] In Woodward's conclusion, he believed that "there should be enough intrigue and ill will to keep everyone in the jazz press employed for years to come."[8]

This friction between critics and the Jazz at Lincoln Center staff was indicative of larger shifts in the jazz world. There was a cooling of relations between the old colleagues Gary Giddins of the *Voice* and Stanley Crouch, depicted by Woodward as "the two smartest jazz critics in American journalism"[9]—itself a debatable accolade, as there were other gifted critics. Giddins had been the driving force behind the American Jazz Orchestra housed at Cooper Union, in direct competition with Lincoln Center. However, his orchestra had risen and fallen, while

Lincoln Center's jazz program had kept rising—a spectacle difficult for Giddins to endure, as he himself admitted.[10]

Woodward noted that the first of two big-band battles between the Carnegie Hall Jazz Band and the Lincoln Center Jazz Orchestra had been "no contest."[11] The Carnegie Hall Jazz Band played contemporary music by Wayne Shorter and Miles Davis tunes with ease, grace, and warmth, while the Lincoln Center Jazz Orchestra had shown off professionalism and swing, with a feeling of self-confidence and a sense of purpose. The band had clearly rehearsed a great deal to achieve such brilliance.

"Marsalis deserved acclaim for such excellence. His players respond in kind to his utter self-assurance and drive," Woodward wrote to end his article. "No one has worked harder over the last 10 years to bring jazz to kids who might not otherwise hear a lick. He probably knows more about the trumpet than anyone alive, and he shares what he knows. After his concerts he can be found counseling anyone who brings his or her horn. As he says, 'You won't find a musician who spends more time with the public than I do. I'm always available.'"[12]

The big-band competitions between Lincoln Center and Carnegie Hall were no contest in another way. Wynton went to play with Jon Faddis's band at least once, and Faddis sometimes cooperated with the Lincoln Center Jazz Orchestra to the extent of leading it on tours. Neither he nor Wynton considered themselves competitors. Faddis had tremendous admiration for Wynton and vice versa.

"The missteps that have dogged Jazz at Lincoln Center for the past year can seem, in the context of a performance, more farcical than sinister," concluded Woodward.[13]

Fanning the charges of political and racial bias at Lincoln Center was Gibson's dismissal of David Berger in January 1994. (Rob Gibson later reflected, "If a white guy fires a white guy, how is that anti-white? I never understood that.") But Berger remained loyal to Wynton and was even quoted as saying, "People criticized us for not having enough white musicians. I'll be honest. Some of the white guys were hired by Wynton over my objections. We always hired the people we thought would be the best musicians."[14] So, at least from Berger's point of view, his dismissal was not an attempt to maintain an all African-American outfit— or even for Wynton to further consolidate his power.

Despite the retraction of Gibson's inflammatory letter, the Lincoln Center Jazz Orchestra did indeed change as time went on: All the older musicians left, with the exception of Joe Temperley. By 1998, he was the only one in his generation still with the band. At the time he had received the letter, he didn't join the people who hired a lawyer to contest the firing. Temperley recalled, "I accepted it. I could understand their position at Lincoln Center. I've been playing a long, long time. I can see how they want to have a younger band, that it makes sense to get a younger band. You have to bring young people into the music. Wynton tries to do it. A lot of young people can play. . . .

"It was a drag, of course, to think you're going to lose your job. But it's very understandable. There has to be younger blood in to play the music, or you'll have hundred-year-old men, two thousand-year-old men, Mel Brooks and all them, playing jazz. And you can't have that. You have to bring in young people to play it. It's a tradition. And who's going to carry on the tradition? Basie and Ellington, Dizzy and Charlie Parker are all gone. That was a different thing. That was then. This is now."

Temperley perceived that criticisms of Wynton diminished as the 1990s progressed, and that Wynton had mellowed over a period of time: "He still gets a lot of barbs from different critics, but it doesn't bother him. He just goes straight ahead." Another observer thought that Wynton hadn't mellowed so much as he had become calmer, more easefully decisive, and more sure of himself. As for charges of racism, Temperley had heard some remarks but hadn't paid much attention to them, because he hadn't experienced that kind of thing from Wynton at all. "He's very loving toward me and my wife," Temperley noted. "He's a perfect gentleman to both of us, and we have a wonderful relationship with him at all times. I find him to be a very bright, articulate man and by far the finest musician that I've ever encountered. . . .

"His aims and his goals and all the things happening at Lincoln Center, especially his promotion of Duke Ellington's music in high schools, that's a wonderful thing. . . . He's a fountain of knowledge and wants to keep working and learning. He inspires you because he works himself; he doesn't sit back and rest on his laurels. . . . He just gets on with what he's doing.

"The thing about Wynton is, he has a very superior intellect. He's a very intelligent man apart from being a great musician. People say that people with opinions are opinionated. People call me opinionated because

I have opinions. But what do they call people who don't have opinions? They call them waffles. If you don't have opinions, you're a wimp. Where's the happy medium?"

———————

A second controversy erupted when Wynton reacted to a favorable review of James Lincoln Collier's book *Jazz: The American Theme Song*, which appeared in the *New York Times Book Review* on November 21, 1993. In this book, Collier emphasized the importance of whites in developing early jazz styles, implicitly criticizing those who believed that African Americans had created jazz.[15] Collier had long been a thorn in the side of some jazz critics who found his writings to be demeaning toward African-American musicians—as well as frought with inaccuracies, particularly his biographies of Duke Ellington and Louis Armstrong. Stanley Crouch had been one of Collier's most vocal critics.

In response to the review of Collier's book, Wynton wrote a letter to the editor of the paper, charging that the book "is yet another example of the impoverished state of criticism that obscures the quality and honor of this art." Furthermore, "His biographies of Louis Armstrong and Duke Ellington are filled with errors."[16] Wynton took a dim view of Collier's ideas, as well as his factual mistakes. In his letter, Wynton challenged Collier to join in a public debate with him.[17] Collier agreed to do it.

In a glib, slick announcement of the upcoming debate on Sunday, August 7, 1994, to be held at the Stanley Kaplan Penthouse in Lincoln Center, *New York* Magazine characterized both men as "obstinate and pompous." As for their musicianship, Wynton was a "virtuoso," while Collier was "a fair trombonist; no Jack Teagarden." (Collier is an amateur jazz trombonist who plays around New York City but makes no claims to being on the level of a professional musician.) The magazine also suggested that Wynton was a charming, if perhaps somewhat polemical, speaker.[18]

Collier undoubtedly underestimated the strength of his opponent in accepting the challenge to a debate. In an advance interview, Collier said, "What I want to avoid is just speechifying. But I have no idea what I'm in for. Your guess is as good as mine."[19]

If he had read Wynton's letter to the editor carefully, in which Wynton called Collier "this viper in the bosom of blues and swing," Collier might have prepared himself for a very bad storm or even backed away and let it blow over. The intensity of feeling in the jazz community was apparent when the two showed up for the confrontation to face a standing-room-only audience; many prominent jazz writers were in attendance.

Loren Schoenberg, a close friend of Wynton and Stanley Crouch in the 1990s, recalled how Wynton bested Collier in the debate. Schoenberg said, "The main thing was that Wynton had marshaled an incredible amount of hard evidence to refute all these spurious claims by Collier about Armstrong, about Armstrong's 'problems'. It began with Collier noting how Louis Armstrong had gotten lost playing the blues on King Oliver's famous record of 'Chimes Blues.' In the audience were dozens of musicians and serious jazz fans. And it was obvious to everyone that Collier had turned the beat around in his head. It was Collier who was lost . . . and not Louis. It was beyond debate. Collier wouldn't give it up, even in the face of [many] musicians. . . .

"Then Wynton put up on a screen a picture of something maybe from 'Gray's Anatomy,' a picture of facial muscles, and he used this to refute Collier's claims about Armstrong's embouchure. Wynton demonstrated beyond a doubt that Louis couldn't have done what Collier claimed he did. Again, Collier wouldn't give it up. Wynton pointed to this muscle, this muscle, this and this muscle, and said, 'What you're saying is impossible.'

"And the capper was when Collier began lecturing Wynton about the complexities of race relations in New Orleans. Wynton took exception to some of Collier's statements about Creoles. At which point Collier cited some study he had found. Wynton flashed on the overhead screen a picture of his grandparents; and said, 'Mr. Collier, this is my grandfather, he was a Creole. Now, what are you going to tell me about Creoles? I'm from New Orleans.' And again Collier would not give it up. . . . So it was a very strange evening in some ways."

Schoenberg's account was clearly completely pro-Wynton. Jeff Taylor, another writer who attended the debate, had a different view of the proceedings: "The exceedingly testy audience, clearly in Marsalis's camp, was out for blood, loudly cheering the trumpeter's comments and rudely interrupting Collier in mid-sentence. During the ensuing debate, which lasted well over two hours, the sparks flew, but each participant made valid points. Marsalis, drawing upon his prodigious talents as a working musician and his eloquence as a speaker, severely undermined

Collier's analyses of recordings by Ellington and Armstrong. [Wynton] clearly illustrated, for example, that Collier had misinterpreted the rhythmic structure of Armstrong's 1924 'Chimes Blues' solo. Yet Collier managed to show the breadth of his own work, which, although often accused of inaccuracies, is based on years of studying primary sources.

"Marsalis began by criticizing specific passages of Collier's books, but the discussion soon drifted to other topics, including the volatile issues of class and education among black jazz musicians. Perhaps the tensest moments came when Collier openly questioned Marsalis's motives in his role at Lincoln Center, noting that the trumpeter has been criticized for refusing to acknowledge the historic importance of white jazz musicians in shaping the center's programs and for supposedly giving himself commissions. Marsalis eloquently refuted these accusations, as the air of belligerence rose to a fever pitch, fed once again by the audience's indignation.

"On leaving, I overheard one critic ask another, 'Well, who won?' As I walked toward the subway, I couldn't help think that such a spectacle leaves us all losers, including the participants." Taylor would have preferred that the participants had worked together. "But such a public display of hostility benefits no one. Rather, it does an injustice to the great American art form to which both Collier and Marsalis have devoted the better part of their lives."[20]

Taylor was not alone in leaving the penthouse with an unsettled feeling. One official of Lincoln Center who had been there, and who did not really have any background in the issues raised, recalled only that Wynton "demolished" Collier—"which is not to say there's not another side to this issue."

It was a difficult night. Nobody had mentioned that in his writings, Collier, to his everlasting credit, had said Armstrong was the primary influence for everyone in American popular music. He taught everyone. Whatever Collier's shortcomings as a critic, the debate did little to settle some of the lingering concerns about the Lincoln Center program and Marsalis's role as one of the protectors of the jazz canon.

"Once the debate was over, I was glad it was over," Wynton reminisced. "I regretted doing it. I didn't feel any sense of pride about it at all. None." Wynton had gone to debate about music, he said. As it turned out, "It's not like I felt celebratory. I thought the whole thing was pitiful."

Four years after the debate, Collier adamantly refused to discuss it. A shopper hoping to buy his books in 1998 had difficulty finding them in New York bookstores. One prominent store's information clerk said the store couldn't get any copies of Collier's books from distributors; the books were out of print. Schoenberg and Crouch, among others, were glad to hear that the books were scarce, although the shortage may have been a temporary situation.

CHAPTER NOTES

1. Richard B. Woodward, "The Jazz Wars: A Tale of Age, Rage, and Hash Brownies." *Village Voice*, August 9, 1994.
2. One writer claimed that his mind turned virtually to rubble from the brownies, which he suggested were laced with hashish. It's really inconceivable to imagine that Marilyn Laverty would serve hashish-laced brownies to people without telling them. It is especially hard to believe that she would do this to people who not only could sue her but could also write about their experiences and forever impugn the sanity of the people connected with Jazz at Lincoln Center.
3. Richard B. Woodward, "The Jazz Wars: A Tale of Age, Rage, and Hash Brownies." *Village Voice*, August 9, 1994.
4. Ibid.
5. Ibid.
6. Ibid.
7. Ibid.
8. Ibid.
9. Ibid.
10. Gary Giddins, "Shackling Surprise." *Village Voice*, October 12, 1993.
11. Richard B. Woodward, "The Jazz Wars: A Tale of Age, Rage, and Hash Brownies." *Village Voice*, August 9, 1994.
12. Ibid.
13. Ibid.
14. Ibid.
15. Another prominent jazz writer, Gene Lees, published at about the same time his book *Cats of Any Color*, which furthered the argument that both whites and blacks contributed to jazz history—and implicitly criticized the polarization that Lees and others felt was occurring among the races in the jazz world.
16. Wynton Marsalis, "A Viper in the Bosom of the Blues." The *New York Times*, December 19, 1993.
17. Some people gossiped that Stanley Crouch may have written the letter to the editor that challenged Collier to the debate. But that is highly unlikely; Wynton was fully capable of finding his own voice in all kinds of situations.
18. "Fast Track." New York, August 8, 1994.
19. Robert Miller, "Debate Pits Jazz Voices." *Danbury News-Times*, July 31, 1994.
20. Jeff Taylor, "Encounters With Jazz." *I.S.A.M. Newsletter*, 24 (1), Fall 1994.

MORE FRIENDS AND LOVERS

Wynton's personal life has often taken a backseat to his musical one. He has that in common with jazz musicians since the beginning of jazz's existence. The road becomes their real home. And, with the many temptations of the road, it is not unusual for musicians to have several long- and short-term affairs. A few years before Candace Stanley and Wynton split up for good, he began affairs with several women, at least two of whom he had known for a long time.

One affair was very short-lived, consisting of about three rendezvous over a period of years beginning after Wynton moved into his Lincoln Center condominium. That woman had maintained a chaste friendship with him for the previous decade. Then one night their relationship changed. "I can't explain why," she would recall, "I wasn't expecting any romance with him." But when she went to visit him in his apartment, "things took a more romantic turn."

Her feelings for him had always felt like love to her, even though she had never had any basis for her feelings "in terms of anything he had done. It was just sort of an unconditional deep admiration. He doesn't have to do anything for me," she said. Her friendship with him had taught her a great deal about how love should be. Her past relationships with other men had been "totally possessive and crazy."

The morning after the first time they made love, Wynton had to run to catch a plane. "I wasn't even sure he had my phone number. He would always give me his changing phone numbers." But it turned out that he did have her number, because he called her.

Although their friendship lasted, their intimacy didn't. By 1998, when she visited him in his apartment, she got a long hug, and that was all. "So it's just one of those things. It's a friendship, because we're not intimate," she said. "I don't take any neglect personally, because I know the book by Duke Ellington, *Music Is My Mistress*. I have read Wynton's writings and the way he studied Duke Ellington's music and his book. He studied it the way other people study the Bible. I may be Wynton's friend and in his life, but he's not going to stop for me."

They still talked several times a year, usually because she called him. "We talk about deep things, personal things. I see more maturity and warmth and compassion in him. Earlier in his life, he was a lot more cavalier and aloof—and selfish, too, in a big way. I envy that passion he has for music. Just to have that drive and love for something! His apartment is like a musicians' hostel. Trumpet players, young ones, seem to congregate around him. . . .

"Sometimes I wonder if I even know him at all," she mused. "Sometimes I wonder if he cares a lot more deeply about things he pretends not to care about. . . . He has a nonchalance about everything," she noticed, including his attitude toward awards, but he actually paid very close attention to the details affecting his life as well as his music directly.

"During the years of our friendship, I got indications that he has felt that I am important to him. He at times has been my highest and strictest confidante." She could tell him about her problems—with work and with men. Once, after their intimacy had been over for a while, she was having a problem with a boyfriend; she called Wynton. He told her she could stay in his apartment. When she went there, he made up a bed for her, talked to her for quite a while, then went back to his own room. Another woman was waiting for him. He said he was sorry to his former lover, who didn't mind the situation at all.

"Even though he's critical and has harsh opinions, he can be so supportive and nonjudgmental. So there's a very enriching component, a mutual love and acceptance that friends have. I experienced that in a profound sort of way, but I felt that he really belonged to the world. Even if he allowed me to share in his life, it was because I invited myself along. He was receptive. Sometimes I did call, and he invited me over.

"The neatest part," she said, was that she "shared his music over the phone a lot. . . . He would play chords [on the piano] and sing melodic parts. He might even ask me to sing something to do with what he was playing. It was very enriching for me. When we visited over the phone, some of our conversations might be personal talks. I could share some very personal things. He was very supportive. When I alluded to things, he would probe. And I would tell him very intimate things. He could be a good listener and a supportive friend.

"Stories come to mind. He took off from a studio break to play a basketball game. It was during the *Tune in Tomorrow* session. Wynton had been daring somebody all day to try to beat him at basketball." And so, during the dinner break, he and the fellow and the woman and a girl-friend of hers had hurried out to a basketball court at the Meridien Hotel. "It was a crazy, whirlwind thing, a hectic thing. That man has a lot of energy."

At one time, the woman, who, like so many of Wynton's friends and associates, had met Candace Stanley, thought Candace was a really won-derful person, "just a joy to know. I could be totally envious that she was where I once wanted to be. But I was very happy for her and genuine in my feelings about her."

The woman eventually began dating a man with whom she thought she might have a lasting relationship. She hoped so. But from time to time she wondered about Wynton and whether she was just one of many women in his life.

There was another woman whom Wynton had met in the South early in his career. For about six years, she saw him occasionally when he played in the city where she lived. Then she moved north for a good job opportunity in 1988. "I heard he was going to be performing at the Grand Opera House in Wilmington, Delaware, and I tracked him down and got his phone number in New York before the concert. I told him I was in the area and was interested in going to hear him play. He said he would have tickets there for me. I traveled to Wilmington [from a city near New York], and I had tickets and a backstage pass in an envelope. I sat and looked at the first half of the concert. I went backstage during inter-mission. That's when things really changed.

"He stared at me a lot that night. There were a lot of people in the room and a lot of food and people making noise. I was standing across the room from him. We just kept staring at each other. I stayed backstage for the second half of the show. The pianist had a solo during that half. And Wynton came downstairs. We were in one of the dressing rooms. He was circling me, walking around, looking at me. And we were silent and just vibing. I stayed that night in the hotel. He gave me the key. And that's when it all started. The change in the relationship."

He was traveling extensively at the time, but she was able to connect with him, she said. "If I called, his people knew he was always interested in talking to me. It was no problem to get to speak to him in Paris, Australia. We have a very compassionate, strong emotional bond to one another. It's pretty deep, but it gets complicated because of everything that has happened."

They didn't just become lovers, she said. "He talked to me about everything. When anything major happens to him, he tells me." When someone sent him a death threat once—she thought it was in 1996—he told her. "'Lovers' does not capture what we are. The bond that we share is everlasting," she said. "I can tell him anything. And if I feel something is serious or deep or life-changing, I have to call him and tell him about it.

"There was a time when I had a relationship and got very hurt by it," she recalled. "Wynton came to me and comforted me. It was very deep, because it was so special. He came to the city where I live, and it's hard to get him to go anywhere if it's not pertaining to his tours or his work. And he came and pampered me. It was the most wonderful thing I had ever experienced. We spent a couple of holidays together. One year we spent Thanksgiving and Christmas together, probably in 1995."

Once he left a message—a trumpet solo, and no words—on her answering machine. "He serenaded me. I took that tape out of that machine and saved it." Once, when she was running an event at her company, he came to give a speech for about an hour to help her. "It was an incredible success. He talked about how democracy on the bandstand can be translated to the workplace, and how in jazz performances, if something doesn't sound right, he tries to find out if he or his band members are contributing to the problems. And in the workplace, if something is going wrong, instead of pointing a finger, figure out if you're contributing to the problem. So to me, that's special."

They met on the fly, as it were—she drove to hear him play in various theaters, when he was performing at a reasonable distance from her apartment. Once she invited the entire band to her apartment, where she cooked jambalaya, corn on the cob, and corn bread for them. One year she saw him once a month. Either she would go to New York for a night, or he would come to her apartment. Once they saw each other only for intermission when he was performing at Princeton.

"That's how strong our relationship was," she said. "Even if we only had half an hour, we appreciated that. A lot of times he was so busy, he wouldn't be home until ten at night, and then out at dawn. Or I would have to leave at 5:00 A.M. to be at work. We would squeeze in time when we could. One time he asked me to go to see him in D.C. He was depressed. I drove to D.C. to see him. The next day I probably had to go to work. We never had a whole day to spend together. I've seen him in many different states and Canada, all kinds of places.

"My life has been so enriched by the experiences I have had with him, not only because of the musical performances, but also just because of the person he is and the conversations he and I have had. He adds a whole dimension to my life. The average person wouldn't understand the relationship. They would say it's nothing deep. 'He just wants to screw you.' But they don't know him.

"I think the most important thing I have gotten from the relationship is the knowledge I have gotten from him," she reflected. "His perspective on life is so deep. No one else in my life has given me what Wynton has given me. He is that unique. He's compassionate and incredible." When she wanted to leave her corporate job and start her own business, Wynton encouraged her. Without that encouragement, she might never have done it. But she did accept the challenge, and she was working very hard to make it succeed.

She had no expectations that Wynton would make a long-term commitment to her. "We're close friends first, and lovers second. Wynton is married to his music. But if he were ever to marry someone, chances are that would be me. . . . Wynton won't get married because he doesn't think he could give me what I want from a husband. It would be unfair to me. And you can understand it, given his schedule. He has said it would get better. 'I'll stop overcommitting,' he has said. But that's not going to be true. I have not stopped my life because of him. I didn't put my life on hold for a dream. But it has been incredible," she says, "which is why I can't let go of it."

She had been through "some very deep things emotionally," she said, and shared them with him. "Like reactions from me. Like the Victoria thing. Jasper is two now."

At the same time he was seeing this woman, Wynton had been having an affair with Victoria Rowell, an Emmy-winning actress on *The Young and the Restless* on CBS, among her other credits. A few stories linking them appeared in the newspapers in New York. One said that the couple was engaged; another said that Victoria was expecting Wynton's child. That story was true. Wynton was in Europe when the story appeared. He called his girlfriend to see how she was taking the news. "He knew it would have a profound effect on me and be very hurtful," she said. "He called me and sat on the phone with me until I wanted to hang up. I'm tolerant and understanding of everything, because I know how he feels about me. And if anything hurt me, it wasn't intentional. We're very involved in each other's welfare."

But the woman immediately began to cry when he told her the news that Victoria Rowell was pregnant. She had actually known that Wynton and Victoria were friends. "I saw their picture in his house. There wasn't a whole lot of noise about that." But the pregnancy was a different matter. "He said, 'I'm sorry, I never meant to hurt you. Please get over this.' He even told my mother, when he saw her down South, and asked her to ask me to please get over it. My mom said, 'How do you expect her to feel?'"

On the phone he kept saying to her, "I don't mean to hurt you. Please don't cry.' And he just hung onto the phone. That's not like him. There was a lot of silence and my sobbing, if you will. He stayed on the phone until I said, 'Okay.' Usually he ends the conversation. And that helped to ease the pain. Something like that call—it shows when somebody cares about you."

She was not the only girlfriend Wynton told about Victoria's pregnancy. Another girlfriend simply said, "Oh," in a way that cut him to the quick. "It was like a razor blade," he would remember.

Jasper Armstrong, as the child was named, was born on December 26, 1995. He lives with his mother in Los Angeles. Wynton's and Victoria's relationship as lovers was not long-lived. However, probably because of Jasper, the connection between Wynton and Victoria continued. Wynton visits his son in Los Angeles and waits for the day when Jasper will be old enough to come to stay with him often. Wynton took Jasper to New Orleans to stay with his parents for two weeks during the Christmas season in 1997.

Jasper also came to stay with Wynton for four days around Christmastime the next year. Slender, with fashionably cropped bleached blond hair, and very pretty, Victoria left Jasper in Wynton's apartment, where friends—a budding screenwriter, a cook, and photographer Frank Stewart—came and went. When Victoria left, Jasper began to cry loudly.

Wynton picked him up, hugged and kissed him, and walked around the apartment with Jasper's legs wrapped around him; Wynton was trying to calm the child down.

But Jasper didn't quit crying and calling out, "I want my mommy."

Finally, Wynton said, "I want my mommy, too; I'm going to cry, too." He gave a resounding holler. Everybody laughed, including Jasper. For a while the crying stopped.

When Wynton had to go out to a sound check for a performance around the corner at Alice Tully Hall, he told Wynton, Jr., and Simeon, also spending the weekend with Wynton, to take care of Jasper. Wynton, Jr., with a sweet, quiet demeanor, resembled Candace. Simeon seemed to blend the looks of his parents. Jasper looked exactly like Wynton.

Wynton always admired Victoria. Not only was she beautiful, but "she is extremely strong, very intelligent, and independent," he said. He knew she had survived a difficult childhood. For one thing, she had one white parent and one African-American parent. She had weathered those complications well and had grown up to win several awards for her acting skills. And she could write; she wrote one story for a women's magazine about the complexities and rewards of raising her own child of mixed race. (When she met Wynton, she already had a daughter, Maya, whose father was white.) Wynton was particularly admiring when he read one of her stories. "Shit, you can write like that? And you're spending your time [fooling with my nerves?]" he said, joking with her.

He really liked women with Victoria's attributes—"women who are really strong and intelligent like my mama," he said, "who have that type of power, and that type of magisterial beauty. I like a woman with a lot of fire. That's how Victoria is. She has a lot of heat in her. And she is very committed to a lot of things—like her commitment to foster kids. Above all, she loves her kids.

"I have been lucky with Victoria and Candace. Above all of our personal situations, we are concerned with our children. Our kids never have to go through any dumb shit on account of us. Like people don't want you to see your children? Or you have to go through changes? We don't have to deal with any of that. I've been very fortunate. Victoria truly looks out for her kids and puts them first. And she has an unbelievable work ethic and stamina. She can be sweet, and she has that fire, too."

Stanley Crouch thought Wynton had never married because he might not have found anyone interesting enough. Wynton said, "I can't say that. I've met plenty of interesting people." He didn't know, he said, if he would get married one day. "Maybe I will do that. Probably, I'm sure I will.

"I think [a relationship with a woman] is a beautiful thing when it works. My whole generation has a problem. I really connect to the over-obsession with sex and the lack of romance that we were given, and that we all have been victimized with, and also the increased rights for women. Once women have the kind of rights that we have today, the whole structure of marriage and family life is going to change. You're going to have a bad period like what we have now. But in the long run it will work out for the better, because the more freedom of choice everyone has, the fuller the life you're going to live will be.

"You have my mother's generation and things they had to do," Wynton said. "Now it's not like that. So in relationships you're going to have a problem, because all of the philosophy and religions are structured that other way. But the new way that will come will be better, because you won't have women sitting around mad all the time. You'll have people choosing to do what they want to do. You'll have another conception of marriage, another conception of a relationship.

"The first thing is: You can't have a society in which, from the time you're twelve, everything is telling you fuck fuck fuck fuck fuck and get as much pussy as you can. . . . You have kids eleven, twelve, thirteen years old, when all they're thinking about is fucking anyway. And you're just selling them this image all the time. 'Get you some pussy. Get you some pussy. Get you some pussy.' I know this, because this is what we did [when we were growing up].

"Then, all of a sudden, after you've lived this whole lifestyle for six or seven years, you're supposed to know what's a serious relationship and be romantic. That doesn't make sense. Those things don't equate with each other. That's your social life that you've lived. You've grown up in the system. And you can't tell a twelve-year-old that pimps are what's happening, and women are bitches, and all that shit they put out here for you, unquestioned, unchallenged. And then you're supposed to be twenty and mature and enter into a holy relationship in the eyes of God. Those things don't equate with each other.

"First it starts off with a premise that sex is wrong, which is a fucked up premise. It's not wrong. It's a beautiful thing. But it's like everything else. You have to know how to balance what you're doing.

But if all you're getting from the time you're twelve is 'Get some pussy,' it's all used to sell shit. Then everybody wants you to go back to ye olden days, an agricultural lifestyle, big families. Why would you think they're going to do that?"

⟶➤●◄⟵

Not only did his girlfriends see him when he could fit them into his schedule, but so did his men friends, some of them in distant cities. Young musicians came and went in his apartment when he was there to give them lessons, take them to the nearby basketball court, or simply talk with them. Some people thought he didn't like to be alone. "It's true," he said. "I was always around my brothers—and everybody."

Wynton kept in touch with his longtime, trusted friends by telephone, and he tried to gather them around him at times: Skip Norris, the successful businessman in Detroit; K—Dr. Ken Mask, the radiologist who settled in New Orleans; Wynton's childhood buddy Larry Dillon, who had given up music and taught tennis in New Jersey; and Tony Parker, the police officer in Chicago—most of them had settled lives in their own cities. Wynton saw them when he passed through; he was eager to include them in his life.

In 1998 Wynton traveled by car to New Orleans, stopping along the way to give a performance. By prearrangement, he met K, and they drove with other friends across the country, through Texas, to California, where he performed and also visited Jasper at Victoria Rowell's house. Wynton and his friends accumulated great memories along the way; they laughed, talked, and ate good meals, K said. What did they talk about? Laugh about? Maybe basketball. It didn't matter. That was the way they had always spent time together, K said. Wynton felt he had actually spent his life like that, alternating between laughing with friends and focusing with absolute seriousness on music.

K claimed that Wynton had a harem of women around the country. "It's true," K said. He was far from the first person to say that.

"It's a lie, and [Wynton] knows it," Skip Norris said.

Wynton thought the notion of a harem was hilarious. He knew he had been fortunate to meet a number of attractive women in his travels. And he appreciated a good story. His brother Branford described the Southerner's spirited approach to storytelling—about anything: "We don't just say it's hotter than hell. We say, 'It's hotter than a cow peeing on a flat rock.' Northerners say, 'It's sure raining out there.' Southerners talk. The shit is just colorful. . . .

"Southern people are just natural born storytellers. In the [PBS] Civil War documentary [by Ken Burns], these professors came on and said that the Civil War was about this, the Civil War was about that. And Shelby Foote, the Civil War historian, came on and said, 'Let me tell you a story.' And that's what the South is about. . . . Wynton got his ability to tell stories from growing up in the South. And in addition there's my father."

Branford was talking about Wynton's storytelling talent, which served him as an educator, but Wynton could use the talent effectively in or about any area of his life. "No matter how sophisticated Wynton's language is, his delivery is incredibly homespun. So no matter how much he's waxing, and whatever the degree of language, whether we're talk about Shakespeare or Wagner or Bulldog Slim—Bulldog Slim is just a Southern name, something steeped in traditional Southern negritude— he tells the story in a style that makes people immediately comfortable. Even if you have to tell a little lie, as good storytellers do, which sometimes he has been known to do, you have to get the point across, to stretch the truth with a little taste," Branford said.

JAZZ AT LINCOLN CENTER: A FULL CONSTITUENT

With hindsight, Rob Gibson would feel extremely proud of the way that he and Wynton ran Jazz at Lincoln Center together. They talked to each other three or four times a day on the phone and spent a couple of hours a day discussing their activities. As artistic director of Lincoln Center, Wynton was scheduled to spend about six months on the road that year; Gibson programmed all the activity in conjunction with Wynton and arranged all of the itineraries.

Nat Leventhal knew that Gibson and Wynton often talked at three or four o'clock in the morning. Puzzled about when they slept, Leventhal figured they were simply used to the jazz life with late-night gigs. Or maybe it was just that they were young. In any case, Leventhal was amazed at what they accomplished; the jazz program was the biggest success story at Lincoln Center in two decades. They had started a new enterprise, become world famous at it, produced best-selling CDs of performances at Lincoln Center, started a national radio broadcast series, carried out international tours, won acclaim from critics around the world, and showed a financial bottom line that satisfied Lincoln Center.

Leventhal thought the program had come along at the right time. Lincoln Center gave jazz a boost. And the brilliance of Wynton and Rob

Gibson together worked magic. "Don't underestimate the importance of Rob Gibson and his partnership with Wynton," Leventhal said, assessing the program. "Rob's one smart cookie and very creative."

Leventhal knew that after Jazz at Lincoln Center became a constituent, it grew much faster than it would have under him. He never would have taken the risks, expanding the program so dramatically each year. He would have been more conservative. "And I would have been wrong," he said. "They know what they're doing. We're the world's most famous jazz program. Who would have believed that in 1987? We were just trying to fill Alice Tully Hall, which was dark in those days."

Leventhal was personally charmed by Wynton's warmth and lack of pretension. Early in 1998, at the annual jazz gala, a fundraiser, Wynton played with the pianist Oscar Peterson to a very quiet, respectful audience at Avery Fisher Hall. A few weeks later, Wynton spoke about the gala at a Lincoln Center board meeting, saying, "My hands were sweating, I was so nervous playing with Oscar Peterson." Leventhal knew Wynton wasn't just trying to ingratiate himself but was truly awestruck by Peterson.

"It's Wynton's humility," Leventhal noted. "He can be very lofty and difficult when he's talking about matters of musical principle. He's loathe to consider compromise. But that doesn't translate into a personal rigidity or heavy-handedness. He couldn't be nicer, and he is committed beyond belief to this music and Lincoln Center. We appreciate it."

Jazz at Lincoln Center was one of Wynton's primary commitments, but not his only one. He had family commitments; his two eldest sons often spent weekends with him, when he was in New York. Wynton liked to stay home with them instead of going out to clubs on his free weekend nights. He noticed similarities between his childhood relationship with Branford and his sons' behavior. Wynton had imitated Branford in many ways.

"My kids do that," Wynton said. "My second son, Simeon, learns from his brother Wynton, and Simeon's always kind of competing with his brother. He's always playing and talking with his brother. He always wants to go places if Wynton is going. Ask Simeon if he wants to do something, and 'Is Wynton going?' he wants to know. I took Wynton on the road without Simeon, and Wynton missed his brother. He wants to be with his brother. Now when they get there, they fight."

Wynton's friends noticed. Wynton had the ability to talk to other people's children on their own level, playfully and affectionately, while he imparted lessons to them. Herlin Riley's eldest son, Merlin, was having problems in school and at home. Herlin thought his son was smart, but manipulative in his own way. "He was fooling around, with so much play in him that he wasn't reaching his full potential," as Herlin described it. Though Merlin had met Wynton a few times, it wasn't until Wynton took his own sons to New Orleans in the summer of 1997 that Merlin got to know Wynton better.

Wynton invited him to go to New York and hang out with him for a couple of weeks. Herlin didn't go along. It was just Wynton, Merlin, and Wynton's sons Wynton and Simeon, who went to museums, Harlem, and wherever and whatever Wynton thought he and the kids would enjoy. Herlin never knew exactly what Wynton talked about to Merlin, but when Merlin went home to New Orleans, Herlin noticed a change. Merlin seemed more serious. When he returned to school, Herlin didn't have to ask him if he did his homework. He just automatically did it. The school stopped calling the Rileys about Merlin's behavior problems. He didn't have any. He went from C's and D's to A's and B's on his report card. When Herlin told Wynton, Wynton said he had taken other kids under his wing, acted as a mentor, and gotten results most times. Herlin was sure nothing was 100 percent. But you couldn't tell that from Merlin.

"So," Rob Gibson continued, with pride and reverence for Wynton, "he has his own life as Wynton Marsalis, and as a spokesman for jazz music. He has many honorary doctorates. One night in the spring of 1998, he was in Washington, D.C., with Billy Taylor, playing at the Kennedy Center. The night before that, he was at the French Embassy in Washington, doing a benefit for the Duke Ellington High School for the Arts.

"But one of his top priorities, about eight months of the year, is Lincoln Center, of which he is artistic director and leader of the orchestra. A great deal of what Lincoln Center is about is him. And I'm executive director and producer, my exact title. I just call myself director. We have different functions. We program it together, because he's busy, and he doesn't have time to program every single little thing.

"We wouldn't be anywhere near where we are if it weren't for Wynton," Gibson said, "He could be off making millions of dollars playing with a quintet or a septet, but he has chosen to sacrifice financial gain for something that he truly believes in, for, as he put it so aptly to me several years ago, the power that one has as an individual is nowhere near the power that one has as an individual combined with the power and the weight of an institution like Lincoln Center. So if you associate yourself with the institution, which he did, then you have the weight of the institution combined with your own power. Then you can really create some changes.

"We're by far the youngest art form and by far the fastest growing constituent on the [Lincoln Center] campus of the twelve—the first new constituent created by Lincoln Center since 1969," Gibson said.

"Jazz at Lincoln Center has a board of directors, but as far as the people who run it, there's a staff of about thirty-five people who report to me," he said, "and a band of people reporting to Wynton. The day-to-day operations are directed by me, and the operations on the road plus artistic portions directed by Wynton. The board of directors is comprised of people from the media, for example Ed Bradley of CBS, and from the financial community, and from the political world, and many well-known real estate people, and music industry people such as Ahmed Ertegun, who founded Atlantic Records."

All performances at Lincoln Center since 1991 were taped, and thousands of tapes existed by 1998. The number of tapes made in a year varied from fifty to 100, multiplied over the years, for the program's archive.

Jazz at Lincoln Center raised five million dollars for the endowment. Income from the endowment is reinvested in it. Its operating budget comes from ticket sales, and other kinds of earned income, and fundraising from foundations, corporations, and individuals. That money sustains the staff and all the events and programs—everything that Jazz at Lincoln Center is involved in.

There are three primary objectives for Lincoln Center: curatorial, which encompasses the programming objectives; educational; and archival—that is, documentation, which comprises "all our lectures, films, programs, education programs, and over 250 master classes all over the country, and really all over the world," Gibson explained. "Sometimes the documentation is done on video, always on audio." He and Wynton want to make the archive available to future generations. Stanley Crouch, as artistic consultant, "was much more involved in the Classical Jazz period," Gibson explained, "but now his primary job is writing program notes, and he occasionally gives us artistic advice. We also have a Latin music advisor, Rene Lopez, a Latin Jazz authority, who lives in the Bronx; and Phil Schaap, a noted jazz historian and broadcaster; and Albert

Murray, a board member, who gives a great deal of artistic advice. But the program is done by myself and Wynton for the most part."

Whether Wynton had sacrificed millions of dollars that he could have made with his own group to devote himself to Lincoln Center is a fascinating idea, and one that can't be proved or disproved. From all his varied sources of income, said one of his best friends, Skip Norris in Detroit, Wynton was a millionaire several times over. His manager, denying that Wynton is a millionaire, would not reveal his annual income. But Skip Norris said, "One year he worked 306 days, another year 311 days, and [his managers] have really taken care of his money, with wise investments, stocks and bonds, real estate. And he lives modestly." His music products—CDs and videos—probably sold in the neighborhood of 200,000 units a year, with a good recording selling 75,000 or more, Skip estimated.

In 1996 Jazz at Lincoln Center moved from the Rose Building to its own new offices under the fountain in the center's main plaza. The offices are strung out along a corridor, with no windows, and so the interior is decorated in bright colors to make up for the lack of a view. One office, for example, has lime-, purple-, and mustard-colored walls; another has blue and red walls. Wynton's office has bright red walls. There, under the fountain, Wynton can walk to his heart's content from office to office. This is Skain's domain.

Asked for high points of the program, Gibson thought the 1998, nine-week tour around the world for the Lincoln Center Jazz Orchestra titled "All Jazz Is Modern" was one of the most successful projects. "Obviously, I think becoming a constituent at Lincoln Center was a high point," he said. "We have a deep, abiding commitment to do this the rest of our lives. It's a long-term project. And we're just cranking up. [Let's say we're] an elevator in a twenty-story building; we have gone from the ground floor to the mezzanine, with nineteen more floors to go—a long way."

And so it came to pass that, after Jazz at Lincoln Center became a full constituent in July 1996, the number of concerts and events and educational programs kept growing.

One of the crown jewels was the Essentially Ellington High School Band Competition and Festival, which was created to make Ellington's music available to high school students. In his travels, Wynton had been dismayed that high school bands didn't play what he considered to be the best-quality music. He felt they would learn a lot more by playing Ellington's music. So he helped invent a grand remedy. It began in 1996 as a Tri-State Festival in the New York City area, the next year expanded to include schools in the Northeast and mid-Atlantic states, and in 1998 grew to encompass schools from twenty-six states east of the Mississippi River.

As explained in an official Lincoln Center brochure in May 1998, each of 584 schools, which responded to the program's outreach, received a package containing five complete Duke Ellington charts in original arrangements, specially transcribed and published for the program. Then 137 schools sent in applications and tapes of their bands playing three of the compositions. Judges selected fifteen finalists, and those bands showed up to compete at Avery Fisher Hall. The three top-placing bands performed after intermission at an evening concert, after which they received their awards: $8,000 to the first place band, $6,000 to the second place, and $4,000 to the third place, with two honorable mention award winners receiving $2,000 each, and $1,000 to each finalist. The ceremony also acknowledged outstanding soloists and sections in the bands. Each band brought its well-wishers and cheering sections, who expressed their support repeatedly. They even cheered for the rivals whom they liked.

In the spring of 1998, Branford—who helped Wynton judge the initial tapes of the contestants—joined Wynton and the other judges listening to the bands. In the evening, for the first half of the concert, Branford played with the Lincoln Center Jazz Orchestra. Wynton's men wore their usual formal suits; Branford played in his shirt sleeves, a charming touch signifying independence for this interesting man who never likes to play it quite the company way.[1]

For the 1999 season, the centennial celebration of Duke Ellington's birthday, the festival planned to include bands from all fifty states, with about twenty bands to be selected as finalists. A two-day concert was planned for the finalists, expanding beyond the original single-day program.

⸻⸱⸱⸱⸱⸱⸱⸱⸱⸱⸱⸱⸱⸱⸱⸱⸱⸱

Wynton personally continued to receive constant attention in the media and a stream of honorary doctorates from such schools as Rutgers

University and Yale University, whose scholarship he had passed up as a teenager. He was also appointed to prestigious arts councils, among them the New York State Council on the Arts in 1997. But his most significant achievement was winning the Pulitzer Prize in 1997 for his oratorio, *Blood on the Fields*. Wynton had actually composed this work in 1994, when it had its premiere in New York City. Many critics appeared to have missed that single performance. However, one critic, Chip Deffaa, who attended the premiere that year, gave the long piece a very favorable review: "Despite some tedious stretches—the impact of the 2-1/2 hour long work would be heightened by tough editing—this is the 32 year old Marsalis's most ambitious, adventurous and impressive work yet. Some segments . . . are devastatingly brilliant on every level: music, lyrics, arrangement and execution. This is Marsalis's first composition for his big band. I wish he hadn't waited so long to write for big band, because he has an enormous contribution to make. The introductory bars alone were as strikingly original as anything I've heard in years. His uses of color show he has learned well the lessons of Ellington. . . . Marsalis's own solo contributions on trumpet, hot and inventive, also commanded attention . . . ."[2]

After this single performance, Wynton didn't record the oratorio until 1996. At that time, he also planned a 1997 tour for the Lincoln Center Jazz Orchestra to perform it in fifteen cities in the United States and then for two weeks in Europe. The difficult music must have been arduous for him and his group to play night after night.

Wynton explained his composition to Thomas Sancton, who had written the 1990 *Time* magazine cover story on Wynton. Sancton interviewed the composer in Marciac, France, in the summer of 1995.[3] Wynton was enjoying a visit to his favorite jazz festival there, where he had the chance to see a bronze statue erected in his honor.

As Wynton conceived the work, it was both a historical description of the African-American experience and a comment on contemporary life. As he explained, "It's set in slavery times, but it's not about slaves really. It's about today. The only part that's about slavery is the beginning part, which takes place on the slave ship. I use all kinds of music. The basis of it is blues, and also spirituals, which is before the blues. I have things that come out of choral writing, chants, contrapuntal textures. New Orleans-type things, modal progressions, things with chord changes like the standard popular songs, ballads. I have a band set up like a Greek chorus. . . .

"The band speaks. Kind of like a congregation commenting on the action. I try to have some pieces where you go through different moods. Like in the beginning when [singer] Cassandra [Wilson] is supposed to sound like she's losing her mind. It has lots of different things, like shouts and sounds going back to spasm bands. A lot of the stuff is real contemporary."

Wynton explained how the characters were based in history yet expressed contemporary concerns. "Cassandra's character [Leona] poses a question, which is like today, contemporary life. When a woman says, 'Move over,' she doesn't mean move over, she means come closer. You see what I mean? So automatically, you're starting off with this thing that is like a lot of contemporary relationships. It's told from an African American perspective, but really it's the American perspective. That's the basis for a lot of our problems: you're hearing one thing, but what's actually being said is another thing.

"She's on the slave ship, and she thinks she hears a drum. But it's a different drum than a traditional drum. She thinks she hears a drum coming from way back; it's like an ancestral thing. Then the man comes in and she starts to go crazy. She's calling for her mother—she's in a slave ship, man, her hair is stinky, and she's never been on water. She thinks monsters are going to eat her, it's beyond her wildest imagination."

The man who appeared at this point in the work was the character of an African prince. He was played by the singer Miles Griffith, a powerful baritone with a profound experience of singing gospel music.

Wynton noted, "This piece is about [the prince] identifying himself, and about what it takes for him to learn what soul is. He believes he is one thing, but he really is not. He's confused in his identity. And that's about today. . . ."

While the work drew on the jazz tradition, it also used many other musical styles. Wynton said, "It's coming from the perspective of jazz. But it's not something in the contemporary sense of trying to combine all these things into fusion and some new thing. You know, I never really try to do that. It's new because it's never been played this way. With something like this, from the very first piece it's so wild. There's all kinds of sounds, different types of polyphonic things. Five saxophonists playing five totally different lines."

Wynton noted that, in the later parts of the work, he had left a lot of room for soloists, sometimes just blocking out chords for them, the way

Ellington had done for his musicians. He noted, "As the piece progresses, as the characters become freer, there is more room for people to play. In the beginning a lot of it is all written out."

Wynton commented on the relation of composing to performing, "Composing comes out of playing. Because when you play, you hear a lot of different things. If you play trumpet, it all just comes out of the trumpet. It depends on what someone's hearing, you know? Ornette Coleman once came around my house and told me he could hear a lot of different connotations in my playing. It surprised me. Because he's not given to just praising, he's not that type of man. He said it was like language. . . .

"After playing, I'll hear something. They say that Duke used to compose after a gig, when I guess he could still hear all of the music. Monk would sit down and play for a long time; then he would compose."

For Wynton, composing began when he was able to select a form for his work: "I just try to hear, you know, get some type of form and just fill the form in. Everything starts from the form for me. Things like the keys I want to go in, who I want to play what part, like a grid. If it's a real big piece, you have to have that or else it can just meander. A lot of times I write pieces that are real long, but I am very meticulous with the form. I want to make sure that it's unified and integrated. Sometimes I use the melody notes as the basis of the progression. If I have something with different movements in it, I get a key scheme that goes across all of the movements. Maybe I get the key scheme from the notes in the melody. I just try to make sure that I have something coherent. The progressions and the melodies just come to me. I just hear them. . . . "

Wynton believed that his teaching style came out of how he approached performing: "It just comes out of playing. To me, the source of all of your power is the creative playing and the art of music itself. With teaching, you communicate a lot more than just what you tell the students. And I always tell them, when I really criticize them, that I'm coming in the spirit of love. Because they have to know that you're not there to put them down—that you're there to impart some information and that it's not biased. In the service and interest of music, it's coming from a perspective of love and the desire to see them develop. You know, if you've taught a certain number of kids and you have the experience of doing it, you just develop a feeling for it." He attributed his teaching methods, too, to his observations of his father, and Alvin Batiste, Kidd Jordan, Danny Barker, "their way of teaching is just down home."

By that, he meant, "you've got to just love the students and you have to want to communicate that. You also have to know that the communication and interpersonal stuff really comes from God. It's a spiritual thing, really. Teaching is a very spiritual thing. The whole crux of everything is the spirituality. . . . When we were doing *Making the Music*, the twenty-six hour series for National Public Radio, all of the musicians we interviewed said that, if you don't have love in your music, you can't be great."

Wynton took the time to teach because he truly enjoyed it. He didn't do it out of some sense of mission, or to "pass the torch" to younger players. He didn't even believe that was possible: "You can't pass the torch on; somebody has to come up who wants to take it. It's not up to you to do that. If somebody wants to pick up the torch of something, it can be long-dead and they'll pick it up. Picasso used to always say that he could make forms of art come alive that had been dead for a hundred centuries. And he could do that. Like Louis Armstrong—he could just raise sounds from the dead, sounds that hadn't resonated for who knows how many years, and this trumpeter would resonate them. He wouldn't even say that he was trying to do it. But he did it, you know. Things just have a spiritual resonance to them. That's what it's all about."

—————

Through the 1990s, reams of stories came out about Wynton, about the programs presented at Lincoln Center—the joyful Jelly Roll Morton concerts, the elevating Ellingtons, the mixed repertoire concerts, the Wynton Marsalis compositions—the CDs of his works, and the works he composed for other arts programs and companies. Sometimes the reviews were less than jubilant for particular concerts, and some stories contained sniping remarks about Wynton by critics and by musicians, too. Keith Jarrett trivialized Wynton in the *New York Times*. Lester Bowie and Wynton had their own war, as did David Murray and Wynton. But on the whole, Wynton Marsalis on his own and with Jazz at Lincoln Center maintained fine reputations.

The titles of the stories that appeared about Wynton, his performances, his policies for Lincoln Center, and his band give an idea of the varied points of view expressed in the mainstream and music press. There was "Wynton Marsalis: The Professor of Swing," in *Life* magazine in

August 1993. "It's Jazz, Stupid," had a negative slant in November 1993, in the *Village Voice*. "Lincoln Center Jazz Series Draws Flak" came out in the *Detroit Free Press* in 1994. "Marsalis and Critics Lock Horns" was in the *New York Post*, November 1994. "Wynton Marsalis's Evangelical Peal" ran in the *Washington Post* in March 1995. "Stop Nitpicking a Genius" was the title of an appreciative article by Frank Conroy, a well-known writer and one-time jazz pianist, for the *New York Times Sunday Magazine* in June 1995. When Wynton said, "I'm tired of all this stuff they're writing about me. It has nothing to do with music," Conroy quoted a philosophical maxim for Wynton to take to heart: "The dogs bark, but the caravan rolls on." Wynton laughed and said he would have to remember that.

"Watching Wynton" was one article with a negative slant that ran in the *Village Voice* in October 1995. Another that month was entitled "Marsalis and Friends Play Ellington, Selflessly," which appeared in the *New York Times*. "The Marsalises: The First Family of Jazz Is, First, a Family" was published in *Request* magazine in September 1995. *Life* magazine called Wynton one of "The 50 Most Influential Boomers" in July 1995. In June 1996 *Time* magazine included Wynton in a feature story, "America's 25 Most Influential People."

The criticisms of Wynton by the end of the 1990s were, at most, a rehashing. For one thing, Wynton had prevailed, and it was pointless for anyone to keep writing the same complaints, when they didn't change anything. In a private conversation, one critic in his forties, with a generally unflattering view of Wynton, persisted in repeating the usual criticisms of Jazz at Lincoln Center and calling Wynton "a bright young man," when he was nearly thirty-seven years old, not really young anymore. When reporters sat down with Wynton, they found him so agreeable that they said he was mellowing. Some of his friends said the same thing about him, and others, both friends and writers, thought he was the same way he had always been: charming, friendly, outspoken as any person had a right to be, and defensive when he thought he was being maligned.

Wynton himself remained eminently quotable, with his intrinsic, seductive dash: "All you can do is get in the ocean, try to swim, look at some of the fish, catch somethin' you want to eat, have a good-ass time. You can't make it across. You can't influence it. Its course was set in motion long before you was born. You can't do nothin' but participate in it and love it, because if you hate it, you still got to be out in the ocean."[4]

———⊶⊷———

It wasn't until the CD of *Blood on the Fields*—recorded in 1995 but not released until 1996—that most critics had a chance to assess it; predictably, reactions ran the gamut from negative to superlative. A fine one, which appeared in the *Chicago Tribune*, praised the piece and underscored the importance of the Pulitzer Prize that it had won. The author, Howard Reich, mentioned that Duke Ellington had been denied a Pulitzer in 1965, essentially because of racial prejudice. Reich wrote about Wynton's victory: "From coast to coast, newspapers trumpeted the same remarkable tune: A jazz artist had won a prestigious award hitherto given only to classical musicians. 'Marsalis Swings a Pulitzer,' noted *USA Today*, evoking the jazz idiom with its choice of verb. 'Wynton Marsalis Captures Music Honors; First Jazz Artist To Do So,' said the *Los Angeles Times*.

"But the real significance of Marsalis's award . . . runs deeper than that. By awarding the prize to jazz trumpeter bandleader Marsalis, the Pulitzer board gave the distinctly American art of jazz improvisation a degree of recognition and honor it never had received." Reich went on to say that the oratorio drew on both jazz and classical traditions and therefore represented a broad spectrum of American musical tradition. "[T]o hear [on the CD] Marsalis's radiant trumpet lines" along with the singers Jon Hendricks, Miles Griffith, and Cassandra Wilson, and other performers, and the "resplendent chords and the rhythm section's pervasive swing backbeat was to savor a major composition that could not have been created without improvisation. Further, 'Blood on the Fields' evoked many sprawling jazz pieces that Marsalis and his sidemen have invented over the last decade, from the hypnotic 'Majesty of the Blues' (1989) to the three-CD 'Soul Gestures in Southern Blue' (1991) to the evocative 'In This House/On This Morning' (1994)." The Pulitzer committee also opened the door wide for jazz by changing its rules, providing that improvisation became an accepted part of the Pulitzers from then on. "As the 20th century approaches its end, the development comes not a moment too soon," wrote Reich.[5]

In private, Wynton's recording producer, Steve Epstein, praised Wynton, his work, and of course *Blood on the Fields*. Epstein was impressed by how much Wynton had listened to both classical music and jazz, and "how important Bartók and Stravinsky and Beethoven were, and Pops [Louis Armstrong] and Ellington; they're of equal importance to him," Epstein said. He recalled how he went to a hotel with Wynton, when Wynton was about to record Bach's "Brandenburg" Concerto No. 2; Wynton sat down at the piano and analyzed every chord. "He said, 'Listen to how this motif relates to that, and how this relates to that.' He is so enthusiastic. Like music is oozing from every pore. It puts you in a very good mood."

Having watched Wynton develop from a composer for small groups to large groups, Epstein admired the way his music became, by the time he wrote *Blood on the Fields*, "more complex, more harmonically dense. All of this is an amalgam, a distillation of his listening and playing over the years. And yet his music is still very accessible."

Not everybody involved in the jazz world as listeners and critics liked the oratorio, of course. A curious review, probably one of the worst Wynton ever received for anything he had ever done, came from Gary Giddins. Giddins disparaged the oratorio, harping on its length and musical components, and calling it "an exercise in unqualified hubris...."[6] Giddins didn't even think that Wynton had a right to the Pulitzer Prize for 1996, since the piece had first been performed and recorded in earlier years.

Responding to Giddins's lambasting of the oratorio, Branford Marsalis rose to defend his brother in a letter to the editor of the *Village Voice*: "Reading Gary Giddins's dismal assessment of my brother Wynton's recent masterpiece ... made me realize how pathetic critical evaluation of modern music is today. ... Giddins still insists Wynton's improvisational trumpet style is a mere imitation of older musicians. In reality, Wynton is the one who has extended the vocabulary of jazz and classical trumpet playing over the past 25 years. With a clear tone and soulful execution, he has made an indelible mark on all young trumpeters. ... Though I do not expect Giddins to understand or appreciate music as complex as 'Blood on the Fields,' an unjust music review anywhere is a threat to just reviews everywhere." To which letter Giddins appended his last lick, "I'm as in favor of brotherly love as anyone, but 'soulful execution'?"[7]

Hundreds of events filled the calendar for Jazz at Lincoln Center in the 1990s, more and more with each passing year. It seemed as if the organization had paid attention to some of the reasonable criticisms. (Though Gibson would comment "we've never based the hiring of any musician on skin color." He did recall however such confusing incidents as a 1993 night when ten musicians, all of them black, showed up to play in a concert. Then three nights later, the Jazz at Lincoln Center Orchestra performed with seven whites and eight black musicians.) Two white trumpeters sat in the section at the end of the decade. One, Seneca Black, was in training as a lead trumpeter under Wynton's wing; the second was Ryan Kisor. Ted Nash, a white musician, had joined the saxophone section. Wayne Goodman and Joe Temperley remained. Of course, no white jazz composer's work was slated for a night of tribute in the last days of the millennium, when the 100th anniversary of Duke Ellington's birth dwarfed all other considerations for Wynton and his associates. Yet Jazz at Lincoln Center had very bright prospects, despite whatever limitations of vision occasionally evidenced themselves.

In the winter of 1998, it was announced that the Coliseum at Columbus Circle at 59th Street was going to be torn down, and a new concert hall and rehearsal space erected there. Mayor Rudolph Giuliani stood wholeheartedly behind the plan , with the idea that it would afford more room for the performance of operas, Nat Leventhal said, but the performance space would actually be used extensively by Jazz at Lincoln Center. How extensively? It remained to be seen, and that wouldn't happen until at least 2004, when the building would actually be finished (and Mayor Giuliani would be out of office).

If carping occasionally surfaced about Wynton, the best way for Wynton to handle it was by trying to duck the fray. It could only distract him from music, despite his prodigious ability to concentrate. Gunther Schuller, for one, told Wynton to avoid talking to the press too much. Then Schuller noticed that Wynton kept talking to everyone, drawn to opportunities "like a moth to a flame." Schuller knew the ropes very well. He could cite forty-four instances of having been misquoted in *Time* magazine alone, he said. But Wynton's methods, which had established him as a spokesman, had created a good and brilliant future for jazz (and hadn't hurt his own career at all).

Wynton reflected that he had been motivated by a desire to help jazz musicians like his father, who had so much to give and found so little acceptance. Wynton also wanted to make older musicians proud of him.

Despite the controversies that had beset him, he felt he had done so. "I think it," he told Ed Bradley softly and earnestly on *60 Minutes.*

Branford Marsalis philosophized that he wouldn't want the constant criticism that Wynton faced, nor the responsibility of running a jazz program as far-reaching as the one at Lincoln Center. He said, "I wouldn't want that job for all the tea in China. . . . A lot of people could do it, but not as good as he can. . . . But it's not a job that I would want. . . . I didn't think it was the kind of thing he *would* do. But he can do anything well. What can't he do well? . . . I think that what he has done so far is wonderful."

CHAPTER NOTES

1. That was one of the reasons he had left *The Tonight Show*, he said. But then he had gone on to head the Jazz and New Music department at Sony; of course, there he had plenty of freedom to record artists whom he chose.
2. Chip Deffaa, "Marsalis' 'Blood' Is Full of Life." *New York Post*, April 4, 1994.
3. Thomas Sancton, "A Conversation With Wynton Marsalis." *Jazz Times*, March 1996. The following excerpts are taken from this extensive interview.
4. Touré, "Wynton Marsalis: The Icon Profile." *Icon Thoughtstyle*, August 1997.
5. Howard Reich, "Let Freedom Swing." *Chicago Tribune*, April 11, 1997.
6. Gary Giddins, "Classic Ambition." *Village Voice*, July 1, 1997.
7. "Letters to the Editor." *Village Voice*, July 17, 1997.

APPENDIX

The History of Jazz at Lincoln Center

Classical Jazz

In 1987 the original Classical Jazz at Lincoln Center had a budget of $146,300 for three New York City concerts. In 1988 the figure was $227,600 for four New York concerts. In 1989 the budget was $462,500 for a live national telecast from Lincoln Center and five concerts. In 1990 the budget was $526,100 for six New York concerts.

For the new, year-round *Jazz at Lincoln Center Program*, the budget in 1991-'92 was $1.3 million for seventeen New York City concerts, two Jazz for Young People Concerts, one commissioned composition, three lectures, and six jazz films.

In 1992–1993, the budget rose to $1.9 million for a similar, growing program, with the addition of a thirty-city, Lincoln Center Jazz Orchestra tour, master classes, jazz in the schools sessions, and the release of a CD.

In 1993–1994, the budget was $2.1 million for a similar, growing program and the inauguration of a radio program series, as well as six broadcasts over a local radio station, WQXR, and a second CD release.

In 1994–1995, the budget was $2.4 million for a similar program, with a thirty-two-city LCJO tour, plus a third CD release.

For the *constituency of Jazz at Lincoln Center* beginning officially on July 1, 1996, the aim was to establish the following "chairs":

Artistic Director's Chair, $1.5 million, to support the position of artistic director: "[T]he earnings from the endowed gift will cover the annual expenses associated with the Artistic Director's position, and will allow the establishment of a discretionary fund for the Artistic Director to develop and implement new artistic initiatives," read the official brochure.

The following also appeared in the brochure: The George Weisman Conductor's Chair, $1 million, income from which fund "will help finance the annual salary of the Lincoln Center Jazz Orchestra's conductor and the related expenses of the position during the year."

271

The Lincoln Center Jazz Orchestra Fund, $1 million, to support the orchestra's touring schedule and help subsidize ticket prices in "underserved communities within the United States. . . ."

The Jazz for Young People Concert Fund, $750,000, to "ensure that these highly popular concerts will continue at Lincoln Center."

Education Director's Chair, $500,000, to "coordinate the nationwide expansion of Jazz at Lincoln Center's education efforts, and implement the national High School Band Competition. An endowed chair is required to provide support for this newly-created position."

National High School Band Competition fund, $500,000, to "bring the competition to a wider number of high schools, first in the New York metropolitan area, then across the country."

Transription Fund, $500,000, "to finance [an] annual program to create accurate scores of masterpieces from the jazz canon. Each year, 30 to 50 such transcriptions are needed for the orchestra to continue expanding its repertoire."

The Ellington Transcription Fund was assigned $400,000; the Preservation Fund for the archives, $300,000; the Education Materials Fund, $250,000 "to develop new materials"; the Ticket Subsidy Fund, $250,000 for low-cost tickets for school groups for the regular season and young people's concerts; the New York City Outreach Fund, $250,000, to provide free concerts for people unable to afford tickets; the Lifetime Achievement Award, $250,000, to establish an award "to recognize substantial achievement in the field of jazz"; and the Artistic Initiatives Fund, $100,000, to develop new ideas and directions for Jazz at Lincoln Center.

DISCOGRAPHY

With Wynton as a Sideman

This section is a mere sampling. A reasonable estimate is that Wynton has appeared on scores of albums led by other artists. No complete discography on this aspect of Wynton's career exists.

Wynton Marsalis, (tpt) Bobby Watson (as), Billy Pierce (ts), James Williams (p), Ellis Marsalis (p-1), Charles Fambrough (b), Art Blakey (d), recorded live at Bubba's in Fort Lauderdale, Florida, October 11, 1980, on the Who's Who in Jazz Label, on a release entitled *Wynton*, although this date was actually led in the club by Art Blakey.

"Angel Eyes" (rw, bp out, em in on this song only) "Bitter Dose," "Jody" (bw, bp out), "Wheel Within a Wheel," "Gipsey."

Also, same personnel, date, and place, on Who's Who in Jazz, on a release entitled "The All American Hero."

"One By One," "My Funny Valentine" (rw, bp out), "Round 'Bout Midnight," "Eta or E.T.A.," "Time Will Tell," "Jody (Blakey's Theme)."

Art Blakey in Sweden, Art Blakey and the Jazz Messengers, recorded at Dodra Teatern, Stockholm, Sweden, March 9, 1981, on the Evidence label, with Wynton Marsalis (tpt), Bobby Watson (as), Billy Pierce (ts), James Williams (p), Charles Fambrough (b), Blakey (d).

"Webb City," "How Deep Is the Ocean," "Skylark," "Gypsy Folk Tales."

The Young Lions, Wynton Marsalis (tpt), James Newton (fl), John Blake (vln), Kevin Eubanks (g), Avery Sharpe (b), Ronnie Burrage (d), Bobby McFerrin (vcl). The Kool Jazz Festival, recorded in New York, June 30, 1982, Elektra Musician.

"Endless Flight."

(Newton and Blake out, Chico Freeman (ts) in on "Breakin'.")

Art Blakey and the Jazz Messengers, A La Mode. Recorded live at Keystone Korner, San Francisco, California, January 1982, with Branford Marsalis (as), Wynton Marsalis (tpt), Billy Pierce (ts), Donald Brown (p), Charles Fambrough (b), Blakey (d), Concord Jazz CCD-4196.

"In Walked Bud," "In a Sentimental Mood," "Fuller Love," "Waterfalls," "A La Mode."

The Beautyful Ones Are Not Yet Born, Branford Marsalis (ldr, saxes), Wynton Marsalis (tpt), Robert Hurst (b), Jeff "Tain" Watts (d). Wynton plays on only one track, "Cain and Abel." Recorded in New York, Columbia, 1991.

The Proper Angle, Charles Fambrough (ldr, b), with Kenny Kirkland (p), Branford Marsalis, Joe Ford (saxes), Wynton Marsalis, Roy Hargrove (tpt), Jeff "Tain" Watts (d), Steve Berrios (d, perc), Jerry Gonzalez (tpt, perc). Released in 1991, CTI Records.

Crescent City Serenade, Dr. Michael White (cl, ldr), 1991, Antilles; and "New Year's at the Village Vanguard," Dr. White (cl, ldr), New York, 1992, Antilles.

Note: Among the many other albums that have had a commercial release featuring Wynton Marsalis as a sideman have been "Destiny's Dance" led by saxophonist Chico Freeman on the Contemporary label, and albums by trumpeters Nicholas Payton and Roy Hargrove, singers Teresa Brewer and Shirley Horne. One very amusing sidelight: Wynton played trumpet under the pseudonym of E. Dankworth on Marcus Roberts's first CD, "Deep in the Shed," which was on the Novus label and at this writing is out of print.

With Wynton Marsalis as Leader

All are on Columbia unless otherwise noted. The primary, though not only, source for jazz recording dates and other information is *The Jazz Discography*, by Tom Lord, Vol. 13, Lord Music Reference, Inc., West Vancouver, B.C., Canada, published by that company and Cadence Jazz Books, Cadence Building, Redwood, NY 13679. Another work, which was referred to by the compiler of this discography, and which occasionally disagrees on dates with Tom Lord's book, is *70 Years of Recorded Jazz, 1917–1987*, by Walter Bruyninckx, privately published by the author, address Lange Nieuwstraat, 2800 Mechelen, Belgium. Shore Fire Media in Brooklyn, New York, Wynton Marsalis's publicity firm headed by Marilyn Laverty, has also provided some discographical details and support. According to Rob Gibson, several thousand tapes, which have had no commercial release, and with Wynton as leader, exist in the archives of Jazz at Lincoln Center.

God Rest Ye, Merry Jazzmen, Wynton Marsalis (tpt), Branford Marsalis (ts), Kenny Kirkland (p), Clarence Seay (b), Jeff "Tain" Watts (d). Recorded in New York, June 1981.

"We Three Kings of Orient Are."

Wynton Marsalis, Wynton Marsalis (tpt), Branford Marsalis (ts, sop), Kenny Kirkland (p), Clarence Seay (b), Jeff "Tain" Watts (d). Recorded in New York, August 1981.

"Father Time," "I'll Be There When the Time Is Right,"

(Seay out, Charles Fambrough (b) in on "Twilight.")

Wynton Marsalis, Branford Marsalis, Herbie Hancock (p), Ron Carter (b), Tony Williams (d), Recorded in Tokyo, 1981.

"RJ," "Sister Cheryl," "Who Can I Turn To When Nobody Needs Me?" (bm out), "Hesitation (Hancock out).

Fathers and Sons, Wynton Marsalis (tpt), Ellis Marsalis (p), Branford Marsalis (ts, as, sop), Charles Fambrough (b), James Black (d). Recorded in New York, 1982.

"Twelves It," "A Joy Forever," "Nostalgic Impressions," "Futuristic," "Lush Life."

Note: According to Bruyninckx's *70 Years of Record Jazz, 1917–1987*, this album was recorded in New York in April 1981. It took up one side of an LP, and saxophonists Chico and Von Freeman recorded for the other side.

Think of One, Wynton Marsalis (tpt), Branford Marsalis (sop, ts), Kenny Kirkland (p), Phil Bowler, Ray Drummond (b), Jeff "Tain" Watts (d). Recorded in New York, February 15 and 18, 1983.

"Knozz-Moe-King," "Fuchsia," "My Ideal," "What Is Happening Here?" "Think of One," "The Bell Ringer," "Later," "Melancholia."

Hot House Flowers, Wynton Marsalis (tpt), Branford Marsalis (sop, ts), Kent Jordan (alto fl), Kenny Kirkland (p), Ron Carter (b), Jeff "Tain" Watts (d), Charles Libove (vln), plus strings, double reeds, and other brass. Recorded in New York, May 30–31, 1984.

"Stardust," "Lazy Afternoon," "For All We Know," "When You Wish Upon a Star," "Django," "Melancholia," "Hot House Flowers," "I'm Confessin'."

Black Codes from the Underground, Wynton Marsalis (tpt), Branford Marsalis (sop, ts), Kenny Kirkland (p), Charnett Moffett (b), Ron Carter (b), Jeff "Tain" Watts (d). Recorded in New York, January 11 and January 14, 1985.

"Black Codes," "For Wee Folks," "Delfeayo's Dilemma," "Phyrzzinian Man," "Aural Oasis," "Chambers of Tain," "Blues" (wm, cm only).

J Mood, Wynton Marsalis (tpt), Marcus Roberts (p), Bob Hurst (b), Jeff "Tain" Watts (d). Recorded in New York, December 17–20, 1985.

"J Mood," "Presence That Lament Brings," "Insane Asylum," "Skain's Domain," "Melodique," "After," "Much Later."

Standard Time: Vol. 1, Wynton Marsalis (tpt), Marcus Roberts (p), Bob Hurst (b), Jeff "Tain" Watts (d). Recorded in New York, May 29–30, 1986 and September 24–25, 1986.

"Caravan," "April in Paris," "Cherokee," "Goodbye," "New Orleans," "Soon All Will Know," "Foggy Day," "The Song Is You," "Memories of You" (p solo), "In the Afterglow," "Autumn Leaves," "Cherokee" (2nd version).

Live at Blues Alley, Same personnel as above. Recorded live at the club in Washington, D.C., on December 19–20, 1986.

"Knozz-Moe-King," "Just Friends," "Knozz-Moe-King" (interlude), "Juan," "Cherokee," "Delfeayo's Dilemma," "Chambers of Tain," "Juan (E. Mustaad)," "Au Privave," "Knozz-Moe-King" (interlude), "Do You Know What It Means To Miss New Orleans," "Juan (Skip Mustaad)," "Autumn Leaves," "Knozz-Moe-King" (interlude), "Skain's Domain," "Much Later."

Thick in the South: Soul Gestures in Southern Blue, Vol. 1, Wynton Marsalis (tpt), Joe Henderson (ts), Marcus Roberts (p), Bob Hurst (b), Jeff Watts (d), Elvin Jones (d). Recorded in New York, probably in 1987.

"Harriet Tubman," "Elveen" (Watts out, Jones in), "Thick in the South," "So This Is Jazz, Huh?," "L.C. on the Cut" (Watts out, Jones in).

Intimacy Calling, Standard Time Vol. 2, Wynton Marsalis (tpt), Wessell Anderson (as), Todd Williams (ts), Marcus Roberts (p), Reginald Veal (b), Herlin Riley (d). Recorded in New York between September 1987 and August 1990.

"When It's Sleepy Time Down South," "You Don't Know What Love Is," "Indelible and Nocturnal," "I'll Remember April," "Embraceable You," "Crepuscule With Nellie," "The End of a Love Affair," "East of the Sun" (wm out), "Lover," "Yesterdays," "Bourbon Street Parade."

(Bob Hurst in, Veal out, Jeff Watts in, Riley out on "What Is This Thing Called Love?")

The Majesty of the Blues, Wynton Marsalis (tpt), Teddy Riley (tpt), Freddie Lonzo (tbn), Dr. Michael White (cl), Wessell Anderson (as), Todd Williams (ts, sop), Marcus Roberts (p), Danny Barker (bjo), Reginald Veal (b), Herlin Riley (d). Recorded in New York, October 27–28, 1988.

"The Majesty of the Blues," "Hickory Dickery Dock," "The New Orleans Function: The Death of Jazz" (Riley, Lonzo, and Barker in), "Premature

Autopsies" (Riley, Lonzo, Barker in), "Oh, But on the Third Day (Happy Feet Blues)" (Riley, Lonzo, Barker in).

Crescent City Christmas Card, Wynton Marsalis (tpt), Wycliffe Gordon (tbn), Alvin Batiste (cl), Wessell Anderson (as), Todd Williams (ts, sop, cl), Joe Temperley (bar, b-cl), Marcus Roberts (p), Reginald Veal (b), Herlin Riley (d), Kathleen Battle (vcl). Recorded in New York, January 24–25, and April 3–4, 1989.

"Carol of the Bells," "Silent Night" with Battle, "Hark the Herald Angels Sing," "Little Drummer Boy," "Let It Snow! Let It Snow! Let It Snow!," "'Twas the Night Before Christmas," "God Rest Ye Merry Gentlemen" (wm, wg, wa, jt out).

Ben Riley (d) in, Herman Riley out; Batiste, Temperley, Battle out; Jon Hendricks (vcl) in.

"Jingle Bells," "Sleigh Ride" (with Hendricks), "We Three Kings."

Wynton Marsalis (tpt), Wycliffe Gordon (tbn), Wessell Anderson (as), Todd Williams (sop).

"Tannenbaum."

Wynton Marsalis (tpt), Marcus Roberts (p), Reginald Veal (b), Herlin Riley (d).

"Winter Wonderland," "O Come All Ye Faithful" (p solo).

Uptown Ruler: Soul Gestures in Southern Blue Vol. 2, Wynton Marsalis (tpt), Todd Williams (ts), Marcus Roberts (p), Reginald Veal (b), Herlin Riley (d). Recorded in New York, probably 1989–1990.

"Psalm 26" (Williams and Riley out), "Uptown Ruler," "The Truth Is Spoken Here," "The Burglar," "Prayer," "Harmonique," "Down Home with Homey," "Psalm 26."

Levee Low Moan: Soul Gestures in Southern Blue Vol. 3, Wynton Marsalis (tpt), Wessell Anderson (as), Todd Williams (ts, sop), Marcus Roberts (p), Reginald Veal (b), Herlin Riley (d), recorded in New York, probably 1989–1990.

"Levee Loan Moan," "Jig's Jig," "So This Is Jazz, Huh?," "In the House of Williams," "Superb Acting."

Standard Time, Vol 3: The Resolution of Romance, Wynton Marsalis (tpt), Ellis Marsalis (p), Reginald Veal (b), Herlin Riley (d). Recorded in New York, circa 1990.

"In the Court of King Oliver," "Never Let Me Go" (rv, hr out), "Street of Dreams," "Where or When," "Bona and Paul," "The Seductress" (rv out), "A Sleepin' Bee" (wm out), "Big Butter and Egg Man," "The Very Thought of You," "I Cover the Waterfront," "How Are Things in Glocca Morra?" (rv, hr out), "My

Romance" (em piano solo), "In the Wee Small Hours of the Morning" (rv, hr out), "It's Too Late Now" (em piano solo), "It's Easy To Remember."

Live in Swing Town: Wynton Marsalis Septet, Wynton Marsalis (tpt), Wycliffe Gordon (tbn), Wessell Anderson, Walter Blanding (saxes), Marcus Roberts (p), Reginald Veal (b), Herlin Riley (d). Probably recorded in New York in the 1980s, circa 1987. On the Jazz Door label.

"The Legend of Buddy Bolden," "Swingdown Swingtown," "Highrise Riff," "Cherokee."

Note: This recording was possibly done without the knowledge of Marsalis, since it was not on Columbia.

Tune in Tomorrow, an original soundtrack, with Wynton Marsalis (tpt), Wycliffe Gordon (tbn), Wessell Anderson (as), Todd Williams (ts, sop, cl), Harvey Estrin (as-I), Alvin Batiste (cl), Dr. Michael White (cl-VI), Herb Harris (ts), Joe Temperley (bar), Marcus Roberts (p), Warren Bernhardt (org-II), Lucky Peterson (org-III), Reginald Veal (b), Herlin Riley (d), Johnny Adams (vcl-IV), Shirley Horn (vcl-V). Recorded in New York, circa 1991.

"Big Trouble in the Easy" (VI), "Kings of the Garden District" (wb-org solo), "Crescent City Crawl" (III), "Alligator Tail Drag" (VI), "May Be Fact or Fiction" (IV, VI), "Social Soft Shoe," "Mama Leona," "I Can't Get Started" (V), "The Grand Marshall" (ab out, VI in), "The Ways of Love," "On the Eve of Entry," "Don't Run From Fun," "Albanians" (ab out, I in), "Sunsettin' on the Bayou" (ab out, VI in), "The Ways of Love," "Double Rondo on the River" (VI).

I Like Jazz Two, with Wynton Marsalis (tpt), unknown personnel. Live performance, New York, probably 1991–1993. This appears on Columbia album CK57295.

"Embraceable You."

Portraits By Ellington, the Lincoln Center Jazz Orchestra, with Wynton Marsalis, Umar Sharia, Lew Soloff (tpt), Marcus Belgrave (tpt, flueghn), Norris Turney, Frank Wess (as), Bill Easley (ts, cl), Todd Williams (ts), Dr. Michael White (cl), Joe Temperley (bar), Wycliffe Gordon, Britt Woodman (tbn), Chuck Connors (b-tbn), Sir Roland Hanna (p), Reginald Veal (b), Kenny Washington (d, timp), Milt Grayson (vcl), Andy Stein (violn), Steve Nelson (vibes), Paul Meyers (g), David Berger, (cond). Recorded at Alice Tully Hall, Lincoln Center, August 10–11, 1991.

"Portrait of Louis Armstrong,'" with tpt solo, Marsalis, and Gordon out, Connors in; "Thanks for the Beautiful Land on the Delta,'" with ts solo, Williams, and Gordon out, Connors in; "Portrait of Bert Williams," with tpt solo Belgrave, cl solo Bill Easley, tbn solo Baron; "Bojangles," with ts solo Williams, cl solo Easley, p solo Hanna; "Self Portrait of the Bean," with ts solo

Williams; "Second Line,'" with cl. solo Dr. Michael White, tpt solo Marsalis, and Gordon out, Connors in; "Total Jazz (Final Movement of Portrait of Ella Fitzgerald)," p solo Hanna, tpt solo Belgrave, cl solo Easley, tbn solo Gordon, ts solo Williams; "Liberian Suite," I. "I Like the Sunrise," vcl Grayson, bar solo Temperley; II. "Dance No. 1," tpt solo Marsalis, ts solo Williams: III. "Dance No. 2," cl solo Easley, vibes Nelson, IV. "Dance No. 3," violn solo Stein, bar solo Temperley, tpt solo Soloff, V. "Dance No. 4," timp solo Washington, VI. "Dance No. 5," bar solo Temperley, tbn solo Baron, tpt Marsalis.

˙ From New Orleans Suite

Blue Interlude, Wynton Marsalis Septet, with Marsalis (tpt, p), Wycliffe Gordon (tbn), Wessell Anderson (as), Todd Williams (ts, sop, cl), Marcus Roberts (p), Reginald Veal (b), Herlin Riley (d). Recorded in New York, 1992.

"Brother Veal," "Monologue for Sugar Cane and Sweetie Pie" (Wynton Marsalis only), "Blue Interlude (The Bittersweet Saga of Sugar and Sweetie Pie)," "And the Band Played On," "The Jubilee Suite": "Day to Day," "Running and Rambling," "Grace"; "Sometimes It Goes Like That."

In This House, On This Morning, Wynton Marsalis Septet, Wynton Marsalis (tpt), Wycliffe Gordon (tbn), Wessell Anderson (as), Todd Williams (ts, sop), Eric Reed (p), Reginald Veal (b), Herlin Riley (d), Marion Williams (vcl). Recorded in New York, May 28–29, 1992, and March 20–21, 1993.

"Part I":

"Devotional, Call to Prayer, Processional, Representative Offerings, The Lord's Prayer."

"Part II":

"Hymn, Scripture, Prayer, Introduction to Prayer, In This House, Choral Response, Local Announcements, Altar Call, Altar Call (Introspection)."

"Part III":

"In the Sweet Embrace of Life Sermon, Father, Son, Holy Ghost, Invitation, Recessional, Benediction, Uptempo Posthude, Pot Blessed Dinner."

Citi-Movement (Griot New York), Wynton Marsalis (tpt), Wycliffe Gordon (tbn), Wessell Anderson (as), Todd Williams (ts, sop), Herb Harris (ts) (on "I See the Light" and "Curtain Call" only), Eric Reed (p), Marcus Roberts (p on II only), Reginald Veal (b), Herlin Riley (d). Recorded in New York, July 27–28, 1992.

"Cityscape": "Hustle Rustle," "City Beat," "Daylight Dinosaurs," "Down the Avenue," "Stop and Go," "Nightlife-Highlife."

"Transatlantic Echoes": "How Long?," "I See the Light" (two versions), "Duway Dialogue," "Dark Heartbeat," "Cross Court Capers," "Bayou Baroque," "Marthaniel" (II), "Spring Yaounde."

"Some Present Moments of the Future": "The End" (II), "The Legend of Buddy Bolden," "Swingdown, Swingtown" (II), "Highrise Riff" Parts I, II, III, IV.

"Modern Vistas (As Far As the Eye Can See)."

"Curtain Call" (II).

They Came To Swing, a CD released by Columbia in 1994, featuring the Lincoln Center Jazz Orchestra and various Marsalis groups. It was recorded live during a period spanning three years.

"Take the A Train," recorded October 10, 1992, Poughkeepsie, New York. The Lincoln Center Jazz Orchestra, Wynton Marsalis, Marcus Belgrave, Lew Soloff (solo), Joe Wilder (tpt), Art Baron, Wycliffe Gordon, Britt Woodman (tbn), Joe Temperley (bar), Jerry Dodgion, Norris Turney (as), Bill Easley, Todd Williams (ts), Sir Roland Hanna (p), Reginald Veal (b), Herlin Riley (d), David Berger (conductor).

Same CD, "Black and Tan Fantasy," October 13, 1992, McCarter Theater, Princeton, New Jersey. Same orchestra and personnel. Marsalis (solo).

Same CD, "Express Crossing," Wynton Marsalis Ensemble, January 14, 1993, New York State Theater, Lincoln Center, New York, Wynton Marsalis (tpt, solo, music dir), Marcus Printup (tpt), Wycliffe Gordon, Ronald Westray (tbn), Todd Williams (ts), Wessell Anderson (as), Kent Jordan (piccolo), Victor Goines (bar), Eric Reed (p), Reginald Veal (b), Herlin Riley (d), Robert Sadin (cond).

Same CD, "Light Blue," August 3, 1993, Alice Tully Hall, Lincoln Center, New York City. Wynton Marsalis (solo), Marcus Printup (tpt), Ronald Westray (tbn), Walter Blanding, Jr. (ts), Herb Harris (sop), Wessell Anderson (as), Victor Goines (bar), Marcus Roberts (p, music dir), Billy Higgins (d).

Same CD, "Jelly, Jelly," Lincoln Center Jazz Orchestra, recorded February 17, 1994, Garther Auditorium, Cleveland Museum of Art, Cleveland, Ohio. Jon Faddis, Ryan Kisor, Nicholas Payton, Marcus Printup (tpt), Art Baron, Jamal Haynes, Ronald Westray (tbn), Joe Temperley (bar), Jesse Davis (solo, as), Jerry Dodgion (as), Bill Easley, Joshua Redman (ts), Marcus Roberts (p, music dir), Chris Thomas (b), Lewis Nash (d), Milt Grayson (vcl), Robert Sadin (cond).

Same CD, "Things To Come," Lincoln Center Jazz Orchestra, same place, date, and personnel. Faddis (solo).

Same CD, "Boy Meets Horn," Lincoln Center Jazz Orchestra, recorded October 13, 1992, McCarter Theater, Princeton, New Jersey. Marcus Belgrave,

Wynton Marsalis (solo), Lew Soloff (tpt), Art Baron, Wycliffe Gordon, Britt Woodman (tbn), Joe Temperley (bar), Jerry Dodgion, Norris Turney (as), Todd Williams (ts), Sir Roland Hanna (p), Reginald Veal (b), Herlin Riley (d), David Berger (cond).

Same CD, "Lost in Loveliness," Lincoln Center Jazz Orchestra, February 15, 1994, Hill Auditorium, University of Michigan, Ann Arbor, Michigan. Jon Faddis, Ryan Kisor, Nicholas Payton, Marcus Printup (tpt), Art Baron, Jamal Haynes, Ronald Westray (tbn), Joe Temperley (bar), Jesse Davis, Jerry Dodgion (as), Bill Easley, Joshua Redman (ts), Marcus Roberts (p, music dir), Chris Thomas (b), Lewis Nash (d), Milt Grayson (vcl), Robert Sadin (cond).

Same CD, "Back to Basics," Wynton Marsalis Big Band, April 2, 1994, Alice Tully Hall, Lincoln Center, New York City. Wynton Marsalis (cond, primary solo), Russell Gunn, Roger Ingram, Marcus Printup (tpt), Wayne Goodman, Wycliffe Gordon, Ronald Westray (tbn), Victor Goines (ts, cl), Robert Stewart (ts), Wes Anderson (as), James Carter (bar), Eric Reed (p), Reginald Veal (b), Herlin Riley (d).

Same CD, "Tattooed Bride," Lincoln Center Jazz Orchestra, Hancher Auditorium, University of Iowa, Iowa City, Iowa, February 11, 1994. Jon Faddis, Ryan Kisor, Nicholas Payton, Marcus Printup (tpt), Art Baron (solo), Jamal Haynes, Ronald Westray (tbn), Joe Temperley (bar), Jesse Davis, Jerry Dodgion (as), Bill Easley, Joshua Redman (ts), Marcus Roberts (p, music dir), Chris Thomas (b), Lewis Nash (d), Robert Sadin (cond).

Joe Cool's Blues, recorded in New Orleans, April 12 or June 14, 1994, and in Brooklyn, New York, August 25, 1994. The Wynton Marsalis Septet, Wynton Maralis (tpt), Wycliffe Gordon (tbn), Wessell Anderson (as, sop), Victor Goines (ts, cl), Eric Reed (p), Ben Wolfe (b), Herlin Riley (d).

"Linus and Lucy," "Buggy Ride" (wg out), "On Peanut's Playground," "Wright Brother's Rag," "Little Red-Haired Girl," "Snoopy and Woodstock," "Why, Charlie Brown," "Joe Cool's Blues (Snoopy's Return)" (wg, wa, vg out).

Jazz and *Jump Start*, two ballets by Wynton Marsalis, released on one CD in 1997. Both recorded by the Lincoln Center Jazz Orchestra.

Jazz: 6-1/2 Syncopated Movements, recorded in New York on Jan 23, 1993. Wynton Marsalis, Marcus Printup (tpt), Wycliffe Gordon, Ronald Westray, (tbn), Todd Williams (ts, sop, cl), Wessell Anderson (as, sop), Victor Goines (bar, b-cl), Kent Jordan (piccolo, fl), Eric Reed (p), Reginald Veal (b), Herlin Riley (d), Robert Sadin (cond).

"Jubilo (The Scent of Democracy)," "Tick-Tock (Nightfalls on Toyland)," "Trail of Tears (Across Death Ground)," "Express Crossing (Astride Iron Horses)," "'D' in the Key of 'F' (Now the Blues)," "Ragtime," "Fiddle Bow Real."

Jump Start - The Mastery of Melancholy, recorded in Los Angeles on August 17–18, 1995. Wynton Marsalis (cond, tpt) on "Bebop," Ryan Kisor, Marcus Printup (tpt), Wessell Anderson (as, sop), Victor Goines (cl, ts, sop), Ted Nash (ts, sop), Gideon Feldstein (bar, b-cl), Wycliffe Gordon, Ronald Westray (tbn), Kent Jordan (fl, picco), Eric Reed (p), Ben Wolfe (b), Herlin Riley (d), Branford Marsalis (sop on "Root Groove" only), Harry "Sweets" Edison (tpt solo on "Jump" only).

"Boogie Woogie Stomp," "The Dance," "Slow Drag," "Habanera," "March," "Gagaku," "The Spellcaster," "Bebop," "Root Groove," "Jump."

Blood on the Fields, for which Marsalis won the Pulitzer Prize in 1997, had its premiere performances on April 1–2, 1994, at Lincoln Center. Produced by Steve Epstein, Marsalis's usual producer at Columbia for both jazz and classical recordings, the three-and-a-half-hour-long oratorio was recorded in the Grand Hall of the Masonic Grand Lodge in New York on January 22–25, 1995, and was released in 1996.

Wynton Marsalis, Russell Gunn, Marcus Printup (tpt), Wessell Anderson (as), James Carter (bar, b-cl, cl), Victor Goines (ts, sop, cl, b-cl), Robert Stewart (ts), Walter Blanding, Jr. (sop) on "Work Song (Blood on the Fields)," Wayne Goodman, Ronald Westray (tbn), Wycliffe Gordon (tbn, tuba), Michael Ward (vln), Eric Reed (p), Reginald Veal (b), Herlin Riley (d, tambourine), Jon Hendricks, Cassandra Wilson, Miles Griffith (vcl).

Disc One: "Calling the Indians Out," "Move Over," "You Don't Hear No Drums," "The Market Place," "Soul for Sale," "Plantation Coffle March," "Work Song (Blood on the Fields)."

Disc Two: "Lady's Lament," "Flying High," "Oh We Have a Friend in Jesus," "God Don't Like Ugly," "Juba and a O'Brown Squaw," "Follow the Drinking Gourd," "My Soul Fell Down," "Forty Lashes," "What a Fool I've Been," "Back to Basics."

Disc Three: "I Hold Out My Hand," "Look and See," "The Sun Is Gonna Shine," "Will the Sun Come Out?," "Chant to Call the Indians Out," "Calling the Indians Out," "Follow the Drinking Gourd," "Freedom Is in the Trying," "Due North."

Midnight Blues—Standard Time Vol. 5, with Wynton Marsalis (tpt), Eric Reed (p), Reginald Veal (b), Lewis Nash (d). Recorded in New York, September 15–20, 1997. Released in 1998.

Marsalis's original composition is the title tune, plus "Ballad of the Sad Young Men," "My Man's Gone Now," "After You've Gone," "Baby, Won't You Please Come Home," "I Guess I'll Hang My Tears Out to Dry," "It Never Entered My Mind," "Spring Will Be a Little Late This Year," "You're Blase," "Glad To Be Unhappy," "I Got Lost in Her Arms," "The Party's Over."

Marsalis Plays Monk—Standard Time Vol. 4, Recorded in New York, released in 1999.

Sony has announced that it plans to release twelve new CDs by Marsalis during 1999, nine jazz oriented and three classical.

———————

Note: The Rutgers University Institute of Jazz Studies has compiled a list of albums on which Wynton Marsalis plays, apart from his work on the Columbia label, and apart from the non-Columbia albums already mentioned in the above discography. The list is as follows:

CDs

"The Modern Jazz Quartet and Friends," Atlantic, issue no. 82538.

"Black Box of Jazz," Disc One, a Castle CD, issue no. 4501; "Black Box of Jazz," Disc Two, Atlantic, issue no. 4502.

"Black Box of Jazz," Atlantic, Disc Four, issue no. 4504.

"Classic Hoagy Carmichael" (3CDs), Smithsonian, issue no. 38.

"Monterey Jazz Festival, 40 Legendary Years, 1958–1996," Warner Bros., issue no. 46703.

LPs

"Jazz Brass," (4LP Box #2), Franklin Mint, issue no. 90.

"Classic Hoagy Carmichael (4LP Box), Smithsonian, issue no. R 38.

———————

Note: Marsalis has made a number of recordings and tapes still not released; one of his compositions, "Sweet Release," done for a ballet, numbers among the works that have had no commercial release yet.

———————

Note: Marsalis has been included in compilations (e.g. "I Like Jazz Two!", Columbia), with his live performance of "Embraceable You" done at the Village Vanguard, and with no other information about the recording date except that it was pre-1993.

CLASSICAL RECORDINGS

The European classical music career of Wynton Marsalis has not been included in any detail in this biography. However, his European classical music recordings are listed here, with recording dates noted if known by author.

Haydn/Hummel/L. Mozart Trumpet Concertos, National Philharmonic Orchestra, with Raymond Leppard, conductor. Recorded at EMI Studio One, Abbey Road,

London, December 15–17, 1982. Released in June 1983.

Baroque Music for Trumpet, with music by Handel, Purcell, Torelli, Fasch, Molter, English Chamber Orchestra, with Raymond Leppard, conductor, and Edita Gruberova, soprano. Recorded at St. Barnabas Church, London, April 4–6, 1984. Released in September 1984.

Three Favorite Concertos, with Yo-Yo Ma, Cho-Liang Lin, National Philharmonic Orchestra, Raymond Leppard, conductor. Recorded at EMI Studios One, Abbey Road, London, December 15–17, 1982.

Jolivet/Tomasi: Trumpet Concertos, with the Philharmonia Orchestra, Esa-Pekka Salonen, director. Recorded at Walthamstowe Town Hall, England, June 9, 11, and 13, 1985. Released on CD, January, 1986.

 Wynton Marsalis (tpt), "Concerto for Trumpet and Orchestra," by Henri Tomasi, and "Concertino for Trumpet," by Andre Jolivet.

Carnaval (cornet music), recorded in Rochester, New York, with the Eastman Wind Ensemble, Donald Hunsberger, director. Recorded September 13–15, 1985. Released on cassette, February 1987, on CD 1988.

Variations sur "Le Carnaval de Venise," "The Debutante," "Believe Me, If All Those Endearing Young Charms," "Grand Russian Fantasia," "Moto Perpetuo, Op. 11," "'tis The Last Rose of Summer," "The Flight of the Bumblebee" from "Tsar Saltan," "Napoli-Variations on a Neapolitan Song," "Fantaise Brilliant," "Sometimes I Feel Like a Motherless Child," "Valse Brillante" (Sounds from the Hudson).

Baroque Music for Trumpets, with the English Chamber Orchestra, conducted by Raymond Leppard. Recorded at St. Barnabas Church, London, February 2–5 and March 31–April 3, 1987. Released February 1988. Concerto for 2 Trumpets and Strings in C Major, RV537, by Antonio Vivaldi; Concerto for 3 Trumpets and Orchestra in B-flat Major by Georg Philipp Telemann; Canon for 3 Trumpets and Strings by Johann Pachelbel; Concerto for Trumpet and Orchestra in D Major by Michael Haydn; Concerto for Trumpet and Orchestra in D Major by Georg Philipp Telemann; Sonata for 3 Trumpets and Orchestra in A Major by Heinrich Von Biber.

Portrait of Wynton Marsalis. Released on CD in 1988. A reissue.

Baroque Duet with Kathleen Battle. Recorded in 1992. Released May 1992. Conductor John Nelson, orchestra of St. Luke's, New York. Several pieces by Alessandro Scarlatti, J.S. Bach, George Frideric Handel.

On The Twentieth Century, Wynton Marsalis, trumpet, Judith Lynn Stillman, pianist. Recorded in Princeton, New Jersey, January 21–24, 1992. Released on CD and cassette, September 1993.

"Piece en forme de Habanera" by Maurice Ravel, "Intrada" by Arthur Honegger, "Triptyque" by Henri Tomasi, Sonata for Trumpet and Piano by Halsey Stevens, "Eiffel Tower Polka" by Francis Poulenc, "Legende" by Georges Enesco, "Rondo for Lifey" by Leonard Bernstein, "Rustique" by Eugene Bozza, Sonate für Trompete und Klavier by Paul Hindemith.

The London Concert. Released on CD and cassette, 1994; on laser disc 1995; on VHS tape, 1995. Newly recorded version done on February 17–23, 1993. Of Marsalis's first album, this one done with the English Chamber Orchestra, of works by Haydn/Hummel/L. Mozart, with the addition of Johann Friedrich Fasch.

In Gabriel's Garden. Recorded at St. Giles Church, June 19–23, and 25, 1995. Bach, Purcell and Torelli, with the English Chamber Orchestra, Anthony Newman, conductor; featuring Bach's *Brandenburg* Concerto No. 2 and Mozart's "Rondeau," Cripple Gate, London, England. Released on cassette May 1996, on CD 1997. Wynton Marsalis, piccolo trumpet.

Rondeau from "Suites de Symphonies, Premier Suite, Fanfares," by Jean-Joseph Mouret; "The Prince of Denmark's March," by Jeremiah Clarke; Sonata in D Major, G.5, by Giuseppe Torelli; "An Ayre," by Jeremiah Clarke; Sonata No. 2 in D Major for Trumpet, Strings and Basso Continuo, by Henry Purcell; "Rondeau from Abdelazar," by Henry Purcell; Sonata a5 No. 1 in D Major, AT.V.1, by Giuseppe Torelli; Rondeau, by Jean-Francois Dandrieu; Sonata in D Major, G.6, by Giuseppe Torelli; Prelude from "Te Deum," H. 146, by Marc-Antoine Charpentier; "Sinfonia con tromba in D Major," T.V.8, by Giuseppe Torelli; "Trumpet Voluntary," by John Stanley; "Brandenburg" Concerto No. 2 in F Major, BWV 1047.

GRAMMY AWARDS FOR JAZZ AND CLASSICAL RECORDINGS IN CHRONOLOGICAL ORDER

1983, Best Jazz Instrumental Performance, Soloist, for "Think of One."

1983, Best Classical Performance, Instrumental, Soloist or Soloists with Orchestra, *Concert for Trumpet and Orchestra in E Flat Major*, L. Mozart.

1984, Best Jazz Instrumental Performance, Soloist, *Hot House Flowers*.

1984, Best Classical Performance, Instrumental, Soloist or Soloists, for *Wynton Marsalis, Baroque Music For Trumpet*.

1985, Best Jazz Instrumental Performance, Soloist, *Black Codes from the Underground*.

1985, Best Jazz Instrumental Performance/Group, *Black Codes From the Underground*.

1986, Best Jazz Instrumental Performance/Group, *J Mood*.

1987, Best Jazz Instrumental Performance/Group, for *Marsalis Standard Time Vol. 1*.

NOMINATIONS FOR GRAMMY AWARDS

1982, Best Jazz Instrumental Performance, Soloist, *Wynton Marsalis*.

1983, Best Jazz Instrumental Performance, Group for *Think of One*.

1983, Best Classical Album, *Haydn Concert for Trumpet and Orchestra*.

1984, Best Instrumental Composition, *Hot House Flowers*.

1984, Best Classical Album, *Wynton Marsalis, Baroque Music for Trumpet*.

1986, Best Jazz Instrumental Performance, Soloist, *Insane Asylum*.

1986, Best Instrumental Composition, *J Mood*.

1986, Best Classical Performance, Instrumental Performance, Soloist or Soloists with or without an Orchestra, *Tomasi Concerto for Trumpet and Orchestra/Jolivet Concerto No. 2 for Trumpet, Concertino for Trumpet, String Orchestra, and Piano*.

1987, Best Jazz Instrumental Performance Soloist, *Marsalis Standard Time Vol. 1*.

1990, Best Jazz Instrumental Performance, Group, *Standard Time Vol. III, The Resolution of Romance*.

1992, Best Jazz Instrumental Solo, *Blue Interlude*.

1992, Best Instrumental Composition, *Blue Interlude*.

1995, Best Instrumental Composition Written for a Motion Picture or Television, *Buggy Ride*.

VIDEOGRAPHY

All Sony except if otherwise noted:

Jazz at the Smithsonian—Art Blakey, a Jazz Messengers concert, with Wynton Marsalis (tpt), Branford Marsalis (sax), and others, on Kultur Video, 1982.

Trumpet Kings, Jazz Images, Inc., 1985. (Burrill Crohn, producer.)

Wolf Trap Salutes Dizzy Gillespie, with Dizzy Gillespie (tpt), Benny Carter (arr, comp, as), Wynton Marsalis (tpt), Oscar Peterson (p), and others, Music Video Distribution, 1987.

Portrait of England: Treasure Houses. Released in 1989.

Marsalis: Blues and Swing, live performances and workshops at the Duke Ellington School of Music in Washington, D.C., and Harvard University, 1989.

Dizzy Gillespie All Star Tribute, marking the seventieth birthday and fiftieth anniversary of Dizzy's professional career as a musician, with Dizzy, Freddie Hubbard, and Wynton Marsalis (tpt), and others, on laser disc, Pioneer Label Entertainment, 1989.

Griot New York, a collaboration between Garth Fagan Dance Company, the Wynton Marsalis Septet, and sculptor Martin Puryear, 1991.

Baroque Duet, Kathleen Battle (sop), Wynton Marsalis (tpt), CD, cassette, and laser disc, 1992, 1993.

Carnegie Hall Christmas Concert, with Wynton Marsalis (tpt), Kathleen Battle (sop), and Andre Previn (cond), 1992.

Leonard Bernstein Place, seventy-fifth birthday tribute for the late composer and conductor at Alice Tully Hall, with actress Lauren Bacall, violinist Isaac Stern, Wynton Marsalis, singer Phyllis Newman, and others, Kultur Video, 1993.

The London Concert. Same as the CD in 1994. See Classical Recordings.

Marsalis on Music, videos with Wynton, conductor Seiji Ozawa, and cellist Yo-Yo Ma, on Well Spring Media:

"Why Toes Tap," 1995.

"Tackling the Monster: Wynton on Practice," 1995.

"Listening for Clues: Wynton on Form," 1995.

"Sousa to Satchmo," 1995.

Storyporch with Wynton Marsalis. Released in 1995.

Accent on the Offbeat. Wynton Marsalis's music for the ballet, *Jazz*, in collaboration with Peter Martins of the New York City Ballet Company, Sony, mid–1990s.

———◆———

No date is available for "Swing Into Christmas," with Marcus Roberts (p), Wynton Marsalis and Terence Blanchard (tpt), and others.

———◆———

Undoubtedly many informal videos, which are not commercially available, exist of Wynton Marsalis in performance. On one such video, done by jazz filmmaker Burrill Crohn, circa 1980, New York City, Wynton plays "Cherokee" at a Brass Conference, where he was introduced with praise by trumpeter Lew Soloff.

AUDIO DOCUMENTARIES ON CASSETTE

National Public Radio's series "What Is Music?" won a Peabody Award in 1996.

Titles dated 1995 are The New Orleans Cradle, The Spanish Tinge, The Functions of Jazz, Louis Armstrong, Inside the Blues, Blues Conquers All, What Is Swing?, The Battle, Jazz and the American Popular Song, Duke Ellington, The Jazz Vocalist, The Jazz Ballad, The Big Room: Avant-Garde Jazz.

Titles dated 1996 are Duke Ellington's Harlem Suite; Miles Davis; What Is an Arrangement?; King Drum; Jazz: Alive and Well; Personality in Jazz; Culture and Race in Jazz Music; No America, No Jazz; What Is Bebop?; Who Was Monk?; What Is a Solo?; What Makes a Great Solo?; What Is Fusion?

National Public Radio's Making the Music Teachers' Kit, a handbook with two cassettes, aimed at middle-school students, is based on the Peabody Award–winning series.

Jazz from Lincoln Center, which has won a Peabody Award, sometimes has featured Marsalis on programs. The tapes are in the Jazz at Lincoln Center archives.

BOOKS

By Wynton Marsalis:

Marsalis on Music. New York, London: W.W. Norton and Company, 1995. The companion to the Public Television series, including a CD.

Sweet Swing Blues on the Road, New York, London: W.W. Norton and Company, 1994. With Frank Stewart's photographs.

Children's books by other authors about Wynton Marsalis:

Craig Awmiller. *Wynton Marsalis: Gifted Trumpet Player.* Children's Press, October 1, 1996. A picture story biography for children ages 9–12.

Veronica Freeman Ellis. *Wynton Marsalis.* Contemporary Biographies Series. Austin, Texas: Raintree/Steck Vaughn Co., 1997. For children ages 9–12.

Margaret Gay Malone. *Jazz Is the Word: Wynton Marsalis.* Benchmark Biographies Series, Tarrytown, N.Y.: Marshall Cavendish Corp., January 1998.

INDEX